The Catholic Priesthood - A 360 Degree View

Bevil Bramwell OMI

Catholic Distance University

Other books by Bevil Bramwell OMI

The Laity: Good, Beautiful and True – Hans Urs von Balthasar's Theology of the Laity

The World of the Sacraments: A Catholic Theology of the Sacraments

Catholics read the Scriptures: A Commentary on Benedict XVI's *Verbum domini*

John Paul II's *Ex Corde Ecclesiae* – The Gift of Catholic Universities to the World

Acknowledgements

Many people have been very helpful readers including colleagues at Catholic Distance University such as Elizabeth Shaw, James Kruggel, Stephen Bozza, David Bonagura, Carole Brown, Christine Wood, Alyssa Thorell, Charles Rieper and a fellow Oblate Fr. Leo Perez. Thank you too to priest friends for the discussions and the laughter.

Abbreviations

CD Christus dominus

CIC Codex Iuris canonici

DI Dominus Iesus

DV Dei verbum

EDE Ecclesia de eucharistia

GL I Glory of the Lord volume 1

GS Gaudium et spes

LG Lumen gentium

PO Presbyterorum ordinis

RH Redemptor hominis

RP Reconciliatio et paenitentia

SS Spe salvi

TD I Theodrama I

VD Verbum domini

Contents

My people are ruined for lack of knowledge!
Since you have rejected knowledge,
I will reject you from serving as my priest.

Hosea 4:6

Introduction

The priestly nature of the Catholic Church is one of the marvels of this world. Humanity is meant to offer sacrifice to Almighty God who loves mankind so completely. The Church is hierarchical (from the Greek *iereus* – priest) for reasons that have to do with the nature of the presence of Jesus Christ in the Church. Jesus Christ is holy, authoritative and prophetic in his own life, in his Church and through his Church into the world. The Bishop and his priests participate in Christ's sanctifying, leading and teaching work in the Church.

Generally, to truly appreciate the priesthood and not confuse it with what religions do, one must know that Catholicism is a way of life and is not reducible to a religion.[1] It is not reducible to what various cultural trends would like it to be. Hence, the episcopate must be appreciated through the lens of the Catholic faith. This means drawing out the theology of the priesthood using the Scriptures and the Tradition (history) of the Church.

This book examines the continuing priestly presence of the glorified Christ in the world. It focusses on the theology of the priest as the Bishop's assistant with his various relationships to the Bishop, the Laity and the world at large. In fact, priests "in a certain way make him [the Bishop] present in every congregation." (PO 5) The study of priesthood also includes some reflections on the spirituality of the priest, his intellectual world and his pastoral work. Finally, it includes some thoughts on who the priest will meet in his work and the issue of same-sex attraction and the priesthood.

The Catholic priesthood is a sacrament, a Sacrament of the Community, with all that that involves including a terminology that has to be learned. The priesthood is a sign of what it signifies, in this case, it signifies the presence of the priestly grace and activity of Jesus Christ acting through a particular man in the Church, as he goes about his day of spreading Christ's knowledge, grace and prayer around the community. Furthermore, the sign causes what it signifies. The laying on of hands by the Bishop brings about the transformation of the candidate into the priestly delegate of the Bishop. As John Paul II explained: "By its very nature, the ordained ministry can be carried out only to the extent that the priest is united to Christ through

---

[1] Joseph Cardinal Ratzinger, *Truth and Tolerance: Christian Belief and World Religions*, San Francisco: Ignatius Press, 2004, 50.

sacramental participation in the priestly order, and thus to the extent that he is in hierarchical communion with his own Bishop." (PDV 17)

Now, Christ's knowledge was deliberately mentioned because historically "the Christian faith is not based on poetry or politics. It is based on knowledge."[2] This is an important point to recall when Clergy and Laity want to turn the Church into a political agent or as a cover for political agents. These dreams are congruent with the anti-intellectual revisions of Christianity caused by the Enlightenment.

In every age, the idea of what the Catholic priest is, has to be re-learned, in conscious opposition to the prevailing streams of secular thought. Even non-Catholics have really strong opinions about what a priest "should" be. Secular thinking in the US is largely a child of the Enlightenment. In the seventeenth century, the Enlightenment was an intellectual current in European culture, and it was, and still is, viciously hostile to the Church and to the supernatural dimensions of the world. The heritage of the Enlightenment still continues with the expectation that, among other things, Clergy should be invisible, and they ought to limit their public role because society-at-large is to be led and inspired by the self-appointed cultural elite, with the Clergy playing no part at all. Some Clergy quietly go along with this expectation!

Another negative result of the Enlightenment is the illusion that there are dozens of 'reasonable' philosophies and the one that a priest chooses is not particularly important. This ignores the fact that there is only one way of knowing that is most congruent with how human beings are created to function and it involves faith and reason—something that the Church and the Jewish people before them have known for millennia. For reasons that will become apparent, knowing is rooted in the fact that "creation be a mirror (sacramental image) of the Creator's own thought" in the orders of creation and redemption.[3] This applies to the operation of the faithful individual's mind. Lastly, when the individual takes in the truth, he/she is encountering God.

Unfortunately, the ersatz philosophies get carried consciously or unconsciously into the thought-world of the seminary by some of the faculty and staff. In addition, many Clergy get their courses at universities where even the disciplines themselves are laid out according to agnostic Enlightenment principles more related to offering what the professor thinks and is interested in at the moment rather than what the Church

---

[2] *Truth and Tolerance*, 170.
[3] International Theological Commission, "The Reciprocity between Faith and Sacraments," 4.

thinks. This happens to varying degrees. Clergy then unquestioningly use these philosophies in their preaching and charitable work.

Allied to these major distortions of thinking, some priests themselves import ideas from Protestantism or even pagan religions to visualize what being a minister entails.

This work will stay with the theology of Catholic priesthood and not follow cultural stereotypes and stereotypes from ecclesial communities (in Benedict XVI's sense) or pagan religions.[4]

Furthermore, many have a justifiably jaundiced view of the priesthood because of the Clergy's accrual of wealth and power. Historically, the problem is that since Constantine, many Clergy were civil officials as well, rulers of cities and even provinces. This is insofar as civil and religious roles could be separated in times before the separation of Church and State. Such Clergy had great administrative power and corresponding possibilities for accumulating wealth. The habit continued long after the civil service by the Clergy ended. The fact that power and wealth has *no intrinsic* connection with the priesthood is painfully obvious in the Scriptures and the Tradition but it took a long time for it to become a conscious principle for some Clergy.[5] Fortunately, in every age, the sin of clericalism has always been obvious to some groups of religious and secular Clergy.

Theologically, "power is connected with humanity's original sin and concupiscence."[6] What von Balthasar is referring to is the original reach for power in the question of eating the fruit in the Garden of Eden. The serpent says: "You certainly will not die! God knows well that when you eat of it your eyes will be opened and you will be like

---

[4] Ecclesial communities are those communities who do not have all the signs of a Christian Church. Cf. *Dominus Iesus*: "ecclesial communities . . . have not preserved the valid episcopate and the genuine and integral substance of the Eucharistic mystery, [and] are not Churches in the proper sense; however, those who are baptized in these communities are, by Baptism, incorporated in Christ and thus are in a certain communion, albeit imperfect, with the Church." (*Dominus Iesus* 17)

[5] The rise of the secular nation-states forced Clergy to realize that they do not need secular power to serve the faithful well. Hence, for example, John Paul II's instruction to Clergy to refrain from holding civil office. In some form, the principle had long been in Canon Law. For example: "Clerics are forbidden to assume public offices which entail a participation in the exercise of civil power." (canon 285.3)

[6] Hans Urs von Balthasar, "Women Priests?" *New Elucidations*, San Francisco: Ignatius Press, 1986, 197.

gods, who know good and evil." (Genesis 3:4, 5) The question of power will return frequently in this text.

One lingering remnant of attachment to the civil world might well be the massive salaries that some priests receive for their work, say in the Bishops Conference or in the Vatican. They seem to operate on the secular business model rather than following any Christian considerations. Or they work from the illusion that they are some-kind of royalty with salaries to match. Why can such Clergy not simply earn what most pastors earn? Laypeople would be happier knowing that their donations are going to the charities and other tasks for which it was originally intended rather than paying for Clergy.

The recent abuse and sexual scandals have caused many to be sceptical of Catholic Clergy. This is a perfectly valid reaction even though it is only a small minority who have done these heinous things. This monumental issue remains to be fully dealt with and yet without a pause, the Church also has to deal with the fall-out from a pandemic and people doing without liturgies for months. Then, on top of that, there is the very real need to respond to the problems of racism in the country.

One final issue—that is rarely if ever mentioned—is the problem of a priest/Bishop belonging to a political party or even supporting a political party. The way that the Catholic priesthood is constituted in Scripture and Tradition by the Holy Spirit, is turned into a pretzel when a priest participates in a political party. The problem is: whose thinking is he following? Is he saying in fact that Christian morality is not absolute? In our historical period, this particularly applies to committing to a leftist party because of the Left's fundamental thinking blatantly contradicts the whole intellectual and moral framework of Catholicism. The traditional intellectual framework of Catholicism—alluded to above—fits the full functioning of the human being according to revelation.

For example, the Council said: "Man achieves [his/her] dignity when, emancipating himself from all captivity to passion, he pursues his goal in a spontaneous choice of what is good, and procures for himself through effective and skillful action, apt helps to that end."(GS 17)[7] Feelings are not the root of a moral decision. Just a reminder: over the last century, the Left has killed hundreds of millions more people than the

---

[7] Cited in John Paul II's *Veritatis splendor*, 42.

4

so-called Right. This must be a clue that there is something wrong with its basic principles.

The Left does not work with actual universal concepts, regardless of the words that they use. In vast contrast, Catholicism works with universal concepts drawn from the real—from the revelation in creation or in salvation history. So, just to take one example, Catholicism has the principle that human beings are precious, no matter at what stage of life they find themselves. Not so on the Left. In Catholicism, and hence universally, the value of human beings does not vary according to what others want it to be at the moment, or which group is being courted politically by the elite. (See Chapter Nine)

Based on this principle: One cannot associate with appalling practices such as racism and abortion. More about that later. This even means voting for a candidate who supports these things. There is no way to tailor one's vote: "I support this but not that part of the party's policy." Not surprisingly, this dilemma arises from the Enlightenment one of whose purposes is to dismantle the Church. The Enlightenment sets up situations to damage the Church. Clergy who play into this tactic are not helping to develop the Church. The priestly stance described here is one of the features of the separation[8] that priests undergo when they are taken over by Christ.

These are some of the intellectual challenges to passing on the valid concepts of the priesthood—a topic to which we shall be returning. Knowing these challenges is crucial to building the priestly mind, if it can be called that. Speaking about priests, Hans Urs von Balthasar explained the 'priestly mind' in this way:

> The action and the suffering of the 'representative' [of Christ] has an inner effect on the persons in whose place he stands. Thus it is highly significant that the God who has reconciled the world to himself has entrusted the Apostles, and in a wider sense, the Church of Christ, with 'the ministry of reconciliation' (II Corinthians 5:18), 'the message of reconciliation' (5:19), so that they can 'work with him' (II Corinthians 6:1) in the world in implementing this reconciliation.[9]

---

[8] Jean Galot, *Theology of the Priesthood*, 205.
[9] Hans Urs von Balthasar, *Theodrama – Theological Dramatic Theory III. Dramatis Personae: Persons in Christ*, San Francisco: Ignatius Press, 1992, 121.

5

Just what has to be reconciled will be the topic of Chapter One. Now, continuing with von Balthasar's line of thought, it follows that: "While the aim of this collaboration, of course is to spread the peace of Christ (bought on the Cross) among men, to all individuals and groups, it is peace that can only be shared by each person entering into the mind of Christ."[10] Both Clergy and Laity are called to this entering in.

What this means will be explained in the rest of the book, but one must start by acknowledging that the meaning of priesthood lies in the mind of Christ himself. The Catholic priesthood is not a job or a part time occupation, it is being called and given the sacramental grace to plunge into the Priesthood of the Christ himself.

---

[10] Ibidem.

Chapter One: The Mystery of Iniquity

Grace to you and peace from God our Father and the Lord Jesus Christ, who gave himself
for our sins that he might rescue us from the present evil age in accord with the will of our
God and Father.
(Galatians 1: 3, 4)

(1) The Present Evil Age

It would be more straightforward to learn the theology of the priesthood if one
lived under Nazi or Soviet occupation or under some other leftist government–
as Karol Wojtyla did, for example![11] Then, one could get a feel for the
priesthood while surrounded by menacing evil and by people's frightening
capacity to collaborate daily with that evil. (Obviously the practical horrors
would be incredibly difficult but the theology of the need for the presence of
Christ would be readily apparent!) The theology would not remain resting in
books, books that can be closed at will. The experience would offer the
appropriate context for understanding the drama of the life and work[12] of the
effective Catholic priest. The fact remains that people *still* are surrounded by
evil and by people's collaboration with evil, even though Christ is victorious and
even if it is not fashionable to say so! This is the dramatic world of the Catholic
priest. However, studying the priesthood from such a perspective is still possible
if one is deeply spiritually aware. Vatican II, for example, deliberately noted the
evils in the world at the time. Aside from being correct because it is based on
revelation, this perspective of Christ working in the midst of evil has the added

---

[11] The concept of the Left that is being used here is tied to the original Jacobinism in the
French Revolution. They were the early Left. See Chapter Nine. That chapter also explains
the only valid alternative to the Gnosticism and Jacobinism of the Left. This arrangement of
concepts has nothing to do with the Democrat and Republican polarisation in the US. The
descriptions here do not line up with the major political parties in the US. This is because the
two possible political options either of love or of power involve human beings and humans
always try to mix approaches under the illusion that they are personally above both and can
competently cherrypick aspects of one or other approach and mix them together. Actually,
they do not have a neutral vantage point at all.
[12] The work of a priest includes being the public face of the Church serving the mission of the
Bishop. It includes prayer, celebration of the sacraments, education of parishioners, leading
people to holiness, speaking out about using proper anthropology in public contexts, visiting
the sick, burying the dead. Don't forget parish administration!

advantage of seeing the glory of what God is doing and taking the value of God's revelation and his redeeming and sanctifying gifts very seriously.

Generally speaking, the approach used here holds that the *context* of a concept is essential if one wants to understand all the dimensions of that concept. The context includes the metanarrative and metaphysics involved. This point will appear again and again. The study of the priesthood as it functions in a context of good and evil is just one illustration.

At least superficially, the priesthood has often been seen as a life of gold cufflinks, good meals and a nine-to-five job! This is no longer generally true. The so-called 'John Paul II priests' coming out the seminaries during and after John Paul II's pontificate definitely have different expectations. Then, also, recent scandals have hopefully put paid to the illusion of the priest as not answerable to anyone once and for all. First and foremost, they should be answerable to the traditional theology of the priesthood. Now to some of the theology . . .

(2) The Deformation of Creation

To start with, the *Catholic Catechism* explains that: "To try to understand what sin is, one must first recognize the profound relation of man to God." (CCC 386) The Second Vatican Council described the relationship: "man would not exist were he not created by God's love and constantly preserved by it; and he cannot live fully according to truth unless he freely acknowledges that love and devotes himself to his Creator." (GS 19) This relation is the key to understanding human existence in general. Men and women are sustained and loved in their relationship with God. When a person acknowledges this love and consciously focuses his/her existence on attending to the God who is creator and redeemer, then he/she comes to a more profound life.[13] This is the first principle needed in a discussion of sin.

John Paul II offered a second essential principle—the interconnectedness of all humanity in sin:

> one can speak of a communion of sin, whereby a soul that lowers itself through sin drags down with itself the Church and, in some way, the whole world. In other words, there is no sin, not even the most intimate and secret one, the

---

[13] Cf. Psalm 16:11: "You will show me the path to life, fullness of joys in your presence, the delights at your right hand forever."

most strictly individual one, that exclusively concerns the person committing it. With greater or lesser violence, with greater or lesser harm, every sin has repercussions on the entire ecclesial body and the whole human family. According to this first meaning of the term, every sin can undoubtedly be considered as social sin. (RP 16)[14]

The wonderful gift of humanity's interconnectedness unfortunately grounds a communion of sin, just as, conversely, and fortunately, it is part of the foundation of a communion of grace where all can help each other on so many levels.[15] Then, John Paul II expanded on the meaning of social sin:

the term 'social' applies to every sin against justice in interpersonal relationships, committed either by the individual against the community or by the community against the individual. Also social is every sin against the rights of the human person, beginning with the right to and including the life of the unborn or against a person's physical integrity. Likewise, every sin is social when it is against others' freedom, especially against the supreme freedom to believe in God and adore him; social is every sin against the dignity and honor of one's neighbor. Also social is every sin against the common good and its exigencies in relation to the whole broad spectrum of the rights and duties of citizens. The term social can be applied to sins of commission or omission—on the part of political, economic or trade union leaders, who though in a position to do so, do not work diligently and wisely for the improvement and transformation of society according to the requirements and potential of the given historic moment; as also on the part of workers who through absenteeism or non-cooperation fail to ensure that their industries can continue to advance the well-being of the workers themselves, of their families and of the whole of society. (RP 16)

---

[14] The interconnectedness of humanity by nature is fundamental to everything that a priest does and is basic to the functioning of the presbyterate and its relation to the Bishop and the hierarchy's relation to the world. It is the presupposition of whatever the priest does. Whomever he is dealing with, he is already connected to them by nature, by grace and by being a sinner.

[15] This is the distinction found in Saint Augustine's City of God/ City of Man. The distinction is found in Book XI of his *Concerning the City of God against the Pagans*, London: Penguin Books, 2003, 429ff. Cf. "Streams of the river gladden the city of God, the holy dwelling of the Most High." (Psalm 46:5)

The social network of sin rests on the communal nature of human being, in all of its aspects, and the concept illuminates the logic of large areas of the pastoral work of the priest as he promotes people's withdrawal from the communion of sin and brings them to participate more deeply in the communion of grace—and progresses in his own participation in the latter as well! One could write an essay just on how this concept of social sin indicates how we are going to be politically active or not. This point will return in the discussion of the intellectual component of the life of the priest.

These two anthropological principles help clarify the understanding of sin as it is presented in the scriptures.

(3) In the Word of God

Looking at a tiny part of the scriptural record: Historically, the scriptures are partially the story of how God opposes human sin in the world. To take one example: God said to Ezekiel: "Son of man, I am sending you to the Israelites, a nation of rebels who have rebelled against me; they and their ancestors have been in revolt against me to this very day." (Ezekiel 2:3) God was describing a sinful people through the mouth of his prophet. There are dozens more examples. The scriptures illustrate the communal nature of sin and how God confronts it, in this case by sending a prophet. In the New Testament, God sends the Prophet, Jesus Christ and, from then on, Clergy participate in his prophetic work after his Resurrection. God himself frequently used the terms 'rebellion' and 'revolt' to refer to the people's sins. In such cases, the people were willfully acting against their fundamental relationship with God and against their own best interest.

In the New Testament, Jesus explained what he is to the world using the metaphor of darkness and light: "The light will be among you only a little while. Walk while you have the light, so that darkness may not overcome you. Whoever walks in the dark does not know where he is going." (John 12:35) Moreover, the darkness "hates the light, and does not come to the light." (John 3:9) The theme of revolt is cast in terms of the world's hatred of the light. This hatred means that the priest will experience all kinds of opposition to his work ranging from simply being ignored to being physically threatened or imprisoned.

10

Then, even more bluntly, using the term 'war', the *Book of Revelation* says that even before time itself, "war broke out in heaven; Michael and his angels battled against the dragon. The dragon and its angels fought back." (Revelation 12:17) This struggle had terrible consequences that were already known and felt in the Old Testament where "by the envy of the devil, death entered the world, and they who belong to his company experience it." (Wisdom 2:26) Returning to the larger subject, a properly pastoral priest is ordained as an instrument of light[16] and the stakes are far higher than most modern ideas of the priesthood would even suggest! Of course, then too priests also face their own repeated personal revolt against God.

(4) Christian Prayers

Appropriately enough, the common prayers of the Church accurately portray the human situation. For example: "To thee do we cry poor banished children of Eve, to thee do we send up our prayer mourning and weeping in this valley of tears." (Hail Holy Queen) Each day, people pray in the Our Father, "deliver us from evil." There is also the petition: "Pray for us sinners, now and at the hour of our death," in the Hail Mary.

In Church liturgy, the Eucharistic liturgies take pride of place. To be prepared to participate in the celebration, after the opening greeting, for example, the priest introduces the Penitential Act saying to the people: "let us acknowledge our sins and prepare ourselves to celebrate the sacred mysteries." Evidently sin interferes with everything even with one's participation in the Eucharist. The community's prayer of confession then follows and concludes with the priest's petition: "May almighty God have mercy on us, forgive us our sins, and bring us to everlasting life."[17] Thus the community prepares herself to sing the Gloria in praise of the Lord God. Even in that prayer there are the words: "you take away the sins of the world, have mercy on us."[18]

---

[16] Cf. Preface, *Mass of Ordination*, speaking of the priests, "they are to renew *in his name*, the sacrifice of human redemption." *The Roman Missal*, New Jersey: Catholic Book Publishing Corp 2014, 1004.

[17] The Catholic Church, *The Roman Missal*, New Jersey: Catholic Book Publishing Corp, 2011, 367.

[18] Ibidem, 374.

The prayers[19] at Mass repeatedly announce the inescapable role of God in the salvation of humanity and the whole of creation. The priest's Prayer over the Offerings recognizes, in one instance, that "we have no merits to plead our cause." In fact, everyone finds themselves in this situation. One might look at the priest's private prayer before he shows the Body and Blood of Jesus Christ to the people: "Lord Jesus Christ . . . free me by this your most holy Body and Blood, from all my sins and from every evil; keep me always faithful to your commandments, and never let me be parted from you."[20] In the prayer, the priest humbly acknowledges his own unworthy state, something that is glaringly evident in the light of the Real Presence of the Body and Blood of Christ there on the altar. This prayer also serves to sum up the existential tension in the priest's own life. He has the grace of Baptism, Confirmation and Ordination and yet he still commits sins and trips himself as he tries to work as a priest.

Lastly, in the Eucharistic celebration's Prayer after Communion, the priest asks, for example, that: "You may teach us to judge wisely the things of earth and hold firm to the things of heaven." The community asks God for salvation because there is no other avenue to salvation. With these words, people also get the standard of life clear, namely, they grasp that some things have eternal value, and some do not. This is crucial for Clergy and Laity alike, but especially for those Clergy who, for some reason, are attached to clothes, or who 'have to' know the best wines, or who think a priest has a special social status.

Of course, sin is mentioned in many types of eucharistic celebrations: The various Commons of the Blessed Virgin Mary, just to choose some examples among so many, contain the petitions: "may [we] with the help of her intercession rise up from our iniquities." (Common 2)[21]; "may [we] be freed by her motherly intercession from all evils on earth" (Common 8)[22] and so on. The prayers illustrate the concern about

---

[19] This was a constant theme in the Old Testament too: "Keep me safe, O God; in you I take refuge." (Psalm 16:1); "Blessed the one whose help is the God of Jacob, whose hope is in the Lord, his God." (Psalm 146:5); "Our soul waits for the Lord, he is our help and shield." (Psalm 33:20)
[20] *The Roman Missal*, 520.
[21] *The Roman Missal*, 895.
[22] *The Roman Missal*, 901.

the immersion in evil that is so often our lot and they also illustrate the way out of this communion of evil.

Catholics only begin to understand their real situation from God's revelations about the nature of the world and the nature of evil. This understanding grounds the priest's intellectual framework and is vital for the intellectual honesty of his pastoral work.[23] (See Chapter Nine.)

(5) The Concept of Evil and its Origin

A real obstacle to our understanding lies in the nature of evil itself. More explicitly:
> We cannot illuminate the *mysterium iniquitatis* in a way that would render its darkness light, even for our understanding, aided as it is by faith. It is part of iniquity's 'night', and even our understanding 'stumbles because of the lack of light' (Cf. John 11:10)[24]

In other words, there is an intellectual barrier to forming a complete theory of evil. This is yet another reason for valuing the Church's normal approach to epistemology—that is the way of knowing that involves both faith and reason. The intellectual barrier implies that priests be very careful what they choose to say and do, for example in pastoral initiatives otherwise they might be committing sin or leaning towards sin. They might reject initiatives simply because they do not want to do them even though people need them for good theological reasons—not allowing Eucharistic adoration might be one example. They might advocate political policies because they feel that they ought to, to look good. Clergy might assume that their parish is hostage to *their* personal understanding of things rather than being committed to the Church's understanding of things. Pastors might avoid dealing with certain individuals because they do not want to make the effort to understand them. Both priests and Laity are very much subject to a lack of spiritual light.

One can however make certain isolated statements about evil.

To start with, the description of Christ as the Light is singularly helpful. Christ called himself "the Light of the world." (John 8:12) The opposing darkness hates the light and it is that hatred that is of interest now. Von Balthasar again: "The concept of hatred, the open, aggressive opposition to that love which characterizes God in his economic and Trinitarian self-giving (I John 4:16) brings us right to the heart of this

---

[23] The intellectual dimension of salvation is an essential part of one's knowledge of salvation. This has to be emphasized in a country where the Church often seems to be about building institutions which is easier than consistently teaching the truth.

[24] Hans Urs von Balthasar, *Theodrama - Theological Dramatic Theory V: The Last Act*, San Francisco: Ignatius Press 1998, 203.

mystery."[25] Hatred is the opposite of love. (People can also hate truths that the Church teaches.) The Trinity acts completely out of love. It can do no other! The Church is constituted by that love through Jesus Christ even though the Church has many sinful members.

The concept of the good is essential to understanding the purpose of love. Love involves bringing about the good—as understood from revelation and not as learned from a philosopher no matter well-meaning. This is the work of those who serve the light such as priests. Of course, they must know what the good is. They do not have to like it. They just have to act according to the good because their authenticity as human beings depends on it.

Starting with God as the Good, Thomas Aquinas argued that logically, "there needs to be a universal good to which we trace back all goods. This universal good can only be the very thing that is the first and universal efficient cause." (*De malo*, q.1 answer)[26] Each particular thing comes from the universal good, God, who alone is good. (cf. Mark 10:18) But if someone is not all good as God is then "so far as he is lacking in goodness, and is said to be evil." (ST II I 18 1) Both the nature of evil and the notion of God as the source of all good can never be far from the priest's thoughts as pastor of his flock. His decisions must always lead to the good—as it is understood by the Church. His actions cannot use bad means to get to the good either. Of course, this means that the priest has to ask the Church what is good since he will not always know immediately. This takes humility!

For the priest as a pastor, everyone is a creation of the *good* God, hence, for example, Paul could say: "Owe nothing to anyone, except to love one another; for the one who loves another has fulfilled the law." (Romans 13:8) This is the fundamental principle of people's activity. It is how they relate to each and every person. One should expect this from every priest and every layperson, and one should expect it always—in every interaction inside and beyond the Church. The priest or layperson never leaves the Church and so is the face of the Body of Christ in each situation.

On the other hand, personal human subjects can and do lack some good. So, to complete the point that Thomas was making: "I say that evil is not an entity, but the subject that evil befalls is, since evil is only the privation of a particular good." (*De malo* q.1 answer) To discuss evil then, one has to deal with subjects who have been deprived or have deprived themselves of some good—that is they have sinned. This conclusion was already suggested by the quotation from the Book of Wisdom (above) that explained that "by the envy of the devil, death entered the world, and

---

[25] Ibidem.
[26] Thomas Aquinas, *On Evil*, Richard Regan trans., Oxford: Oxford University Press, 2003.

they who belong to his company experience it." (Wisdom 2:26) The clouding of intellect and will is part of the experience: "How profound your designs! A senseless person cannot know this; a fool cannot comprehend." (Psalm 92:67)

An angelic subject can sin and thus become evil. Hence Satan! This has consequences for humanity too, in that, as Peter explained about the Devil to the audience of his letter: "Be sober and vigilant. Your opponent the devil is prowling around like a roaring lion looking for [someone] to devour." (I Peter 5:8) As if unpacking this statement, the Second Vatican Council would later note,

> that world which the Christian sees as created and sustained by its Maker's love, [has] fallen indeed into the bondage of sin, yet [is] emancipated now by Christ, who was crucified and rose again to break the stranglehold of personified evil, so that the world might be fashioned anew according to God's design and reach its fulfillment. (GS 2)

The 'fashioning anew' means Christ's redemption of the individual is realized existentially in time and the re-fashioning of the world takes place each time one cooperates with grace and thinks, acts or meets someone with grace. Christ's redemption even regulates one's speech, for example, private and public: "No foul language should come out of your mouths, but only such as is good for needed edification, that it may impart grace to those who hear." (Ephesians 4:29)

(6) Mankind and Sin

The council did not give much detail about the emancipation from sin in temporal terms. However, they did lay out the central principle: "The council brings to mankind light kindled from the Gospel and puts at its disposal those saving resources which the Church herself, under the guidance of the Holy Spirit, receives from her Founder."(GS 3) The saving resources are available in real time. Emancipation from sin comes from knowing the truth of the Gospel and the grace of Jesus Christ. This will be important for a complete grasp of the wide-ranging spiritual and social scope of the work of the priest. The priest is one of those instruments bringing the saving resources—grace and truth—of the Church to his people and to the world generally.

In the morality of human actions, the human subject and what he/she does when acting, are closely interconnected. There are three points to be noted when considering the morality of a human action. In the words of the *Catechism*: "A morally good act requires the goodness of the object, of the end, and of the circumstances together." (CCC 1755) When the individual pursues understanding of the morality of his actions, all three of the elements of his action have to be correct to bring about a moral act. This then is the graced human person acting in the glorious freedom of the sons of God. But if one of the elements is missing: for example, if the object of the act is immoral then the act is immoral. If the end of the act is immoral then the act is immoral. If the circumstances are not moral, then the act is immoral. (Context again!)[27] Very importantly, having a positive intention—meaning well or simply having empathy—is not enough to make an act a positively moral act. This is crucial to know when the individual reflects on his/her intended action. Once again, feelings are not the issue.

Then further, the Tradition tells us that there are grave acts that are always illicit: blasphemy, perjury, murder, adultery and abortion. This list alone makes choosing a political party much more difficult, for example. Morally, can one join a party that promotes these intrinsically evil acts? Lastly, "one may not do evil so that good may result from it." (CCC 1756) These four points about the morality of actions should be chiseled in stone at the entrance to each church. They will constantly be significant for understanding the priest's life particularly as regards his social, sacramental, intellectual and spiritual life.

The four aspects of a human action (goal, means, circumstances and intention) form the context of the action. Identifying each one of them is important in order to completely comprehend what is going on. 'Am I adding to the communion of sin or the communion of grace?' Then too, human actions always have a larger horizon and that is the promotion of humanity at large by the standards of revelation. This is one of the consequences of the ontological interrelation of all human beings.

The Second Vatican Council described the horizon of the work of the council, and consequently, as it happens, of priests and Laity, in the following words: "the human person deserves to be preserved; human society deserves to be renewed. Hence the focal point of [the council's] total presentation [of their teaching] will be man himself, whole and entire, body and soul, heart and conscience, mind and will." (GS 3) The council's total humanitarian concept then appears in one form in the document *Gaudium et Spes*—a map, by the way, for much of the faithfully realized intellectual and pastoral world of the priest. Interestingly, this totally humanitarian perspective is the horizon that views one kind of political activity as moral and gives the lie to other kinds of political activity. It is baffling why Clergy will readily support Marxist style organizations when Marxism is anti-human and anti-religion.

When using the resources of the Church, the heart of the matter for a priest is to simply know what the preservation of the authentic humanity of each person in a

---

[27] This becomes important in the discussion on politics. Leftist thinking always seems to leave out some of the inconvenient circumstances. All of the shouting around electric cars, for example, ignores the fact that they will need to get their charge from somewhere. Coal-fired power stations perhaps? All of the celebration around abortion, ignores the fact that people die as a result. They are dying for someone's convenience.

particular situation means and also what it means in society and nationally. This will be important for the discussion of the social and political views of the priest and his congregation. The preservation of humanity for God involves opposing evil in *all* of its forms including not supporting questionable organizations. This fundamental point is only fully understood through the Church's study of the revelation that she safeguards and of which she is the sole authentic interpreter. Using this source is fundamental to being a believer. In other words, knowing the way the Church knows, that is through the metaphysics of human existence is essential for grasping the meaning of situations! Trying to work merely from cultural trends, social fads or what tickles one's fancy, misses most of the picture of how humanity is to be developed and preserved.

The promotion of humanity is part of the great hope put forward by the Church. Woe to the priest who poisons this hope wittingly or unwittingly. In Benedict XVI's words: "Paul reminds the Ephesians that before their encounter with Christ they were 'without hope and without God in the world' (*Eph* 2:12)." (SS 2) It is part of the hope that the priest repeatedly evokes in his people. Benedict XVI again: "To come to know God—the true God—means to receive hope." (SS 3)

Returning to our present theme, article two of *Gaudium et Spes*, recalls the effects of evil in the world using the terms "bondage" and "stranglehold," that vividly evoke experiences and humanly created situations that clearly contradict the promotion of humanity. Human immanence means that, each day, human beings are poised between the world bristling with evil and the world that is becoming part of the New Creation through the power of the Holy Spirit. The way that Saint Augustine described the situation twelve hundred years ago was to say:[28]

> Come now, O wretched mortals take heed that the wicked spirit may never foul this habitation, and that intermingled with the senses, it may not pollute the sanctity of the soul and becloud the light of the mind. This evil thing creeps stealthily through all the entrances of sense: it gives itself over to forms, it adapts itself to colors, it sticks to sounds, it lurks hidden in anger and in the deception of speech, it appends itself to odors, it infuses tastes, by the turbulent overflow of passion, it darkens the senses with darksome affections, it fills with certain obscuring mists the paths of understanding, through all of which the mind's ray normally diffuses the light of reason.[29]

Centuries later, when Thomas Aquinas himself quoted these words, he concluded that "the devil has the power to move the will and so directly causes sin." (ST II I

---

[28] Fonteius of Carthage.
[29] Saint Augustine, *Book of the 83 Questions*, Q. 12, *The Fathers of the Church 70*, Washington DC: Catholic University Press, 1982, 43.

17

q.80 a.1) In other places, Thomas qualified this statement. Having the power does not mean that he uses it! So, in his *De Malo*, Aquinas concluded: "God is the author of our good acts both as external persuader and internal mover, while the devil causes sin only as external persuader, as I have shown."(*De malo*, q. III, a.14) This is a reference to the personified evil opposing the good of God and his Creation.

Lastly, the Fourth Council of the Lateran (1215) explained how the devil came about: "The devil and other demons were created by God [as] naturally good, but they became evil by their own doing." (Chapter 1)

(7) Conversion

Building on what was said above, there is still one problem: according to John: "If we say we have no sin, we deceive ourselves, and the truth is not in us." (I John 1:8) There is still the daily struggle with sin. In Psalm 51, the psalmist describes his experience:

> Have mercy on me, God, in accord with your merciful love;
> in your abundant compassion blot out my transgressions.
> Thoroughly wash away my guilt;
> and from my sin cleanse me. (Psalm 51:2, 3)

Then, in the words of the *Catechism*:

> the new life received in Christian initiation has not abolished the frailty and weakness of human nature, nor the inclination to sin that tradition calls concupiscence, which remains in the baptized such that with the help of the grace of Christ they may prove themselves in the struggle of Christian life. (CCC 1426)

Hence, one has to deal with the question of conversion in human beings, Clergy and lay.

Conversion is where the individual comes to accept a new horizon of meaning through grace where God is the center of one's life. It is shifting from merely seeking to have one's appetites satisfied to holding actual values. This is moral conversion. On the other hand, as a state of being, it develops over time. Hence: "Evolutionary religious conversion is the fruit of what Augustine called cooperative grace, and what later medieval theology called actual grace, the gradual movement toward a complete transformation of one's being and living."[30]

The *Catechism* explains the 'gradual movement' as follows:

> Christ's call to conversion continues to resound in the lives of Christians.

---

[30] R.T. Lawrence, "Conversion, II (Theology of)." *New Catholic Encyclopedia*, 2nd ed., vol. 4, Gale, 2003.

This second conversion is an uninterrupted task for the whole Church who, 'clasping sinners to her bosom, (is) at once holy and always
in need of purification,
and follows constantly the path of penance and renewal. This endeavor of con version is not just a human work. It is the movement of a
'contrite heart,' drawn and moved by grace to respond to
the merciful love of God who loved us first." (CCC 1428)

Hence, one can say that, crudely put, even though they are baptized, people start out as 20-minute Christians that, initially, can summon up the courage to love their neighbor for 20 minutes a day. Here love is Christian love, where

Love is patient, love is kind. It is not jealous, [love] is not pompous, it is not inflated, it is not rude, it does not seek its own interests, it is not quick-tempered, it does not brood over injury, it does not rejoice over wrongdoing but rejoices with the truth. It bears all things, believes all things, hopes all things, endures all things. Love never fails. (I Corinthians 13:4-8)

The rest of the day Christians treat their neighbors the same way as those who have turned their wills from God. They gossip about them; look down on them; shun the people that their social group teaches them to shun; they cheat on their taxes; they do illegal things to make money; they are solipsistic in their thinking; act arbitrarily etc. etc. Some Clergy do the same. Everyone who does things like this is adding to the communion of sin. One thing to note in a person's lack of conversion and the lack of working on conversion is 'God help you' if you meet them outside of their 20 minutes of acting Catholic!

The marvel is that the Catholic way of life can actually heal this predicament. The principle of loving your neighbor is still fundamental. Gloriously, no one is a problem when they *do* function as Catholics, loving their neighbour and so on. However, they may have malicious people creating problems *for them* because of the darkness of the society generated by the malicious.

Hopefully, the '20-minute Christian' gradually grows to being loving for longer and longer periods each day. The Christian learns not to blindly follow his/her upbringing or culture or circumstances and chooses to find out how to be loving in each situation. This takes conversion of heart. This is not a change in the abstract but in the person who is roused by grace "from his anonymity and self-absorption into self-awareness," which then opens him to accepting "the word meant for him by God and the work that God wishes to accomplish in him."[31] This is not a generic vocation but a personal one assigned by God to this individual personally for some purpose.

---

[31] Hans Urs von Balthasar, "Conversion in the New Testament," *Explorations in Theology IV: Spirit and Institution*, San Francisco: Ignatius Press, 1995, 252.

The previous paragraphs described what the dynamics of the lives of the faithful in a Catholic community look like in real time. The facts on the ground have to be emphasized because theologies of community are always written in terms of absolutes. They are expressed as if everyone involved is a Christian and works hard to operate as a Christian twenty-four hours a day. Of course, in many cases this is not true. However, the absolute views of the dynamics of Church community are very useful for getting an initial understanding. Personal conversion is quite another matter. Both priests and laypeople who are interested have to know what the goals for Catholic community are, for their own conversion and to help the community move closer to the absolute Christian description of the community.

(8)   The Realm of the Spirit of God

In perhaps one of the best metaphors that he used to refer to Satan, Jesus gave the Parable of the Strong Man. The Pharisees had charged Jesus that he was casting out demons by the power of the Prince of Demons. (Matthew 12:24) Jesus' response was: "How can anyone enter a strong man's house and steal his property, unless he first ties up the strong man?" (Matthew 12:29) This line follows Jesus' statement about he himself being "the finger of God." Jesus is the one who successfully opposes the 'strong man'.

Jesus is the one who 'binds up the strong man'. The strong man is, of course, Satan. However, this does not terminate the activity of the 'strong man'. As von Balthasar was careful to note: "Jesus leaves his own in this world (John 17:11, 15), and the world remains the sphere of influence of the evil one. (I John 5:19)."[32] Again, this particular action of Jesus is significant for grasping the nature of the day-to-day life of the priest. Through the Church and hence through the Bishop and their assistants the priests, Christ sets up a sphere of holy influence and welcomes everyone into it.

In another metaphor, Jesus Christ is the "finger of God," from his saying in the Gospel of Luke that: "if I drive out demons by the finger of God, then the kingdom of God has come upon you."(Luke 11:20) Interestingly, the phrase 'the finger of God' occurred long before, in the *Book of Exodus*, when the author spoke of how the writing on the stone tablets was made. (Exodus 31:18) The actions of the finger of God prepared the tablets and resulted in the physical presence of the law in the world to teach the law to the People of God—anticipating the physical presence of God in the Incarnation! The laws expressed God's mind concerning human life—structuring the morality of the human context. However, it was not possible to obey

---

[32] Hans Urs von Balthasar, *Theodrama III: Dramatis Personae: Persons in Christ,* San Francisco: Ignatius Press, 1992, 477

the law without help. According to Paul: "what the law, weakened by the flesh, was powerless to do, this God has done: by sending his own Son in the likeness of sinful flesh and for the sake of sin, he condemned sin in the flesh." (Romans 8:3)

Further, the laws stand whether the Jews obey them or not. If they do not obey then the laws stand in judgment over them. More definitively, Jesus, the Divine Word himself, now glorified, stands in the world, through his Body the Church. This form of presence is key to understanding of the power of the concrete presence of the priesthood—an important concept to retain so that the priesthood does not simply become a function or an idea of what would be nice. It represents God's intrusion into the world in a whole new way according to parameters chosen by God to reach his people.

Lastly, underlying the flesh and blood presence of Jesus is the realm of the Spirit in this world: Paul explained: "We have not received the spirit of the world but the Spirit that is from God, so that we may understand the things freely given us by God." (I Corinthians 2:12) The Spirit provides the interior depth to human beings of the concrete physical presence of sacramental realities.

(9) Temptations

Despite being in the sphere of the Spirit, Jesus' followers are nevertheless still subject to temptations in the world. Most of these do not come from Satan but from the *self-love* of the individual.[33] Aquinas explains: "That man [who] inordinately desires a temporal good and it proceeds from this that he inordinately loves himself." (ST 1a2ae 77:4) The individual is created to do the will of God, pure and simple. When that happens then he is living a truly free life, an ordered life, a just life. In contrast, by being drawn to a temporal good (something that is good in itself) inordinately (in the place of God), or contrary to the will of God, the individual is tempted. This can be due to many factors including the individual's past indulgence in this particular good.

Courageously facing temptation is a test of one's faithfulness to Christ. The daily challenge is to decide whether to go along with the values of the world ("The spirit of the world" (I Corinthians 2:12)) and the 'strong man', or does he reaffirm his commitment to Christ. There are many factors here but chief among them is the individual's level of egoism and resulting self-love. The love of self, and one's indulgence of self, take away from a full commitment to Jesus Christ. (Cf. Luke 9:62) Pastorally, many spiritual writers offer complete training programs for the priest to overcome egoism and truly care for his flock and also to work to remove them from

---

[33] The temptations of the individual are usually only remotely due to Satan due to his temptation of Adam and the resulting inheritance of concupiscence that all individuals have.

the sphere of the Evil One by freeing them from their love of self. (*The Imitation of Christ* by Thomas á Kempis is just one example.)

Experiencing temptation is routine and it occasions the deeper and deeper discernment of who is one's Father, God himself or Satan. Jesus explained this in the Gospel of John:

> Jesus said to them, "If God were your Father, you would love me, for I came from God and am here; I did not come on my own, but he sent me. Why do you not understand what I am saying? Because you cannot bear to hear my word. You belong to your father the devil and you willingly carry out your father's desires. He was a murderer from the beginning and does not stand in truth, because there is no truth in him. When he tells a lie, he speaks in character, because he is a liar and the father of lies. (John 8:42-44)

Using each temptation as the occasion for a discernment in faith, one develops the repose to be found in Jesus Christ when confronting his own temptations. (Cf. Matthew 4) He was confident in his commitment to the will of God. Ultimately, Jesus says: "The Lord, your God, shall you worship and him alone shall you serve." (Matthew 4:10) This is the fullest answer to the egoism and self-love that are part of the prevailing culture in this world.

(10) Redemption

The wonder of redemption lies at the heart of the Christian message. The Second Vatican Council described redemption as follows: "To men, dead in sin, the Father gives life through Jesus Christ, until, in Christ, he brings to life their mortal bodies." (LG 4) Redemption is that dramatic. It means life rather than death. Among other ways, Christ extends his saving power in history (or time) through his Body the Church. In fact, the council could also have been speaking about the *role* of the Church herself, when it said that "by its example and its witness it accuses the world of sin and enlightens those who seek the truth." (LG 35) There is a part for the priest here!

Then further, regarding each individual Catholic, the council went on: "Christ has communicated this royal power to his disciples that they might be constituted in royal freedom and that by true penance and a holy life they might conquer the reign of sin in themselves." (LG 36) The 'royal freedom' given to the faithful means that they are potentially in the reign of grace and are able to oppose the strong man. And lastly, given the special *secular* situation of laypeople:

> let the Laity also by their combined efforts remedy the customs and conditions of the world, if they are an inducement to sin, so that they all may be conformed to the norms of justice and may favor the practice of virtue rather than hinder it. (LG 36)

Also, in a privileged way, in the liturgy of the Church, the intent of existentially opposing sin comes to the fore. So, for example, on the Friday of the First Week of Advent, the priest prays in the Collect: "Stir up your power, we pray, O Lord, and come, that with you to protect us, we may find rescue from the pressing dangers of our sins, and with you to set us free, we may be found worthy of salvation."[34] The setting-free, the new freedom that comes with grace, means that the individual gets into living a life of ongoing conversion. The priest too will require some conversion himself. According to the *Catechism*:

> For the authenticity of the Catholic message, it requires men who are themselves undergoing conversion. The whole point of conversion is accomplished in daily life by gestures of reconciliation, concern for the poor, the exercise and defense of justice and right, by the admission of faults to one's brethren, fraternal correction, revision of life, examination of conscience, spiritual direction, acceptance of suffering, endurance of persecution for the sake of righteousness. Taking up one's cross each day and following Jesus is the surest way of penance. (CCC 1435)

The Second Vatican Council itself expected this effort at conversion to influence everyone so that "even the program of [lay] secular life lets them express it by a continual conversion and by wrestling 'against the world-rulers of this darkness, against the spiritual forces of wickedness.'" (LG 35)[35]

These few sentences briefly summarize some of the theological issues involved in redemption from the individual's perspective. Notably, everyone is intimately involved in working for the conversion of themselves and others. As the *Catechism* shows (CCC 1435), conversion is one of the more evident features of every situation where devoted Catholics are to be found.

The *Catechism* (above) listed the wide range of features of conversion. These will appear again and again as the priest relates to his Bishop, to laypeople and how he acts in society. The backdrop to the discussion of the role of conversion in the life of the priest and the Laity, is the ever-present question: under whose power do I want to live, the strongman or God? (See Ignatius of Loyola's *Meditation on the Two Standards*!)

(11) Intellect and Will

No explanation of the effects of evil would be complete without the mention evil effects on the powers of the soul.

---

[34] Catholic Church, *The Roman Missal*, New Jersey: Catholic Book Publishing Corp., 2011, 8.
[35] Quoting Ephesians 6:12

It is not possible to understand what happens to human beings in the plan of salvation unless it is appreciated that human beings' two major powers are those of the intellect and the will. The intellect is going to be mentioned frequently because Catholicism is intellectual, in the proper sense. In the words of Aquinas, "there is one special mode [of God being in all things] belonging to the rational nature wherein God is said to be present as the object known is in the knower, and the beloved in the lover." (ST I q. 43 a. 3) In other words, knowing the truth is knowing God. The individual stands or falls on knowing the truth. This fact becomes of major significance when discussing, for example, the individual's political views. His/her views cannot be based on falsehoods. His/her political allegiances cannot be to people who lie or who are violent. Doctrinally too, the wrong doctrine leads to the wrong god. Another reminder from Aquinas: "the rational creature by its operation of knowledge and love attains to God Himself." (ST I q.43 a.3) This is a core principle in Catholicism!

Now, even after redemption, concupiscence (effects of original sin) remains, and sin remains, and these change the powers of the human being himself. This fact is not appreciated by some Clergy or Laity otherwise there would be fewer rationalizations starting with words like "I think . . ." and a lot more "Catholic doctrine says . . ." One hears this rarely enough. Technically, the good of human nature involves three goods: (i) the good of human nature regarding its principles, that is the principles of human nature and the properties that come from them such as the powers of the soul; (ii) the inclination to virtue; (iii) "the gift of original justice," (ST II-I q. 85 a. 1) Then, in Aquinas' summary, sin has the following effects on these goods: "the first-mentioned good of nature is neither destroyed nor diminished by sin. The third good of nature was entirely destroyed through the sin of our first parent. But the second good of nature, viz. the natural inclination to virtue, is diminished by sin." (ST II-I q.85 a. 1) It is damaged.

However, the powers of the soul (the intellect and the will) are also changed by sin via the operation of the passions. Just look at two of the questions that Aquinas poses: "(1) Can a passion of the sensitive appetite move or incline the will? (2) Can it overcome the reason against the latter's knowledge?" (ST II-I q.77) His answer is yes to both of them. Without dealing with the details of the argument, apparently sin can affect how one uses one's will and one's intellect. Furthermore, concupiscence affects both intellect and will as well. These concepts are important for the discussion of the various theological relationships that involve the priest and also for the intellectual life of the priest. (Chapter Nine.)

Hence, our knowing and our willing are not as absolute or as accurate as they appear to us to be or as many philosophers imagine their own knowing and willing to be. Quoting the philosopher Ortega y Gasset: concerning such people: "this creature does not '*appeal from his own to any authority outside him.* He is satisfied with himself exactly as he is. . .. He will tend to consider and affirm as good everything he finds within himself: opinions, appetites, preferences, tastes.'"[36] So, there is a powerful reason for humbly going back to Divine Revelation in Scripture and Tradition, for information on what has value and what does not. Reliable information about the fundamentals of human psychology, human nature, human community and society can only come from Scripture and the Tradition. These are not optional resources in the search for understanding. They are essential. Ultimately, the logic of these statements depends on everything being created through the Divine Word. (Cf. John 1:3)

Put in different terms, sin reaches into everything that people think about and choose to do. This is particularly crucial for Clergy and Laity who act as if they are 'certain' that they know better than the Church; Then there are those who don't 'like' tradition. Trying to be totally free of scripture and tradition is not a freedom at all but rather it is cutting oneself off from God who has revealed how best to understand humanity, the humanity that he created. Everything depends on the quality of the person's training. Of course, it is the priest's responsibility to know the teaching of the Church so well that he can teach others. Laypeople have the same responsibility.

If the individual fills in the gaps in his knowledge by imagining things, then he is not being responsible although he is still accountable. The problem is that for him, the implication is that revelation is not all true. This is an Enlightenment stance that unfortunately has nothing to substantiate it except the willfulness of the individual to give his thinking over to an elite or follow some fad, but it is untenable theologically because of the nature of the Church's particular gifts regarding preserving the truth. One of the gifts is that the teaching includes knowing that being authentically human involves knowing the truth and then following it.

(12) The Communion of Sin in practice

No chapter on evil would be complete without at least a reference to the hypocrisy of some Clergy and religious that has been uncovered worldwide with regard to the abuse of children, seminarians, adults and religious sisters and sister candidates. (This is only a part of the enormous amount of abuse taking place in society in general!) Disgusting as this phenomenon is, it is going to shape much of the day-to-day lives of new Clergy as they enter the community of Clergy even if they are not ever involved in abuse themselves.

---

[36] Quoted in George Will's column in the *Washington Post,* "Much of Today's Intelligentsia cannot Think," June 26, 2020.

Hypocrisy is diametrically opposed to good religion. Christianity epitomizes good religion in that it involves the whole human being, bodily and spiritually, as he worships God and seeks the good of all. Quoting Isaiah, Jesus described the pharisees and the scribes as follows: "This people honors me with their lips, but their hearts are far from me; in vain do they worship me, teaching as doctrines human precepts." (Matthew 15:8, 9) The human precepts do not include the light of faith and thus are poorer descriptions or responses to reality. However, Jesus was also referring to the inconsistency, in hypocrites, between the words of the individual about the faith and his/her external actions.

Earlier, John Paul II referred to the 'communion of sin' and that is something that has been exposed in parts of the Catholic Church as well as in various ecclesial communities, institutions and families in the US. The communion of sin includes the communion of concealment and downright denial, as well as that of aiding and abetting the abuse of children and seminarians in the Church. Given the secretiveness in the culture at large beyond the Church, it is not possible to know yet how much the culture of abuse outside the Church institution have contributed to the abuses inside the Church. But here are some suggestive facts . . .

In the general US culture: "1 in 4 women and 1 out of 6 men are sexually abused in their lifetime." (Department of Justice)[37] This is horrifying in itself, and yet it is not even close to being acknowledged and addressed.

In the Church, the John Jay Study reported:

• Dioceses and eparchies reported that allegations of child sexual abuse had been made against 4,692 priests and deacons for incidents that took place while these men were serving in ecclesiastical ministry. Individual survey forms were submitted for 4,557 of these priests. Of these, the statistics in some surveys had to be eliminated because the victim was 18 or older or the date of the alleged incident was prior to 1950 or after 2002.

• Religious communities reported that allegations of sexual abuse had been made against 647 priests who were members of their communities. Dioceses reported a number of additional religious priests, for the study's total of 929 religious priests when the repeated numbers are removed.[38]

---

[37] https://centerforfamilyjustice.org/community-education/statistics/
[38] John Jay College of Criminal Justice – The City University of New York, *The Nature and Scope of Sexual Abuse of Minors by Catholic Priests and Deacons in the United States 1950-2002* USCCB 2004, 24.

To give some context to the above figures, the CARA organization noted that there were 41,399 priests in the US in 2005.[39] In the same year, there were 14,574 permanent deacons. So, in fact, there are many thousands of Clergy who innocently go about their work. Also, there were 18000 Religious Men in the US in 2015.[40] However, not even one occurrence of abuse is acceptable. One must also note that the John Jay figures are for *allegations*. Sometimes one priest or deacon has many allegations against him. Sometimes these allegations are not true.

(13) Conclusion

First, already in the Old Testament, God is unique and sovereign and, in the words of Hans Urs von Balthasar: "Yahweh creates not only light and darkness but also weal and woe (Isaiah 45:7), which means that he is Lord, standing above both of them."[41] The weal and woe that he mentions refers to "light and darkness, order and chaos."[42] The spatial metaphor indicates the sovereign power and authority of God— 'standing above' all of reality. Simultaneously, in this context, the Devil is merely a creature and in no way as powerful as God!

Second: "God formed man to be imperishable; the image of his own nature he made him. But by the envy of the devil, death entered the world, and they who belong to his company experience it." (Wisdom 2:23, 24) Death and other things are in the power of Satan. This is not the place to explore the existence of the Devil in more detail[43].

Third: the Spirit of this world still operates but most sins that man commits are due to faults in the exercise of his own ego. Spirits may suggest things, but he still has his will.

Fourth: our intellects and wills are not as pure or as accurate as they appear. But, of course, one does not know what one does not know.

Lastly, there is the stupendous appearance of Jesus Christ, the Incarnate Son of God, into this world. He is the New Covenant. This glorious event created a remarkable situation, where, in the words of John's Gospel: "the light shines in the darkness, and the darkness has not overcome it." (John 1:5) So, on the one hand, by his presence in human history, Jesus splits the spiritual realm. Evil has not yet disappeared from the

---

[39] Center for Applied Research in the Apostolate, *Frequently requested Church Statistics*, Washington DC, CARA, 2019.
[40] Center for Applied Research in the Apostolate, Special Report, 2015.
[41] Hans Urs von Balthasar, *Theodrama - Theological Dramatic Theory III Dramatis Personae: Persons in Christ*, San Francisco: Ignatius Press, 1992, 475. (Volumes in this series will be referred to by the abbreviation TD.)
[42] From the NAB commentary to Isaiah 45:7.
[43] To do so would be morbid unless one has the vocation and the office of exorcist!

world but the 'finger of God' acts in all who choose to believe in the God of Abraham, Isaac and Jacob. He appears, on earth, in Jesus Christ who is God and man.

Chapter Two Jesus Christ - The Savior

We have seen and testify that the Father sent his Son as savior of the world. (1 John 4:14)

(1) Introduction

The *Letter to the Hebrews* starts with the words:

> In times past, God spoke in partial and various ways to our ancestors through the prophets; in these last days, he spoke to us through a son, whom he made heir of all things and through whom he created the universe, who is the refulgence of his glory, the very imprint of his being, and who sustains all things by his mighty word. When he had accomplished purification from sins, he took his seat at the right hand of the Majesty on high. (Hebrews 1:1-3)

God started revealing himself in what became the Hebrew Testament, in the history of Israel, through various mediators (prophets, priests and kings) and now reveals himself in a profoundly new way through the Incarnation of his divine Son in the history of Israel. He is manifested as the fulfilment of the ancient Old Testament mediatory roles so that *he* is the Prophet, the Priest and the King. These are the ways that God communicates with his people either in the Old Testament or in the New Testament, although in different ways.

In the text from Hebrews, not only is the Son the one through whom the universe was made (cf. John 1:10) but he is the one who achieved the "purification" of humanity, freeing them from sin. Other texts refer to the *sanctification* of the people who have been redeemed. So, for example, the author refers to the "holy 'brothers,' sharing in a heavenly calling." (Hebrews 3:1)

There is ontological symmetry between the creation of the world and the redemption of the world through the Incarnate Word.[44] Paul expressed this symmetry in his letter to the Corinthian Church: "just as in Adam all die, so too in Christ shall all be brought to life." (I Corinthians 15:22) (According to the commentators: 'Adam' is "a common noun for mankind and a proper noun for the first man."[45]) This insight comes to the fore when the Second Vatican Council spoke of the Son and his role in the New Creation in Christ:

---

[44] Thomas Aquinas structured his *Summa* to follow what is found in the Scriptures and the Tradition, so he starts with the fact that everything comes from God (creation) and then is redeemed and returned to God in Christ. This was not an externally imposed structure but the uncovering of the structure of reality itself!

[45] Cf. Comment on this text in *New American Bible*, 1987.

In the human nature united to himself, the Son of God, by overcoming death through his own death and resurrection, redeemed man and re-molded him into a new creation. By communicating his Spirit, Christ made his brothers, called together from all nations, mystically the components of his own Body. (LG 7)

With the life, death and resurrection of Christ, the world became the monstrance of the Divine Son, for the glory of the Father, through the power of the Holy Spirit. In the process, creation is doing what it is meant to be doing, giving glory to the Father. (Psalm 19:1-7) In two sentences, the council neatly summarized the Catholic understanding of who the incarnate Son is, and further, what the Church is, at the same time. Notice the centrality of the role of human nature, this precious thing. This means that pastorally, priests are not dealing with mere human units but with real unique persons who live body and soul in this world and where they are called to live well. Note too how the council used both the terms "Son" and "Christ" and this needs some explanation and that comes in the next section. These concepts move the search for the meaning of the Church and of the Catholic priesthood forward significantly.

(2) The Divine Trinity

The beginning of all reality is God himself. God, dwelling in unapproachable light, is the Divine Trinity of three persons, the Father, Son and Holy Spirit, each possessing the fullness of the one divinity. Through the People of God's history in the Old and New Testaments, the people learned about God as Father, Son and Holy Spirit through their encounters with him. This is not the place to do a detailed theology of the Trinity—one can look in the *Summa Theologica*, or Augustine's *The Trinity*, for that. The next step is to consider the . . .

(3) The Trinity and the World

First, consider Creation itself.[46] In the prologue to his *Commentary on the Sentences* of Peter Lombard. Aquinas quotes the prophet Sirach:

I, wisdom, have poured out rivers. I, like a brook out of a river of mighty water: I, like a channel of a river, and like an aqueduct, came out of paradise. I said: 'I will water my garden of plants and I will water abundantly the fruits of my meadow.' (Sirach 24:40-42)[47]

---

[46] Following Hans Urs von Balthasar, *Theodrama V: The Last Act*, San Franciso: Ignatius Press, 1998, pp.61ff. In the *New American Bible*, the scripture reference is to Sirach 24:30-32.

[47] Thomas Aquinas, *Commentary on the Sentences*, trans. Scott M. Sullivan, at https://scottmsullivan.com/AquinasWorks/Sentences.html

Wisdom is another title for the Divine Son. John the Evangelist simply refers to him as the "Word" with all the theology of him being the *logos* of things that lies behind it. (John 1) Through the Word, Wisdom marks each creature's existence as bearing the "likeness" of the divinity. But when God's Wisdom becomes incarnate as a human being (John 1:14) then "the Son brings [the signs of wisdom] to light."[48] In his life of redemption, the One through whom everything is created now becomes the Redeemer of everything. The one who is first-born in redeemed creation (cf. Colossians 1:15) now "directs into creation those streams of grace—the Church, the sacraments, the various orders of saints—that ultimately 'flow from the wound in his side.'"[49]

Now, already, in the latter parts of the Old Testament, there was mention of the coming of God's anointed One. (In Hebrew, Messiah) In the *Book of Psalms*, for example: "I will bless Zion with provisions; its poor I will fill with bread. will clothe its priests with salvation; its devout shall shout for joy. There I will make a horn sprout for David; I will set a lamp for my anointed." (Psalm 132: 15-17) The 'horn' refers to the anointed one coming from the House of David.

(4) Revelation and Mediation

The concept of creation in the image of God inevitably introduces the topic of God's revelation of himself through his creation and to his creation. Thus, one can distinguish between a human beings' natural knowledge of God and his knowledge of the revelation of God. The distinction is made as follows:

> By natural reason man can know God with certainty, on the basis of his works. But there is another order of knowledge, which man cannot possibly arrive at by his own powers: the order of Divine Revelation. Through an utterly free decision, God has revealed himself and given himself to man. This he does by revealing the mystery, his plan of loving goodness, formed from all eternity in Christ, for the benefit of all men. God has fully revealed this plan by sending us his beloved Son, our Lord Jesus Christ, and the Holy Spirit. (CCC 50)

Expanding on what the *Catechism* says: people can grasp the first order of knowledge somewhat easily by paying reasoned[50] attention to the natural world. If people are not malign, they will uncover some sense of the goodness, beauty and truth of God just from observing the world around them. This is because of the divine imprint on creation because God is the original and eternal One, Good, Beauty, and Truth. By its creation, the world then manifests goodness, beauty and truth itself.

---

[48] *TD V* 61. Von Balthasar again quotes Aquinas' Prologue to the *Sentences*.
[49] *TD V* 62.
[50] This means using reason in the proper sense explained by *Fides et ratio*.

Moreover, there is a second order of knowledge and that is the order of Divine Revelation—also mentioned in the quotation from the *Letter to the Hebrews*. The 'mediators' in the quotation mediate between the order of revelation and the order of creation—the world. In the Old Testament, there were the heads of clans such as Abraham and Moses, for example. They acted as prophets, priests and kings for their people. Then, there were the prophets, and this is apparent in the books of the prophets, for example. There were the kings such as those in the *Book of Kings* and I and II Samuel, for example. In I and II Samuel and *Chronicles*, can be found prophets who also acted as priests, like Samuel and Zadok the priest, just to mention two. The Old Testament mediators were the righteous prophets, priests and kings of Israel.

The complete human response to Divine Revelation involves the individual having the theological virtue of faith. Faith is the graced commitment to God of the complete human being, body and soul. Then, as Thomas Aquinas explained: "in order that a man arrive at the perfect vision of heavenly happiness, he must first of all believe God, as a disciple believes the master who is teaching him." (ST II II q.2 a.3) Importantly, for man to even be able to appreciate what God is revealing, man needs God's grace. The council taught that: "To make this act of faith, the grace of God and the interior help of the Holy Spirit must precede and assist, moving the heart and turning it to God, opening the eyes of the mind and giving 'joy and ease to everyone in assenting to the truth and believing it.'" (DV 5)[51] Within the person, God goes ahead of the operation of the person so that he can grace the person to enable the theological virtue of faith in him/her, to be able to grasp and appreciate what he is revealing. Lastly, God himself is the one who himself interprets what he has revealed. His Spirit in the Church guarantees that the Church comes to the correct meaning of what has been revealed and can do so authoritatively in her Magisterium.

Now for a little history: from about the sixth century before the time of Christ: the Jewish people increasingly expected that at the appropriate point in the future, God would send his Anointed One—also known, from the Hebrew word for anointing, as the Messiah.[52] When this word was translated into Latin, it became *Christus* or in English, Christ.

(5) Jesus Christ
The fullest possible revelation of God to human beings took place in Jesus Christ.

---

[51] Quoting Second Council of Orange, Canon 7.
[52] Isaiah 61:1; Daniel 9:25.

It is clear from the Gospels that Jesus Christ is the incarnate divine Son of God.[53] The Incarnation involves his divine nature and his human nature being united in the person of the Son. Technically, this is called the hypostatic union. This comes from the ecclesiastical Greek for person, *hypostasis*. The one person is that of the Divine Son. This happens at the will of the Divine Father, through the power of the Divine Spirit. The Trinity does not come apart, so to speak.

One question is: why was it the Son and not one of the other divine persons? As was said earlier, God is an eternal unity of three persons, Father, Son and Spirit in one divine substance. (CCC 50)

Starting at the beginning: out of its boundless goodness, the divine Trinity freely creates the world and freely wishes the salvation of the world.

Imagining that just any divine person could have become incarnate, actually diminishes the meaning of the term 'person' by not grasping what the eternal relations between the divine persons mean. They are the foundations of our notion of person. More formally, the mistake is to miss "the relative proprieties of each person."[54] What this means is that the term 'person' as used to describe the nature of the divinity has nuances of meaning that are revealed as salvation unfolds.[55] The nuances show up in the Scriptures and the Tradition of the Church. Finally, the ecclesial definition of a "person" in the Trinity is so specialized,[56] that presenting the theology of the Incarnation has to be done very carefully.

> A divine person: In the Trinity, the persons are the terms (ends) of the divine relations immanent in the one divine substance. In addition, Scripture speaks of things like the names of the persons, as Father, Son and Spirit. Then, in Aquinas' words: "divine Scripture uses, in relation to God, names which signify procession." (ST I q.27 a.1) In other words, some persons proceed eternally from others.

---

[53] "And a voice came from the heavens, saying, "This is my beloved Son, with whom I am well pleased."(Matthew 3:17); "They cried out: 'What have you to do with us, Son of God?'" (Matthew 8:29); "The beginning of the gospel of Jesus Christ [the Son of God]." (Mark 1:1)

[54] Alois Grillmeier, "III Christology," *Encyclopedia of Theology – A Concise Sacramentum Mundi*, Karl Rahner ed., London: Burns and Oates, 1975.

[55] One could also present the explanation of persons and missions in terms of appropriation. Thus: "In appropriation some divine characteristic, activity, or effect that belongs equally to all three persons is thought and spoken of as belonging to one of the three. This manner of thinking and speaking is not merely an invention of men but is sanctioned by God himself, who inspired the writers of the New Testament in their use of appropriation." J.B. Endres, "Appropriation," *New Catholic Encyclopedia*, Detroit MI: Gale, 2003.

[56] The modern sociological and psychological definition of person is totally inadequate and often inaccurate!

Further, the divine Father is the unoriginated origin; the divine Son is eternally generated by the Father and returns all to the Father eternally (filiation). The Holy Spirit is eternally 'breathed' by the Father and the Son (active spiration) and returns all to them eternally (passive spiration). So then, the eternal procession of the Son becomes the mission of the Son to creation and is concrete in time and space (history). And the eternal procession of the Spirit becomes the exercise of divine power where "in the Spirit that which was accomplished by the Son is inwardly appropriated by the redeemed."[57] The concept of these two missions, and our participation in them, is the foundation of the theology of Christ, his Church and his priests. The whole unfolding of salvation in the world is the result of the two divine missions in the world at the will of the Father and for his eternal glory.

This metaphysical thinking leads to the notion of Jesus Christ and his Church bringing about the inclusion of the world in the divine missions. Jesus Christ knew that he was both receiving everything from his Divine Father and returning everything to his divine Father in the power of the Spirit, and he knew this all the time. The priest's participation in the glorified presence of Christ will be treated in the next chapter.

(a) Jesus Christ in History

The New Testament is embodied in the historical figure of this Anointed One, namely in the Jew, Jesus of Nazareth. According to the Catholic Church and the Old Testament, the history of the Jewish people had been moving towards this amazing event when God would manifest himself in history in a new way. By becoming a human being, the Divine Son entered the history of the Jewish people as Jesus of Nazareth. The whole of the Old Testament was straining forward to the moment when he would be born and in fact the Church's study of the Old Testament can teach a great deal about what his life means. Even the Church's writers of the New Testament frequently used the Old Testament to present the meaning of events in Jesus' life.

Introducing the term 'history' points to the fact that to understand Jesus Christ, a hermeneutic of history is needed and it comes back repeatedly in the understanding of the theology of the priesthood.[58] In this hermeneutic, the first

---

[57] Alois Grillmeier, ibidem.

[58] The point here is that one needs an anthropology that is drawn from reality to help clarify the priesthood. This is a theological anthropology and not an anthropology derived from Descartes or Hume or any of the theorists (guessers might be better!) who did not use the revelations about the nature of human beings as their starting point even though revelation is the only valid starting point if one wants one's thought to best conform to reality. In faith, there is a fundamental commitment to the content of revelation being real and meaningful

34

principle is that each individual person lives with a past, a present and a future. Even the divine Jesus Christ himself lives with a human being's past, a present and a future. This was important to the evangelists who used genealogies to situate the history of Jesus. (See Matthew 1:1-17 and Luke 3:23-38.) The Gospel genealogies form part of a stylized history, of course, because they present a *theological* history of Jesus. The mention of 'theology' is crucial here because the concern is much more than the simple idea that events cause other events. Theologically this is salvation history. The genealogies list some major figures in the *history of salvation* of the People of God to situate Jesus in the history of the nation of Israel. This shows both the fullness of his humanity and his destiny to be the one who "will save his people from their sins" through his humanity. (Matthew 1:21)

The second principle is that Jesus Christ and every other person on earth is not a solitary individual isolated in a bubble of selfhood but rather he/she lives in the communion of humanity by sharing in a common human nature and a communion of life for God. Jesus was born in the Old Testament People of God. Before his birth, the People of God already had a more than two-thousand-year history of dealing with God — "I will maintain my covenant between me and you and your descendants after you throughout the ages as an everlasting covenant, to be your God and the God of your descendants after you." (Genesis 17:7) These were God's words to Abraham. Subsequently Paul would say to the Christians "follow the faith of Abraham, who is the father of all of us" in the faith. (Romans 4:16)

These are the basic elements of the historical hermeneutic that the Second Vatican Council gathered together as follows:

> God, however, does not make men holy and save them merely as individuals, without bond or link between one another. Rather has it pleased him to bring men together as one people, a people which acknowledges him in truth and serves him in holiness. He therefore chose the race of Israel as a people unto himself. With it he set up a covenant. Step by step he taught and prepared this people, making known in its history both himself and the decree of his will and making it holy unto himself. All these things, however, were done by way of preparation and as a figure of that new and perfect covenant, which was to be ratified in Christ, and of that fuller revelation which was to be given through the Word of God himself made flesh. (LG 9)

---

and not being interchangeable with secular anthropologies, for example. On the other hand, not believing in revelation impairs the quality of the concepts that one forms. It is surprisingly easy to bend Christian revelation to fit secular (pagan) philosophies. This messes up the quality of preaching, pastoral practice, service to the community etc. and makes them anti-human, non-Christian and untrue.

The council summarized what had been learned about the theological sociology contained in the history of salvation and how the community functions in passing on the faith. These are some fundamental concepts for the theology of priesthood. (See Chapter Four.)

When Vatican II referred to 'this people', they meant the New People of God that was founded from within the Old People of God. This People was founded by Christ through his life, death and resurrection. This People was described by Peter, using terms from the ancient prophecies, as "a chosen race, a royal priesthood, a holy nation, a purchased people . . . who in times past were not a people but are now the people of God." (1 Peter. 2:9-10)[59] Peter used the oracles from Moses' words in the Book of Exodus namely: "You will be to me a kingdom of priests, a holy nation. That is what you must tell the Israelites." (Ex 19:6). The same promise appeared much later in one of the oracles that God spoke through Isaiah: "You yourselves shall be called 'Priests of the Lord,' 'Ministers of our God' you shall be called." (Isaiah 61:6)

Old Testament writers used liturgical terms such as priests and ministers in their descriptions so evidently the language of liturgical activity is significant for understanding the history of salvation (cf. this method was then used in the *Letter to the Hebrews*, for example) as well as for realizing the purpose of the life of a community of people living before God. The concept of liturgy helps clarify the way relationships work in a community that has a transcendent dimension and these are something that the priest has to know about.

(6) Liturgy – The Mystery of Christ

The *Catholic Encyclopedia* says that: "Liturgy (*leitourgia*) is a Greek composite word meaning originally 'a public duty', a service to the state undertaken by a citizen."[60] Transposing the pagan terms into the Christian context, every Catholic (like the citizen of old) has a 'public duty' to make an offering to God for his people and for the world. This is a 'service' that constitutes the community (like the service of the citizens of a state makes the state happen) as the People of God, who are acknowledging and developing their duty towards God and neighbor by participating in the liturgy which then becomes a template of life.

Catholic thought appropriated the term 'liturgy' and redirected it (purifying its pagan aspects) to refer to the public offering of sacrifice to the God who made everything

---

[59] Cf. Isaiah 65:9.
[60] A. Fortesque, "Liturgy," *The Catholic Encyclopedia*. New York: Robert Appleton Company. 1910.

and to whom everything should be returned in thanksgiving (Eucharist). This is the God of Jesus Christ who "made us into a kingdom, priests for his God and Father, to him be glory and power forever and ever. Amen." (Revelation 1:6.) In more formal terms, the Second Vatican Council stated that

> the liturgy, 'through which the work of our redemption is accomplished,' most of all in the divine sacrifice of the Eucharist, is the outstanding means whereby the faithful may express in their lives, and manifest to others, the mystery of Christ and the real nature of the true Church. (SC 1)[61]

But how did the Church-community come about? It came about by the social-spiritual effects of the life, death and resurrection of Christ himself, fulfilling God's moral, cultic and juridical requirements from the Old Testament, from the privileges of his glory.

(7) The Redeeming Savior

Something more about Jesus of Nazareth can be found in St. Paul's writings. His *Letter to the Romans* explains:

> For what the law, weakened by the flesh, was powerless to do, this God has done: by sending his own Son in the likeness of sinful flesh and for the sake of sin, he condemned sin in the flesh, so that the righteous decree of the law might be fulfilled in us, who live not according to the flesh but according to the spirit. (Romans 8:3-4)[62]

Paul has identified the main elements of the Savior's mission: salvation (from Latin - *salvare* to heal) is the act of God through Jesus Christ where Jesus fulfils all the requirements of the Law. Further, Christ's actions express his mission from God. He takes on the sin of the world in his flesh. Finally, Jesus is the beginning of a new life for men and women in the Spirit of God rather than simply in the flesh.

The reflection on Christ here is from the perspective of what he does—his salvific mission. The *Letter to the Hebrews* says: "reflect on Jesus, the apostle and high priest of our confession." (Hebrews 3:1) The word 'apostle' is important. It translates the Greek *apostolos*—the one sent. Paul (above) left some open issues in the quotation from Romans—(i) whose law is it? (ii) who sends Jesus? (iii) Atonement.

---

[61] The council was quoting from the Secret of the Ninth Sunday after Pentecost. The Secret was the priest's prayer at the end of the Offertory before the liturgy was changed after the council.

[62] This text was written in the Church and for the Church. The Church is the only place where Jesus is fully understood.

(i) Whose Law is it?

The term 'law' refers to both the Law given to Moses (the Old Law, which is not abrogated by the coming of Jesus), and the New Law, the law of grace given in Jesus Christ (cf. the Beatitudes in Matthew 5:3-10). Thomas Aquinas spoke of the Old Law in this way: "The old law was given by the good God." (ST II-I q.98 a.2) He further noted that the old law had three parts to it that completely structured the life of Israel: there was the moral law, the ceremonial law and the judicial law. (ST II-I qq. 98-104.) In other words, the ordering of the existence of the People of God has a divinely instituted structure and similarly there is a divinely instituted structure to the existence of the New People of God.

The three types of law shape the three dimensions of the existence and mission of Jesus Christ, and consequently of the Church and its mission. Furthermore, it was and is possible to know the moral law in the Old Testament (the Ten Commandments among the other laws) already from the Natural Law but the supernatural revelation of these commandments was needed to make sure that they were known without error.[63] Turning to the divinely instituted ceremonial law: this was to ensure the peoples' right worship of the True God. Right worship centred on sacrifice and rejected idolatry. Its basic principle was that everything comes from God and can be offered to God. Lastly, the divinely instituted judicial law: it dictated the organization of the Jewish community, especially the judicial system. It recognized the shared humanity of the people and the ways in which they had to act to protect that humanity.

Now in the New Testament: Jesus Christ, who was born in the Old Testament People of God, was born under the Mosaic Law. He came to fulfil the Mosaic Law, not to deny it. (Matthew 5:17) The moral law was specifically retained but within the framework of Jesus' law of love. The goals of the Old Testament ceremonial law were fulfilled by the sacrifice at the heart of the New Testament, the sacrifice of Jesus Christ on the cross.

---

[63] Michael Dauphinais and Matthew Levering, *Knowing the Love of Christ*, Notre Dame IN: University of Notre Dame Press, 2002, 67.

Thirdly, the juridical rules were fulfilled in the New Testament institution of the universal Kingdom (community) of God.[64]

Considering the difference between the Old Law and the New, Aquinas referred to a prophecy in the *Book of Jeremiah*. There God explained that he would make a new covenant with Israel and he described the difference between the Old Testament and the New: "It will not be like the covenant I made with their ancestors . . .." (Jeremiah 31:31) God then continued, describing the New Covenant that he would make: "I will place my law within them, and write it upon their hearts; I will be their God, and they shall be my people." (Jeremiah 31:33) The New Covenant will be of an entirely different nature to the Old. It will be spiritual. With this important conclusion, our study turns to who sent Jesus?

(ii)   Who sent Jesus?

In the first chapter of the *Letter to the Hebrews*, the writer establishes that ontologically Jesus was even superior to the angels. Then chapter three shows the superiority of Jesus to Moses, the great leader. The writer also used the word 'apostle' (*apostolos*) to describe Jesus as one who is sent. (Hebrews 3:1) John the Evangelist expanded on the mission of the Son as follows: "For God so loved the world that he gave his only Son, so that everyone who believes in him might not perish but might have eternal life." (John 3:16) This is the eschatological goal of the Son's mission. It is the divine Father who sends him. In addition, John qualified the goal of the mission in the next sentence: "For God did not send his Son into the world to condemn the world, but that the world might be saved through him." (John 3:17) He means that God intends salvation for all that exists except for the people who rebel.

The fact is that the Father *sends* the Divine Son through the power of the Spirit and in doing so "he establishes, guides and takes responsibility for Jesus' whole existence on earth."[65] In return, Jesus understands his whole existence in terms of having come to do the will of the Father. Importantly then, doing the Father's will is not added-on to whatever else he is doing on his own account according to his own will—as some priests seem to do in

---

[64] See an example of the practical application of the juridical laws in the Kingdom of Saint Louis IX in Andrew Willard Jones, *Before Church and State—A Study of the Social Order in the Sacramental Kingdom of St. Louis IX*, Steubenville: Emmaus Academic, 2017.

[65] *TD III*, 153.

their own lives. In different terms, when Jesus does works, he is doing the Father's works (John 9:4). For example, he speaks the Father's words: "I did not speak on my own, but the Father who sent me commanded me what to say and speak." (John 12:49) In short, he is always doing the Father's will. The same principle applies to the life of a priest so that it remains coherent with his existence in Jesus Christ.

In addition, the life of the one who is sent *recapitulates* revelation.[66] The Father is actually seen in the one who is sent— "whoever sees me sees the one who sent me." (John 12:45) The Father witnesses to himself in the one who is sent. (John 5:37; 8:18) The Father even dwells with the one who is sent. (John 8:16) In fact: "The one who sent me is with me. He has not left me alone, because I always do what is pleasing to him." (John 8:29) In addition, something amazing happens in the one who is sent, the Father is "known" and not just seen. (John 15:21) The Father is also "believed". (John 5:24) And the Father is "honored." (John 5:23) In fact, the Son "is so dependent on the One who sends him that his whole being is in motion toward him."[67]

Moreover, what has been said about the interrelationship between the Father and the Son in the Holy Spirit has all kinds of implications for one (like the priest) who participates by adoption in the One who is sent. The Johannine texts amplify that aspect: the one who participates is "born of God." (John 1:13) He will be "born anew." (John 3:5) Thus, when considering Christ's sending someone who is in his Spirit: the sending is more than a kind of appointment or delegation. It is also total in that he is doing the will of the Father usually mediated through his Bishop.

The one who is sent by Jesus somehow lives an extension of Jesus' own power and mission. However, this is not like someone merely having a conviction that he/she has a mission. Che Guevara thought that he had a mission, but his pathological history means that it was only his own murderous conviction that he was exercising. In salvation history, "this mission could only be fulfilled by stepping beyond what could be achieved within a mortal life" with its mortal abilities.[68] Jesus and his ministers do what

---

[66] Cf. *TD III*, 153.
[67] *TD III*, 153.
[68] *TD III*, 159.

is more than what comes from mere human determination. That word 'more' deserves further explanation.

(iii)   Atonement

To explain the 'more' referred to in the last section: In the quotation from Romans above, Paul says that "by sending his own Son in the likeness of sinful flesh and for the sake of sin, [God] condemned sin in the flesh." (Romans 8: 3-4) God is using his Son to deal with sin, through the power of the Spirit. The Divine Spirit is the one "who is able to accomplish far more than all we ask or imagine." (Ephesians 8:20) The whole Trinity then is involved in removing the sin of the world. On the Cross. God takes on sin in the flesh of Jesus of Nazareth, the Incarnate Son of God. The Incarnation happens through the power of the Spirit.

Atonement is the only theological term that comes from English. It means to be made one. So, in this case, humanity is once more united with God because Jesus has made the satisfaction for our sins. This satisfaction is required because of the workings of Divine Justice. Mankind has revolted against God's Divine Majesty and satisfaction must be made. Now, God is omnipotently merciful, but his mercy does not cancel the need for justice to be satisfied. So, mercy needs to be carefully understood. Hence, "God acts mercifully, not indeed by going against His justice, but by doing something more than justice; thus a man who pays another two hundred pieces of money, though owing him only one hundred, does nothing against justice, but acts liberally or mercifully." (ST I q. 21 a. 3) So, there is no contradiction to speak of a just God and merciful God when speaking of atonement. Aquinas concludes: "mercy does not destroy justice, but in a sense is the fulness thereof." (ST I q.21 a.3)

Now, "'Atone' was coined from 'at' and 'one' and signifies to set at one, to reconcile."[69] It is the answer to mankind's rebellion. Oneness is a recurring theme in Jesus' teaching. It is rooted in the unity of God: "I and the Father are one." (John 10:30) It leads to one believing community: "there shall be one flock and one shepherd." (John 10:16) And: "Holy Father, protect them by the power of your name, the name you gave me, so that they may be one as we are one." (John 10:30) This unity has a fundamental value for the mission of the Church: "that all of them may be one, Father, just as you are in me and I am in you. May they also be in us so that the world may

---

[69] K.F Dougherty, "Atonement," *New Catholic Encyclopedia*, Gale Publishing: Detroit MI, 2003.

believe that you have sent me." (John 17:21) The oneness is oneness with God: "Anyone who loves me will obey my teaching. My Father will love them, and we will come to them and make our home with them." (John 14:23) The divine unity is the foundation of unity in the community, in the mission and of life eternal.

How does one come to his oneness with God? First, he has to have faith: "without faith it is impossible to please him." (Hebrews 11:6) Second, he must know that "at present we do not see 'all things subject to him'." (Hebrews 2:8) Third, the *Letter to the Hebrews* states that Jesus "is the leader of their salvation." (Hebrews 2:10) He is the one working out our salvation in his own being.

As the individual is drawn into the work of Christ, Christ continues his work of reparation and atonement. See, for example: where Paul describes his own experience, namely that "in my flesh I am filling up what is lacking in the afflictions of Christ on behalf of his body, which is the Church." (Colossians 1:24) Christ's work continues right in the process of conversion, healing and inclusion of the individual in the Body of Christ. Notably, not one of the sufferings of the faithful individual is lost, it all furthers the redemption of the world.

Nevertheless, there is always the consequence that: "If we sin deliberately after receiving knowledge of the truth, there no longer remains sacrifice for sins but a fearful prospect of judgment and a flaming fire that is going to consume the adversaries." (Hebrews 10:26, 27) One might always go against the truth of Jesus Christ and apostasize.

(8) Jesus' Life/The Priest's Life

Reflecting on Jesus' life and ministry clarifies that what he does elevates ordinary human existence because he is always following the three kinds of laws—moral, cultic and societal. This specifically is how he constitutes the life and ministry of priests and finally in his glory.[70] After all: "I will give you shepherds after my own heart." (Jeremiah 3:15)

To start with, why did the divine *Son* assume human nature? This is important for the understanding of ministry. Fundamentally ministry has to do with sharing Divine Wisdom and grace. Long before the time of Christ, the prophet Baruch had prophesied about the Wisdom of God. He says that "she has appeared on earth, [and] is at home with mortals." (Baruch 3:38) By 'she,' he was referring to the

---

[70] The word 'minister' comes from the Latin *minus* meaning 'less'. The individual minister is under the authority of another, namely the Bishop. He is the lesser in the relationship.

Wisdom of God, someone who is personified. This is the New American Bible translation. In one translation of the *Summa Theologiæ of St. Thomas Aquinas*,[71] these words come out as: "Afterwards he was seen upon earth and conversed with men." (Baruch 3:38) Here is the answer to the initial question. This is part of what Jesus is adding to his elevation of human existence. (Cf. John 1)

The sense of the translations reveals something else too. God uses the appropriate means of communication to mediate his wisdom and to reach human beings who receive information through their senses. The Incarnate Wisdom of God is 'seen' and 'converses with men'. Note the wonderful condescension of God in trying to reach human beings at their level despite their rebellion. Paul explained the mystery in this way: "Who, though he was in the form of God, did not regard equality with God something to be grasped. Rather, he emptied himself, taking the form of a slave, coming in human likeness; and found human in appearance." (Philippians 2:6, 7) Then the necessary visibility/ audibility of the Savior continues in the visibility /audibility of the Church and through her ministers, her sacraments and her community as well.

Priests would do well to really treasure this principle. It is at the heart of the visibility of Christ's work of salvation and their part in it. The concept severely limits how much priests can try to be upper class and superior or celebrate the sacraments badly or be unseen by those who are sick (instead of personally going and seeing them) or invisible to those who are being taught the faith etc. The giving of salvation audibly and visibly imposes a specific presence, psychology, and intentionality in the day-to-day existence of the Clergy.

The way that Christ's life is sacrificial should indicate how every difficulty that a priest faces, from the ways that his own personality trips him up, to the difficulties in pastoral work and working in a diocese, all become part of his sacrifice to Almighty God. Laity have the same route to follow. Their sacrifices help them develop a lifestyle that takes note of sacrifice and consciously prays to contribute to Christ's sacrifice for the redemption of the world.

Also, Clergy need to communicate confidently. The *Program for Priestly Formation* explains that the candidate should be: "A free person: a person who is free to be who he is in God's design, someone who does not—in contrast to the popular culture—conceive or pursue freedom as the expansion of options or as individual autonomy detached from others."[72] Real freedom grows in real relationships i.e. relationships

---

[71] Second and Revised Edition, 1920.
[72] US Conference of Catholic Bishops, *Program for Priestly Formation*, 2005, article 76, 30.

that are ordered by the will of God. This vital characteristic of true freedom shows why so much time is spent helping the candidate deepen his humanity—learning how to be loving beyond 20-minutes a day, for example. It will become central to the priest's appropriate intellectual development. If a professor served him badly in a particular subject, then he should research what he still needs to read.

The priest has to think in a way that elevates his own humanity and that of everyone around him. This anthropological perspective on the intellect respects "the intrinsic relationship between the knowledge gained in theological preparation and the ecclesial dimensions of priestly service, since the education of a priest is never seen in isolation from the Tradition of the Church."[73] This sentence also comes from the *Program for Priestly Formation*. It sums up the intellectual context of the priest's formation and growth. This particular perspective on priestly knowledge is not simply an option that would be nice if it is achieved occasionally. It is intrinsic to the intellectual development of the priest who is fully functional and maturing intellectually.

Human beings exist and think within a context. The priest's intellect operates within a context. The Tradition of the Church is part of his context. As Vatican II reminded us, the Church's Tradition is part of the stream of revelation that God addresses to us.[74] The other part of revelation, related to it in myriad ways, is Sacred Scripture. Neither is optional for those who wish to think and speak theologically. The authentic priest brings this structure of thinking to every situation.

In addition, Aquinas explains that "Christ's manner of life had to be in keeping with the end of his Incarnation." (ST III q.40 a.1) Jesus' mode of life involved searching out sinners hence he had to be in the streets, the synagogues and the fields. Moreover, not only did Jesus have to be a human to communicate, but as Thomas noted, Jesus was "giving us the example [namely] to go about and seek those who perish, like the shepherd in his search of the lost sheep." (ST III q.40 a.1) Nothing is accidental in Jesus' life. He is always acting with sovereign freedom. Every second he is doing the will of his Father which is the source of true freedom. (Cf. John 4:34)

This is where a caution on social justice work is needed. Obviously social justice is an essential value in society. In many countries, social justice can be expected and indeed demanded of social and governmental institutions that already exist. The

---

[73] Ibidem. article 139, 54.
[74] Cf. Vatican II: "there exists a close connection and communication between Sacred Tradition and Sacred Scripture. For both of them, flowing from the same divine wellspring, in a certain way merge into a unity and tend toward the same end." (DV 9)

problem lies not with social justice but with where it fits into the life of the priest. If it becomes a substitute for worship and prayer, or for associating with the people that he is assigned to care for or to live with there is a problem. If it makes the priest imagine that he is superior to his fellows because he is more woke there is a problem. If it is leads the priest into promoting Leftist principles—if that is even the right word— there is a problem.

Also, Jesus' manner of life included being poor. Thomas again: "It was fitting for Christ to lead a life of poverty in this world." (ST III q.40 a.3) The concept of fittingness is vital for understanding and following Jesus and for a proper spirituality of the priesthood. Something that is fitting demonstrates divine justice. So, clearly the priesthood is associated with a simple life. This is not imposing an alien value on the priesthood. Rather the priest acts in a way appropriate to the matter at hand, namely participating in the presence and mission of Jesus. The life of Saint John Vianney, the Patron Saint of Pastors is just one example of how to do this.

(9) The Mission of Jesus

Studying Jesus from the standpoint of his mission is helpful because it tells a great deal about Jesus himself and it also helps people comprehend the priesthood in the Catholic Church—a Christ-like priesthood with a mission.

Obviously the word 'sending' refers to Jesus[75] being sent by God into the world.[76] However, when he spoke about himself, Jesus also used the word 'coming'.(cf. Matthew 5:17) Because of the particular meaning of the word Messiah (Christ, Anointed One), Jesus' *coming* into the world has to do with being in the 'place' where he does what he was sent to do. In other words, Hans Urs von Balthasar explains that Jesus was "bringing about, in his own person, an ultimate saving event."[77] This is the central mystery of the whole of the plan of salvation. The meaning of Jesus' mission depends on what von Balthasar means in this sentence.

Jesus' self-understanding depended on the purpose of his coming: "I have not come to call the righteous to repentance but sinners." (Luke 5:32) When he called sinners

---

[75] There is only one person, the Divine Son, present in Jesus of Nazareth.

[76] An important consequence of the process of God sending his Son—in other words, the Divine *Word*—means among other things that God himself reveals the meaning of what he is doing. Thus, God reveals who Jesus is, what the Church is and so on. To live an authentic life, people cannot just draw on a sociology, or a philosophy, or what some celebrity thinks when trying to explain who Jesus is. Secular intellectual experiments are no substitute for theology because no faith is involved in the experiments. The priest's accurate grasp of the meaning of who God is, who Jesus is and what the Church and the priesthood are, all depend on this fact.

[77] *TD III* 152.

to repent, Jesus did not intend to abolish any part of the law: "Do not think that I have come to abolish the law or the prophets. I have come not to abolish but to fulfil." (Matthew 5:17)[78] His coming was decisive for sinners: "Do not think that I have come to bring peace upon the earth. I have come to bring not peace but the sword." (Matthew 10:34) Jesus came to bring people to a decision about their relationship to God. The decision divides people between those who live in opposition to God and those who live in alliance with God. (Matthew 10:34) Jesus' coming was such a dramatic event that he described it as "com[ing] to set the earth on fire." (Luke 12:49) Recall John the Baptist's earlier announcement that Jesus was coming to "baptize [you] with the Holy Spirit and with fire." (Matthew 3:11) This is a fire of judgement. (Matthew 3:10) Think of the role of the priest again in all of this! Helping people to understand their rebellion against God. Following God's will leads to a full life. But this life does not go on for ever.

Then too, Jesus describes his mission in terms of service. For example: "the Son of Man did not come to be served but to serve and to give his life as a ransom for many." (Mark 10:45) One particular service was the washing of the apostles' feet in the Gospel of John. It was so important that it replaced the account of the institution of the Eucharist at the Last Supper in John's narrative. Jesus then extended this service to be continued through the apostles: "If I, therefore, the master and teacher, have washed your feet, you ought to wash one another's feet. I have given you a model to follow, so that as I have done for you, you should also do." (John 13:14, 15) This is just one way that the Apostles were included in Christ. The ontological side of inclusion in Christ will be developed in the next chapter.

(10) The Centrality of the Eucharist

In the Church, there are many ancillary organizations like the chancery offices and charitable organizations, but at the core of the Church, the mystery at the heart of the Church, is the Sacrament of the Eucharist itself: "As often as the sacrifice of the cross in which Christ our Passover was sacrificed, is celebrated on the altar, the work of our redemption is carried on, and, in the sacrament of the eucharistic bread, the unity of all believers who form one body in Christ is both expressed and brought about."(LG 3) The council has summed up the celebration of the liturgy of the Eucharist as the dynamic physical and spiritual realization of the Church community and its purpose and mission in Christ.

---

[78] A vital concept for the whole meaning of Jesus' life and the liturgy.

Chapter Three: The Church

"She is the meeting place of all mysteries" Henri de Lubac S.J.[79]

(1) Introduction

No words can capture the wonder of the Catholic Church especially while living in an Enlightenment culture that has reduced the Church to being merely one 'religious' entity among many others with equal rights before the law. Legal rights are certainly necessary and welcome but that is not where a theological presentation starts.

Significantly, Henri de Lubac SJ, the formidable 20th century scholar, started presenting the theology of the Church by reminding his readers to take the "Fathers' habitual manner of thought" seriously.[80] They did not arbitrarily select their way of thinking from a palette of possible choices of how to think, imagining that they were equally valid. The Fathers dealt with heresies on an almost daily basis and as a result they were able to distinguish modes of thinking adapted to the nature of the human being from those that were not. There was also the question of content: the reason for de Lubac's comment was that the Fathers of the Church thought about the Church by drawing on the Scriptures and the Tradition and, significantly, they were also the ones closest in time to when the Scriptures were written.

However, on the issue of method: The Fathers habitually used ontological thinking (*onto* - being) to uncover meaning because, on one hand, the philosophy of the time with its focus on the real was widespread and widely valued.[81] On the other hand, Scripture itself is written in terms of being—more specifically, on man's/woman's being before God.[82] So, despite the claims made at various times in history, the Fathers did not import metaphysics from somewhere 'outside' of man's participation in the history of salvation. The Fathers knew that paying attention to the *whole* of being was how human beings find authentic meaning for themselves.[83] (The question of context again!) Faithful to this method, each Father of the Church attended to the *whole* of Scripture and the *whole* of the Tradition up to his time.

---

[79] Henri de Lubac, *The Splendour of the Church*, San Francisco, Ignatius Press, 1986, 19.

[80] Henri de Lubac, *Catholicism - A Study of the Corporate Destiny of Mankind*, New York. NY: Sheed and Ward, 1950, 18.

[81] This mode of thinking dominated up until the 18th century when the anticlerical Enlightenment shifted the focus off the real to theories of ideas. Subjectivism took over.

[82] Cf. Matthew Levering, *Scripture and Metaphysics - Aquinas and the Renewal of Trinitarian Theology*, Blackwell Publishing, 2004.

[83] The philosopher Pope John Paul II re-emphasized this way of thinking in his *Fides et ratio*, for example.

In contrast with this history, the time between us and them is marked by the Enlightenment. Hence, the US and other 'Enlightenment' countries became trapped in the more superficial languages of politics and occasionally of law. Politicians use language chosen for its effects—this is important when one is looking for power. One has to manipulate those who will cede power to them. Legal language imposes meaning by comparing the Church with similar institutions and of course there is no other institution like the Church. Considering the Church from these limited Enlightenment starting points lacks the spiritual dimension of life and leads to a flawed understanding of the Church.

(2) The Metaphysics of Humanity

De Lubac chose his starting point carefully when presenting the nature of Catholicism.[84] He began with the nature of humanity itself, particularly as regards its natural unity.[85] When considering the Church, the nature of humanity is involved because each individual shares in the one human nature. This is crucial to any discussion of ecclesiology because the Church is about humanity. In this way of thinking, the Church exists precisely to serve humanity by bringing it all into a spiritual unity that it, in the created sense, already shares by the existence of a common nature and history under the one God. The unity of humanity among themselves and with God is wrought by the redemption and sanctification of the world by Jesus Christ through gathering the faithful into the one Church.

Humans are brought together in the Church so that each human being may better worship God in spirit and in truth and serve mankind *in* Christ. This principle is found in both Scripture[86] and the Tradition, where for example, according to the council, "the Church is in Christ like a sacrament or as a sign and instrument both of a very closely-knit union with God and of the unity of the whole human race." (LG 1) The Church as sign and instrument emphasizes the concrete visible side of the Church while including the deepest mysteries of being in Christ through the Spirit.

The Church's whole perspective on her work is toward restoring the unity of humanity[87] with God and each other. This work—including the work of priests—involves breaking down the divisions caused by sin, and restoring humanity's oneness through God's action in Christ, so that the One God may be worshipped by one

---

[84] De Lubac, *Catholicism*.

[85] Cf. Henri de Lubac S.J., "Judaism passed on to Christianity its concept of salvation as essentially social." *Catholicism*, 36.

[86] Cf. Isaiah 66:18-21 and Luke 13:22-30.

[87] Cf. The readings for the Feast of the Epiphany: Isaiah 60:1-6; Psalm 72:1-13; Ephesians 3:2-6; Matthew 2:1-12.

people.[88] Hence, also the problem with introducing divisions into the Church on political grounds!

The unity being treated here is a very special kind of unity. It is a unity at the level of being, where humanity taken as a whole is ultimately the image of the one God too. In the words of Pope Gregory the Great (540 – 604) for example: "the whole of human nature from the first man to the last is but one image of him who is."[89] Most importantly, the fact of this unity is "the foundation in practice of monotheism and its full significance."[90] So, to quote one example: the prayer the *Our Father*,[91] is based on the premise of one humanity under a common divine Father.[92] Then too, this line of thinking undergirds the concept of community as body in what Saint Paul taught the Ephesian Church:

> Christ gave apostles, prophets, evangelists, pastors and teachers, in roles of service for the faithful to build up the body of Christ, till we become one in faith and in the knowledge of God's Son, and form that perfect man who is Christ come to full stature. (Ephesians 4:11-13) (NAB 1970)

The powerful reality of unified humanity as the perfect man in Christ, is the one who is the only one who can offer perfect worship to God, says it all.

Moreover, the hoped-for unity of all humanity in Christ is preceded by the unity of a community in Christ, called the Church. Leftist thinking in the Church militates against this unity by creating divisions, dismantling the doctrines, and making them arbitrary. The Church is tasked with being God's instrument of ever greater unity among human beings. For example, we pray that the Church be "brought to the

---

[88] A more complete anthropology can be found in the *Constitution on the Church in the World*, Part One.

[89] Gregory the Great, *De hominis opificio* c.16 (PG xliv, 188), cited in *Catholicism*. See note 2.

[90] Henri de Lubac, 19. The consequences are too large to go into here but briefly, this means that there is one history of humanity and one history of salvation, the Judeo-Christian one. See Karl Rahner S.J., *Foundations of Christian Faith*, the chapters on General and Special history of Salvation.

[91] Matthew 6:9-6:13; Luke 11:2 – 11:4.

[92] See also: "one God and Father of all, who is over all and through all and in all." (Ephesians 4:6) And: "God is one and will justify the circumcised on the basis of faith and the uncircumcised through faith." (Romans 3:30) And: "He made from one the whole human race to dwell on the entire surface of the earth, and he fixed the ordered seasons and the boundaries of their regions, so that people might seek God, even perhaps grope for him and find him, though indeed he is not far from any one of us. For: 'In him we live and move and have our being,' as even some of your poets have said, 'For we too are his offspring.'" (Acts 17: 26-28)

fullness of charity." (Eucharistic Prayer II) The *Letter to the Hebrews* went into more detail on how exactly this unity came about. The writer says:

> the blood of Christ, who through the eternal spirit offered himself unblemished to God, cleanses our consciences from dead works to worship the living God. For this reason, he is mediator of a new covenant. (Hebrews 9:14, 15)

The New Covenant takes place in Jesus Christ in the union of the two natures—divine and human—in the one person of the Son (hypostatic union) and is the transforming moment in all of history.

The glorious concept of the unity of mankind is significant for what it means for the Catholic priesthood too. The priest is the instrument of Christ the unifier—something that the priest cannot be if he advocates Leftist ideology which requires division.

Thus, in sum then, the Fathers, such as Gregory of Nyssa (c. 335 – c. 395), could say:

> just as any particular man is limited by his bodily dimensions, and the peculiar size which is conjoined with the superficies of his body is the measure of his separate existence, so I think that the entire plenitude of humanity was included by the God of all, by his power of foreknowledge, as it were in one body, and that this is what the text teaches us which says, God created man, in the image of God created he him. For the image is not in part of our nature, nor is the grace in any one of the things found in that nature, but this power extends equally to all the race: and a sign of this is that mind is implanted alike in all: for all have the power of understanding and deliberating, and of all else whereby the Divine nature finds its image in that which was made according to it: the man that was manifested at the first creation of the world, and he that shall be after the consummation of all, are alike: they equally bear in themselves the Divine image. *On the Making of Man* XVI: 17[93]

It is the human's power of understanding and deliberating that chiefly images God in created human beings. Again, the proper operation of the intellect and the will are central. Here, the term 'power' refers to a quality of being itself. The most basic power is the power to exist, thus: "Being and power are identical."[94] This is the first level of power. The second level is the power to act for one's self-preservation. The third is self-determination, the quality that culminates in the giving of oneself. All human beings possess each of these levels at least in some measure. It is the third

---

[93] Gregory of Nyssa, On the Making of Man, *Nicene and Post-Nicene Fathers*, Second Series, Vol. 5. Edited by Philip Schaff and Henry Wace. (Buffalo, NY: Christian Literature Publishing Co., 1893.)

[94] Klaus Hemmerle, "Power," *Encyclopedia of Theology*, ed. Karl Rahner s.j., 1264.

power that is mostly the target of the priest's personal development of his intellect and his will and the core of his work with his people.

Studying unity from a different angle, the concept of a body contributes a great deal to the horizon of the priest's work. The Scriptures and the Tradition of the Church[95] applied the word "body" to the Church to highlight its corporate nature. Unfortunately, the term "corporate" (*corpus* – body – Latin) is one of the words that was taken over by the mercantile culture and so it must be said that the theological meaning of the word is different from its common use.

To show how different it is, one might consider the Church Fathers' notion of the threefold meaning of the word. There are three overlapping meanings of the "body" as it is informed by Jesus Christ. The first meaning refers to the physical flesh and blood body of Christ himself. As John's Gospel described the state of affairs: the Divine "Word became flesh and made his dwelling among us" (John 1:14) in his body.

Then there is the glorified Body of the Risen Lord. This mode of Christ's presence is involved in humanity's unity with Christ and is the way in which believers have communion with the Father through the Holy Spirit in the Church. Believers become the adopted sons of God. (Cf. Romans 8:15) Those who are sons of God receive certain privileges. Pius XII explained that with his glorification, Christ was given a number of privileges. Among other things, "he increased the immense treasure of graces, which, as he reigns in glory in heaven, he lavishes continually on his mortal members" in the Church. (MCC 30) The priest is at least partially involved in handing out this treasure. Another of Christ's privileges was that "all power in Heaven and earth has been given to me." (Matthew 28: 18-20.) These graces he pours out into his Church and beyond.

And finally, the third meaning of the word 'body' refers to the body of Scripture, the body of the Word.[96]

Going back to the second meaning of the word 'body': It refers to the 'Mystical Body of Christ'. In his masterpiece on the Church as the Mystical Body of Christ, Pius XII's encyclical, *Mystici Corporis Christi*, (1943), the pope says:

---

[95] See Vatican II: The Church "has always maintained, and continues to do so, [that the Scriptures] together with sacred tradition, [act] as the supreme rule of faith, since, as inspired by God and committed once and for all to writing, they impart the word of God himself without change, and make the voice of the Holy Spirit resound in the words of the prophets and Apostles." (DV 21)
[96] GL I, 529. This is the doctrine of the Alexandrian School.

The doctrine of the Mystical Body of Christ, which is the Church, was first taught us by the Redeemer himself. Illustrating as it does the great and inestimable privilege of our intimate union with so exalted a head, this doctrine by its sublime dignity invites all those who are drawn by the Holy Spirit to study it, and gives them, in the truths of which it proposes to the mind, a strong incentive to the performance of such good works as are conformable to its teaching. (MCC 1)

The teaching to which he refers can be found, for example, in the Pauline letters, where Paul says: "Now I rejoice in my sufferings for your sake, and in my flesh, I am filling up what is lacking in the afflictions of Christ on behalf of his body, which is the Church." (Colossians 1:24)

The corporateness of the Church in Christ is another basic concept needed to understand the work of the priest. The priest is the one who does his all to bring about a physical and spiritual unity to the Church. He is doing his work to make the corporateness of his parish and his diocese come about.

(3) The Metaphor of "Area"

The metaphor of the Church as Body of Christ can be further analysed using a parallel concept, the metaphor of 'area', as applied to the Church.

St. Paul constantly refers to ecclesial existence as being "in Christ." (eg. Romans 6:11)[97] On the Vigil of Easter, the Church sings of "Mother Church . . . arrayed with the lightning of his glory." (*Exsultet*) Finding language to describe the extraordinary effect of living in Christ is difficult. Back in 1644, the noted French spiritual writer Abbé Pierre de Bérulle suggested that one way would be to explore the concept of the 'acting area' that Jesus opened up in the world by his life, death and resurrection. Von Balthasar sums the concept as follows:

[in] the acting area . . . opened up as the mission proceeds, the 'I of the mission-bearer himself is rendered present; it too becomes an 'area', wherein are found those who have been touched, transformed and resettled in it.[98]

There is an analogy between the 'area' in the world opened up by the actions of Jesus where Christians can act 'in Christ' and the way a stage play advances as its narrative is moved forward by the initiatives of the lead actor. The lead actor opens up the physical, moral, psychological, intellectual and spiritual 'area' for the Christlike actions and words of the lesser actors to make the play proceed to its denouement.[99]

---

[97] Cf. Romans 12:5; 16:3 etc.
[98] See Pierre de Bérulle, *Nous devons nous loger en Jésus Christ*, 1644, cited in TD III, 231.
[99] Cf. Hans Urs von Balthasar, Theodrama III: *Dramatis Personae: Persons in Christ*, San Francisco: Ignatius Press, 1992.

Hence, the way the individual baptized person functions draws its parameters from the way Christ lived (Scriptures) and lives his life in its glorified form in and through the Church (Tradition). The Bishops are part of the ensemble of apostles around the lead actor and in conjunction with the other actors! They take their cues from Christ rather than from some party elite.

From the perspective of the idea of person: The theology of the existence of a baptized person involves a far richer understanding of 'person' than the mere psychological understanding of person as a center of consciousness. For example, Jacques Maritain, a formidable exponent of Thomism, maintained that: "The individual exists for the society, but the society exists for the person."[100] Hence there is a whole social context that is inseparable from the person. He/she is not a monad.

Furthermore, looking into the depths of the person him/herself, "The acting person constitutes himself as a person, as one utterly unique from others, by his freely chosen acts, which are not mere physical events—happenings—but rather constitutive elements of the being of the person." This summarizes the concept of person from the perspective of Karol Wojtla (John Paul II). The individual is constituted as that personal being by his/her actions.

There are also many layers to the sense of person as it is being constituted and elevated by the society formed by Jesus, which is the Church. On the one hand, it refers to an incomparable and unique center of embodied person, and on the other hand, it refers to one who is *in* Christ—as one who has gained a whole new personhood—in the sense of living in a new acting area—in the grace of Christ—for one's specific place in the mission of Christ.

Christ is the finest of all human beings. Hence, there is "in his own person, the realization of the comprehensive and unified idea of the world that the triune God had in the beginning."[101] This follows from what was said about the divine Word above. Turning to Jesus' person and his mission[102], Paul's own life can be used to illustrate what happens when Christ 'takes over' someone's existence:

(1) Paul initially was devoted to the Law and he moved then to faith in Christ, who is the fullest realization of the following of the Law.

(2) Paul remained a conscious deliberative subject, but he was personalized in a new way as one who is in Christ and who acts in Christ's mission. In other

---

[100] Cited by Hans Urs von Balthasar, "On the Concept of Person," *Communio* 13 (Spring 1986), 18.

[101] Hans Urs von Balthasar, *The Christian States of Life*, San Francisco, Ignatius Press, 1983, 192.

[102] "Cf. "As the Father has sent me so I am sending you." (John 20:21)

words, he responds to the love of Christ for him by surrendering himself to Christ and committing himself to the mission of Christ. Thus, "*en* becomes *syn*, a participation in Christ's dying, rising and in his work (*synergoi*)."[103]

Details of the nature of the daily life of the priest begin to surface in these words. After ordination, the priest continues constituting himself by his actions resting in the exchange of grace and truth with Jesus Christ.

In summary: "It is true of all believers that they share this same expropriation; all cease to exist for themselves and acquire personality through being in Christ."[104] They become essentially one human being coalesced and active in Christ even though each is his/her own inviolable center. He/she is not absorbed into Christ so as to disappear. (See Gregory I's comments above) People do not lose their individual consciousness because in fact, Christ "ascended that he might fill all things." (Ephesians 4:10) The emphasis is on filling and not removing! They make a conscious commitment. They take on the mind of Christ in their unique situation. Christ becomes their higher order principle in faith. And so, as a result:

> he gave some as apostles, others as prophets, others as evangelists, others as pastors and teachers, to equip the holy ones for the work of ministry, for building up the body of Christ, until we all attain to the unity of faith and knowledge of the Son of God, to mature manhood, to the extent of the full stature of Christ, so that we may no longer be infants, tossed by waves and swept along by every wind of teaching arising from human trickery, from their cunning in the interests of deceitful scheming. Rather, living the truth in love, we should grow in every way into him who is the head, Christ, from whom the whole body, joined and held together by every supporting ligament, with the proper functioning of each part, brings about the body's growth and builds itself up in love. (Ephesians 4:10-16)

There is a vast ecclesiology in this piece of Paul's *Letter to the Ephesians.* Any priest can continue to deepen his understanding of the workings of the Church by reflecting again and again on this text. In fact, it provides a constant spiritual horizon for every aspect of his work. For one thing, there is the caution against false teaching, something that will become very relevant in the chapter on the intellectual life of the priest. Another example: just the thought that a parish has the duty to build *itself* up in love could spark a whole flood of efforts in building Christian community and spiritual development too.

---

[103] *TD III*, 247.
[104] *TD III*, 248.

Lastly, just as Paul offered a specific example of what it means to be 'in Christ', there are other notable figures in Christian salvation history in the same situation, and one of the prime examples is Mary herself.

(4) Mary

The Church's teaching on Mary is essential when examining the theology of the Church, because Mary

> is the image and beginning of the Church as it is to be perfected in the world to come, so too does she shine forth on earth, until the day of the Lord shall come, as a sign of sure hope and solace to the people of God during its sojourn on earth. (LG 68)

The wonder is that despite the fickleness and sinfulness of many Jews throughout history, the faith that they represented at the time, starting with Abraham was far "too positive and final" to be lost by their sinfulness.[105] The word 'positive' refers to the presence of the good, affirming characteristics of the covenant of God with Abraham. The covenant itself was not an error on God's part nor was it withdrawn. In fact, through the ages, there always was a group of Jewish people who, in the words of the *Letter to the Hebrews*, "did not receive what had been promised but saw it and greeted it from afar and acknowledged themselves to be strangers and aliens on earth." (Hebrews 11:13) They lived in hope! One particular woman belonged to this group . . .

That one person, in the long history of the Old Testament, who was not fickle and who consented in all the purity of her sinlessness to being the mother of the one who "will be great and will be called Son of the Most High, and the Lord God will give him the throne of David his father." (Luke 1:32) These were the words of the Annunciation. They were addressed to Mary, the Mother of God.

Mary saw the faint beginnings of the *realization* of the promise made long before to Abraham. Her consent contained all of what was to happen to her son. It is logical that she should have been judged sinless, since she is the "most blessed." (Luke 1:42) She was the only one who could see the possibilities. So then, in the words of von Balthasar:

---

[105] *TD IV*, 352. Here it is essential to avoid another use of the adjective 'positive' that became current in Germany in the 30's when the government spoke of 'Positive Christianity.' By this, they meant a Christianity that has gone through the Nazi ideological filter so that all traces of Judaism have been removed. The non-ideological meaning of 'positive' is the one used in the text.

Mary's consent represents the pure faith of Abraham and the people; it is the fruit of Israel's positive history, proving that God has not made his covenant for nothing; now the covenant becomes positive reality beneath the cross.[106] However, the description of the role of Mary cannot be simplified to the point where Jesus is the divine one and Mary is the human representative responding positively to Jesus. This is too easy and does not grasp the situation as Scripture presents it. It must be kept in mind that the divine initiative and the complete human response actually take place within Jesus himself, due to the union of the two natures in Christ (hypostatic union). However, Mary represents the fullness of the Old Testament faith (see the Magnificat, for example) and her consent was the "pre-condition" for the Incarnation.[107]

Nevertheless, Vatican II teaching contained this qualification, that:
> The Church does not hesitate to profess this subordinate role of Mary. It knows it through unfailing experience of it and commends it to the hearts of the faithful, so that encouraged by this maternal help they may the more intimately adhere to the Mediator and Redeemer. (LG 62)

Getting into the theology of the relationship between Mary and Jesus Christ, the council explained that: "By reason of the gift and role of divine maternity, by which she is united with her Son, the Redeemer, and with his singular graces and functions, the Blessed Virgin is also intimately united with the Church." (LG 63)

Moreover, any study of the nature of the Church cannot escape examining the intimate connections between Mary and the Church. A fundamental concept lies in the intellectual content of the Catholic faith. (Back to the importance of what is known by the individual!) Von Balthasar's developed analysis of Mary's consent shows why Thomas Aquinas, for example, placed such an emphasis on the intellectual dimension of Mary's consent (above). It was essential "that she should be informed in mind concerning him, before conceiving him in the flesh." (ST III q.30 a.1c) This then led Thomas to assert that—citing Augustine— "Mary is more blessed in receiving the faith of Christ, than in conceiving the flesh of Christ" (ST III q.30 a.1c)[108] He can say this because faith involves intellectual content in addition to assent of the will. Aquinas' alternative expression for Mary's intellectual and volitional conception is that she bears him "in her heart," using the ancient metaphor of the heart. (ST III q.30 a. 1c)

---

[106] *TD IV*, 352.
[107] Ibidem.
[108] The quote from Augustine comes from his *De Sancta Virgine Iii.*

From the overwhelming power[109] of her consent, von Balthasar lists the following consequences:[110]

(1) Her consent continues to pierce her life as a sword. (Luke 2:35)
(2) Her spiritual and physical availability then allows the existence of Jesus in the flesh.
(3) Her consent "prefigures the coming Church of Jesus."[111]
(4) Her consent was still playing out at the foot of the Cross. (John 19:26-27)
(5) Her consent mediates between the faithless ones ("we have no king but Caesar" (John 19:15)) and those who will learn the faith in the future.

Each of these propositions applies equally to every believer. They give a psycho-spiritual map of the dynamics in the spirit of the believer. In addition, the faith in Christ as the meaning of the world will prove to be central to the intellectual life of the priest. (See Chapter Nine.)

A qualifier is needed here: Mary did not leverage God into working for our salvation. At all times, she was abandoning herself to an act of faith in him. Her faith involves her complete submission. Her act of faith is for the service of all of humankind as all complete faith is—important for the perspective that the priest has on his parish. However, there was a sad division in the faith of humanity as the Prologue of John's Gospel shows: "He came to what was his own, but his own people did not accept him." (John 1:11) Then, there were some who did believe because as John goes on to say: "But to those who did accept him he gave power to become children of God, to those who believe in his name." (John 1:12) These individuals, John explains: "were born not by natural generation nor by human choice nor by a man's decision but of God." (John 1:13) They received the gift of faith as pure grace. With Mary and these individuals lie the beginnings of the Church around Jesus Christ and relying on his grace.

Following from this somewhat bare summary and from the parallels between Mary and the Church, one is led to conclude that the Church is *herself* Mother and Virgin too.

(5) Mary metaphysically speaking

Mary's gender grounds the nature of Mary's role that constitutes her more and more as a person. Going back to the Scriptures: the Old Testament describes a long history

---

[109] This power comes from her involvement in the missions of the Son and the Spirit, at the will of the Father.
[110] *TD IV*, 352.
[111] Ibidem.

of God presenting himself as male with respect to his people considered as female. (See the *Song of Songs* as one example. The *Book of Hosea* as another.) In the New Testament, the Savior of Israel is physically present in time as a male. Continuing the form of this trend, the *Letter to the Ephesians* presents the relationship between Christ and his Church in gendered terms: "Husbands, love your wives, even as Christ loved the church and handed himself over for her." (Ephesians 5:25) The author of the letter then explains that Christ "loved the Church and handed himself over to her to sanctify her, cleansing her by the bath of water with the word, that he might present to himself the Church in splendor, without spot or wrinkle or any such thing, that she might be holy and without blemish." (Ephesians 5:26, 27)[112]

This typology of the metaphysically 'male' God with respect to his metaphysically 'female' people entails a further concept—the femininity of the act of faith itself. This is femininity—that is consent and receptivity—at the spiritual level and so is not subject to political considerations about women. Behind this notion is the similarity with the physical manifestation of the feminine in female human beings. But receptivity does not completely define the act of faith, because in a second moment of activity, faith is creatively generative.[113] The unique faithful individual has to take what he/she has received and express it according to his/her own genius in his/her unique situation. So, spiritual 'femininity' is not being reduced to mere receptivity. It is creatively generative in its own way. Moreover, lastly, for reasons that do not matter here, the feminine also involves "that [which] makes a person secure in nature and in being."[114] Briefly this is the ontology of the feminine.

Now, the same three aspects (receptivity, generativity and security in being) can be found in the femininity of the Church.[115] Just as the Old Testament community saw the marital union as describing the 'masculinity' of God with respect to the 'femininity' of the community, the New Testament community has all of that—it has not been abrogated—as well as the concrete living historical role of Mary herself. Only now, the femininity is with respect to God-in-Christ, the one who came as a flesh and blood man. Hence: "Mariology is an inner component of Christology."[116] Each priest

---

[112] Vatican II continued this imagery because of its theological import that is already found in Scripture: "Christ loves the Church as his bride, having become the model of a man loving his wife as his body; the Church, indeed, is subject to its Head. 'Because in him dwells all the fullness of the Godhead bodily,' he fills the Church, which is his body and his fullness, with his divine gifts so that it may expand and reach all the fullness of God." (LG 7)
[113] Hans Urs von Balthasar, "Women Priests?" *New Elucidations*, San Francisco, Ignatius Press, 1986, 189.
[114] Ibidem.
[115] Cf. *TD III*, "Woman's answer," 283ff.
[116] Cf. *TD III*, 175.

ought to examine his understanding of the feminine and the spiritual femininity of his faith. This will lead him to fully develop a spirituality that will make him 'secure in nature and in being' and not subject to the 'slings and arrows of outrageous fortune' (Hamlet).

(6) Inclusion in Christ

By grace, the Bishop, the priest and in fact every baptized person, lives 'in Christ' although in different ways. For example, Paul wrote: "you too must think of yourselves as [being] dead to sin and living for God in Christ Jesus" (Romans 6:11) This 'living in' is the foundation of the Church's understanding of earthly discipleship. Putting it in different terms, after the earthly life of Christ, "earthly discipleship was to become a reality on the basis of the presence, in the Church, of the Crucified and Risen Lord."[117] So then, the Church lives her life in "synchronicity" with the continuing presence of the Crucified and Risen Lord in history.[118]

In other words, God's complete revelation of himself is present in the world in Jesus Christ. He gathered a community around himself, gave them his Spirit, and made them part of his continuing embodied crucified, risen and glorified presence in the world, namely the Church. This body comprises things like the Tradition of the Church, the Scriptures, the Magisterium, and the sacraments. The way that Hans Urs von Balthasar explained it is:

> The mystery of the Church is born when Jesus freely exercises the power he has to 'lay down his life and take it up again' (John 10:8), when he exercises this power by giving this surrender 'for his friends,' (John 15:13) the form of a meal, of eating and drinking his flesh and blood (John 6:55), an act whereby he fills his friends with his own substance, body and soul, divinity and humanity.[119]

Here the Eucharist stands for the whole sacramental system as the sacrament *par excellence*. The sacraments are the results of the power and presence of Christ in the world.

In a primary way, the power and presence of Christ is manifested in the Tradition, the Scriptures and the Magisterium of the Church. The content of each of these phenomena manifests the presence of Christ as the faithful and the ordained participate in them. So, the Church does not confuse the Tradition, the Scriptures or the Magisterium with Christ. Nevertheless, they are closely interrelated and dependent on Christ himself for their full authority, power and meaning because he is present in some way in each of them. Hence, just for one example, the privileged

---

[117] *TD III*, 129.

[118] *Ibidem*.

[119] GL I, 571. The same concept of the realization of the dynamic center of the Church in the Eucharist appears in Saint John Paul II's *Ecclesia de eucharistia*, 1.

place of the interpretation of Scripture lies in the liturgy with all that that means in terms of the activity of Christ in the liturgy. Jesus Christ himself, the interpreter *par excellence* is acting in the liturgy.

(7) Tradition, the Scriptures and the Magisterium

The phrase 'the Tradition of the Church' refers to the whole life of the Church. It expresses, among other things, the historicity of the Church as the Body of Christ includes, as it continues the salvation history of the world, in the history of the world, through the community that Jesus gathered around himself and the eternal validity of the Incarnation for the salvation of mankind. (The very notion of tradition has been done away with in leftist 'theologies' because they want to be the makers of the new 'church'.[120] That is a church with no past except what they allow.)

The Second Vatican Council listed the features of the Tradition:

> what was handed on [i.e. the Tradition – *tradere* – to hand on] by the Apostles includes everything which contributes toward the holiness of life and increase in faith of the peoples of God; and so the Church, in her teaching, life and worship, perpetuates and hands on to all generations all that she herself is, all that she believes. (DV 8)

This includes the Scriptures, in a special way, because the New Testament was written in the Church, the actual books and letters comprising the New Testament were selected by the Church, and the Scriptures are continually used by the Church. In addition to the Scriptures and the Tradition, the salvation history configured around Jesus Christ includes the teaching authority of the Church (Magisterium – *Magister* Latin - master). All three are different manifestations of the presence of the Divine Word in history. In the words of the Council, the

> sacred Tradition, Sacred Scripture and the teaching authority of the Church, in accord with God's most wise design, are so linked and joined together that one cannot stand without the others, and that all together and each in its own way under the action of the one Holy Spirit contribute effectively to the salvation of souls. (DV 10)

Then, by ordination and the granting of faculties by the Bishop, the priest participates in a certain way in this wonderful complex presence of Christ embodied in Scripture, Tradition and magisterium. Each of these is a dimension of the presence of the

---

[120] One can also see this phenomenon in the heresies, in Lutheranism and Calvinism and their offshoots. The issue of tradition is crucial even though popular culture has largely done away with the word. A priest needs to grasp the concept and be committed to it as a true feature of being human and becoming more authentically human. Tradition is also essential to make authentic community happen. The priest rides the wave of the tradition that makes him who he is meant to be and he also bears the tradition in his thoughts and actions.

Crucified and Risen Lord in the Bishop. Any efforts to separate these, for example, claiming not to need a hierarchy, or not to need a tradition, or trying to see Scripture as unconnected to anything else except perhaps a university biblical studies department—each of these efforts denies the interlocking nature of Scripture, the Tradition and the magisterium as they originate in Christ.

The validly functioning priest is a humble servant of the presence of the glorified Incarnate Word in the Bishop and his assistant priests and so serves Scripture, Tradition and the magisterium. They constitute the priest's mode of presence and activity in the world for the whole of his life.

(8) The Mission

The Church, as the extension of the presence of Christ, embodies the mission of Jesus Christ to the world. Everything thus far has been leading up to this point.

The Second Vatican Council noted that there is a mission statement in the Gospel:
> As the Son was sent by the Father, so He too sent the Apostles, saying: "Go, therefore, make disciples of all nations, baptizing them in the name of the Father and of the Son and of the Holy Spirit, teaching them to observe all things whatsoever I have commanded you. (LG 17)

This mission will be examined further under the rubric of priesthood *qua* priesthood. (Chapter Four)

Chapter Four The Priesthood itself

I will give you shepherds after my own heart. (Jeremiah 3:15)

(1) Introduction

The Catholic episcopate (and their assistants the priests) is at the heart of the continuing concrete expression of Jesus Christ in the world, through the Church which is his Body. In the Old Testament, there was a kind of personal priesthood already. The heads of the clans (eg. Abraham) did the priestly actions on behalf of their clans, similarly with the kings (eg. Melchisedek) and many of the prophets (eg. Samuel). With the Mosaic covenant, the men of the tribe of Levi became the designated priests for the people (Exodus 29:9). They offered the various sacrifices during the year for the people. The sacrifices were not their private individually motivated actions but actions for the life of worship and the protection and success of the whole community that was formed as the People of God.

The great difference between the People of God in the New Testament and the Old Testament, is that, for the New People of God, the sacrifice offered to God has already been offered completely and perfectly in Christ. (Hebrews 10:10) The Old Testament priestly figures were, in many senses, figures of Christ pre-figuring his sacrificial work.

(2) Ministerial Priesthood - Christ's sacrificial and servant love[121]

Controversies about priesthood are usually based on theological simplifications, so this section will cover the theology of what is known as the ministerial priesthood in the Tradition.

Terms are very important when discussing the nature of the Catholic priesthood. To start with, the word 'minister' itself:

> In early Latin translations of the New Testament, *ministerium* and its cognates were used to translate *òiakonia* and its cognates, as well as the less frequent *leitourgia*. The best English rendering of *òiakonia* is the word 'service.' The New Testament uses the term for activities in the Church which issue from the graces of the Spirit and build up the body of the faithful.[122]

Etymologically, the word 'ministerium' comes from the word *minus* meaning 'less'. The minister then is someone who acts under the authority and with the power of another—in this case, the Bishop, the successor to the apostles. His work correlates with the work of the *magister*, the Latin for 'master', who is the one who has the

---

[121] Peter M.J. Stravinskas, Homily, April 5 2007, "St. Thérèse of Lisieux: A guide to understand, appreciate the Holy Priesthood," *Catholic World Report*, April 22, 2019.
[122] D.N. Power, "Ministry", *New Catholic Encyclopedia*. 2nd Edition, Detroit MI: Gale, 2003.

power and authority to bring some service about. Scripturally, the *magister,* Jesus says: "You call me 'teacher' and 'master,' and rightly so, for indeed I am." (John 13:13) The magister here is the Bishop who has authority over a piece of territory. He serves the people and institutions in a particular place.

The Greek *diakonia* was used in the original New Testament texts to refer to 'service' and as indicated earlier, service is one of the defining characteristics of who Jesus Christ is. In his own words: "the Son of Man did not come to be served but to serve and to give his life as a ransom for many." (Matthew 20:28) Moreover, the act of service is contained within the evangelical notion of love. As Aquinas described it: we are all under the Good and so, an act of charity to one person is valued "in so far as another [person] tends towards his good by an act of charity." (ST II II q.27 a. 1) This principle underlies the comments about the intellectual life of the Bishop and his priests. They only learn from God what someone's good is.

In addition, New Testament texts refer to Christ as a model and further, they refer to Christ as the source of the priesthood. Firstly, there are instances where these two are closely interrelated, so, for example, "Love one another just as I have loved you." (John 13:34) His meaning is that real love is sacrificial. Then, Jesus puts himself forward as a model.[123] In Mark 10:45: "For the Son of Man did not come to be served but to serve and to give his life as a ransom for many." Here Christ was describing himself as a minister. Then secondly, after his resurrection: "Jesus approached and said to them, 'All power in heaven and on earth has been given to me. Go, therefore, and make disciples of all nations, baptizing them in the name of the Father, and of the Son, and of the holy Spirit, teaching them to observe all that I have commanded you. And behold, I am with you always, until the end of the age.'" (Matthew 28:18-20) With these words, Jesus announced that he is the source of the serving ministerial role for those who participate in his glorious, and mediated, presence like the apostles—the Church.

The Synod of Bishops on the Formation of Priests (1990) detailed the different dimensions of this service:

> the priest minister is the servant of Christ present in the Church as mystery, communion and mission. In virtue of his participation in the 'anointing' and 'mission' of Christ, the priest can continue Christ's prayer, word, sacrifice and salvific action in the Church. In this way, the priest is a servant of the Church as mystery because he actuates the Church's sacramental signs of the presence of the risen Christ. He is a servant of the Church as communion because - in union with the Bishop and closely related to the presbyterate - he builds up the unity of the Church community in the harmony of diverse vocations, charisms

---

[123] Jean Galot, *Theology of the Priesthood,* San Francisco: Ignatius Press, 1985, 25.

64

and services. Finally, the priest is a servant to the Church as mission because he makes the community a herald and witness of the Gospel.[124]

The synod gathered together the three features of the presence of Christ in history and identified them as mystery, communion and mission. Then the priest serves the presence of Christ as he is used by Christ to ensure the manifestation of the mystery of the Church through the sacraments. The priest serves the communion when working for the unity of the Church. Lastly, the priest serves the mission of the Church by spreading the Gospel and creating examples of charity for people to see.

(3) The Anointing -The Meaning of the Sacred Priesthood

The Synod of Bishops stated that priests *participate* in the anointing of Christ. What exactly does this mean? In his instructions to the seventy-two, Jesus himself stated: "Whoever listens to you listens to me. Whoever rejects you rejects me. And whoever rejects me rejects the one who sent me." (Luke 10:16) (Cf. Matthew 10:40) Note the echoes of the concepts of mystery, communion and mission that were laid out above! Vatican II used this formulation in reference to the Bishops given their succession from the Apostles. (Cf. LG 20)

There is a concrete realism to the kind of participation in Christ that Christ himself described and that needs further examination because it has implications for understanding how the priesthood operates. The Catholic priesthood is not a mere delegation or even worse, imagining that some functions are needed in the worshipping community, and anyone can be assigned to do them—a way of thinking in many ecclesial communities.

How did Jesus initiate the participation? The *New American Bible* describes the creation (a deliberate term) of the Twelve with the words: "He appointed twelve [whom he also named apostles] that they might be with him and he might send them forth to preach and to have authority to drive out demons." (Mark 3:14, 15) The word 'appointed' does not carry the same existential weight as the Greek. The Greek text[125] itself uses *epoiesin* which means literally that he 'made' them. So, Jesus *made* the twelve. This term already had Old Testament credentials because it had been used the same way in I Kings 13:33 and II Chronicles 13:9, in the sense of *making* priests. In fact, the Bible refers to God 'making' Moses and Aaron. (I Samuel 12:6)

Jesus gave further indications too, as for example, when he made Simon, James and John, he gave them new names suggesting "a new personality." (cf. Mark

---

[124] Synod of Bishops, Eighth Ordinary General Assembly, "The Formation of Priests in the Circumstances of the Present Day," *Instrumentum Laboris*, 16; cf. Proposition 7.
[125] Nestle Text. Cf. Alfred Marshall, ed. *The RSV Interlinear Greek-English New Testament*, Grand Rapids MI: Zondervan Publishing House, 1970.

3:16:17)[126] In the same text, Jesus also "made twelve [whom he also named apostles] that they might be with him and he might send them forth to preach." (Mark 6:14) Another change that he causes is that they would be sent out—indicated by the name 'apostles.' All twelve received a new name as well. For the Jewish people of the time, the change of name had a great significance. It showed that they had changed their identity, for some reason.

The evangelist further tells us that part of the change wrought by Jesus was that 'they might be with him.' The exclusive privilege of the Twelve was the 'walking with' and the 'being with' Jesus throughout his ministry. (Cf. Mark 3:14; Matthew 26:20; Luke 6:13; John 6:67) Consequently, today's Bishop and his priests are eminently 'with Christ' and therefore much more liable to judgement as a result. Remember again the priest's private prayer before showing the sacred species to the people: "Lord Jesus Christ . . . free me by this your most holy Body and Blood, from all my sins and from every evil; keep me always faithful to your commandments, and never let me be parted from you." The relational language is strong.

The third change caused by the calling of the apostles is the introduction of the name Twelve itself. According to Jean Galot, it "refers to the whole people of Israel, [and] it suggests that Jesus intends to disavow the particularism of a priestly caste restricted to a single tribe."[127] So with the coming of Christ, there was to be a new Israel, also referred to as the "Church". It was to be the new "spiritual Israel."[128]

Importantly, the Twelve had to leave all they had "in order to place their all in Christ and it was into this void that the grace of their office was poured."[129] The character of their being in the world changes. Evidently the scripture texts are offering an *ontological* description of the miracle of the forming of Twelve. This conclusion is valid because, to quote John Paul II: "The Bible, and the New Testament in particular, contains texts and statements which have a genuinely ontological content." (FR 82) The texts refer to an objective reality (beings and ways of being), in this case, the creation of the twelve. The 'twelve' possess a new metaphysical horizon of existence and meaning because they include something of the nature of Christ himself. One thing about the Christ is that: "When Jesus lived on this earth, he manifested in himself the definitive role of the priestly establishing

---

[126] This is not personality in the modern psychological sense but rather personality as the person being graced and elevated to a new ontological level of being that includes the body.
[127] Jean Galot, 73.
[128] Hans Urs von Balthasar, "Office in the Church," *Explorations in the Theology II: Spouse of the Word*, San Francisco: Ignatius Press, 86.
[129] "Office in the Church," 85.

a ministerial priesthood with which the apostles were the first to be invested."[130] This concept can be developed further using the concept of the sacramental character.

(4) Sacramental Character

When Jesus remade the disciples as apostles, he invested them with what came to be called a sacramental character. The word character (seal) was first applied to Jesus himself, "for on him the Father, God, has set his seal." (John 6:27)

Besides ordination to Holy Orders, two other sacraments confer a character as well, Baptism and Confirmation. In them: "the divine plan gains access to the depth of the human self and impresses upon it the project of the whole Christian life that is to unfold."[131] This access occurs superlatively in the priestly character. Hans Urs von Balthasar describes what takes place through these characters as *expropriation*. People who are baptized, confirmed and ordained are expropriated by God more and in different ways so that they live a new vocation where Christ and his life is the "pattern and archetype" of their life.[132] In scriptural terms, "whether [these people] live or die, [these people] are the Lord's." (Romans 4:18) This applies to all those who bear a sacramental character either as one of the baptized, one of the confirmed or one of the priests.

Specifically, regarding the priestly character (a sacramental power): what does it make present? The character is "a holiness, a capacity-to-be-acted upon, a disposition, a figure, a sign that signifies grace, a habitus, a sign of participation in the sacraments, a sign of the profession of faith, a relation, a cultic empowerment."[133] Galot has listed the aspects of the priestly character found by theologians in the Tradition, through the centuries. The character of the priesthood involves these characteristics such that the individual is drawn into the action of the ongoing priesthood of Christ in the world, in all of its many aspects.

Thomas Aquinas explained that "Christ is the source of all priesthood: the priest of the old law was a figure of Christ, and the priest of the new law acts in the person of Christ." (STh III,22,4c.) To emphasize the meaning of the second half of the

---

[130] John Paul II, Angelus (Jan. 14, 1990), 2: *L'Osservatore Romano*, Jan. 15-16, 1990. Cf. *Catechism*: "The three sacraments of Baptism, Confirmation, and Holy Orders confer, in addition to grace, a sacramental character or 'seal' by which the Christian shares in Christ's priesthood and is made a member of the Church according to different states and functions." (CCC 1121)

[131] Jean Galot, 201.

[132] *TD III*, 248.

[133] Jean Galot, 197. In fact, he wrote a book on the sacramental character in history, *La Nature du caractère sacramental*, Paris: Desclee du Brouwer, 1958.

sentence, the *Catechism* explains: "The ministerial priesthood is a *means* by which Christ unceasingly builds up and leads his Church." (CCC 1547)[134] This is the activity of the priest as head. Specifically, he is united with the eternal High Priest, Jesus Christ. (DC 8) (Cf. *Letter to the Hebrews*) Tradition uses the term: *in persona Christi capitis* - in the person of Christ the Head.

This expression refers to what is known as the *capital* (caput - capitis - head) grace of Christ. Christ is the mediation between God and man, which is something that happens in his own being, in the hypostatic union. In Christ, there is both an ascending mediation—"From the heart of Christ, true God and true man, mounts up to heaven an unimaginable supplication . . . of all men . . . on the wings of his own offering, to the heavenly Father," and a descending mediation, where "to such a call God responds by pouring out on the world, through the heart of Jesus opened by a lance, the fruits of the redemption."[135]

Thus, Jesus Christ is the Head of the Church. Bishops, and by association priests, are his face in many ways.

(5) In Persona Christi Capitis

In *Dominicae Cenae*, John Paul II presented some aspects of the priest's relationship with Jesus Christ. John Paul II tried to obviate any attempt to make the act of consecration of the Eucharist into something being done 'in the name of' or 'in place of' Jesus Christ. (DC 8) As usual, the actual theology of something is more complex than popular or political ways of describing things.

To start with, there is a reason for using the term '*persona*': it means a "specific sacramental identification with 'the eternal High Priest.'"[136] The word '*persona*' comes from the ancient word for 'mask' and is barely apt because the notion of 'identification' where the priest *is* Christ, in a certain sense. A more substantial understanding of *persona* comes from Catholic personalism. Briefly: the first two sacraments imprinting a character, each "imprints itself onto the personal self . . . so that it may be realized from within."[137] So, it is not imprinting on the will but on the whole self. Then, the sacrament of Holy Orders "imprints upon the being of the

---

[134] Cf. II Corinthians 2:10: "*Cui autem aliquid donastis, et ego: nam et ego quod donavi, si quid donavi, propter vos in persona Christi.*" *Nova Vulgata Bible.*

[135] Charles Cardinal Journet, *The Theology of the Church*, San Francisco: Ignatius Press, 2004, 51.

[136] Based on the Opening Prayer of the Second Votive Mass of the Holy Eucharist, *Missale Romanum*, 858.

[137] Jean Galot, 201.

baptized person and orientation which commits the whole self to the mission of the priest."[138] That is of a priest with his fellow priests around his Bishop.

Now, a lot depends on the proper comprehension of the concepts of being and self. "The human body is the expression or sign or indeed 'sacrament' of the person, for the human body is an integral and constitutive dimension or aspect of the person."[139] The materialist approaches try to separate person and body so that the body of the priest becomes irrelevant to 'being a priest'. More about that later!

Now back to John Paul II's explanation. The pope says: "the priest celebrant who, by confecting the holy Sacrifice and acting '*in persona Christi*,' is sacramentally (and ineffably) brought into that most profound sacredness, and made part of it, spiritually linking with it in turn all those participating in the eucharistic assembly." (DC 8) This explanation is based on a number of sources, but one appears in Paul's Second Letter to the Corinthians where Paul says: "*eἴ ti kexárisμai ở ὑμᾶς ἐν προσόπω Kpistoû.*" (II Corinthians 2:10) Literally this translates as, "if anything I have forgiven [it is] on account of you in [the] person of Christ."[140] Paul is acting in the person of Christ.

The *New Catholic Catechism* (1992), which is a magisterial document, mentioned the phrase '*in persona Christi capitis*,' to make the perennial theology clear. So, it stated that it is

in representing him that the Bishop or priest acting in
the person of Christ the head (*in persona Christi capitis*) presides over
the assembly, speaks after the readings, receives the offerings,
and says the Eucharistic Prayer. (CCC 1348)

The catechism used the word 'represent' but this must not be understood in the modern sense of standing in for someone else. In the ancient sense, the term means that the person one sees *is* the person who sent him or her. This sense appears in the *Constitution on the Church* where the council fathers taught about the episcopate that "he who hears [the episcopate], hears Christ, and he who rejects them, rejects Christ and Him who sent Christ." (LG 20) It is worth noting that the new presence of Christ in the apostles, Bishops and their priests has traditionally been described as the ordained male person becoming a new being, a concept that fits in here.

---

[138] Ibidem.

[139] W.E. May, "Personalist Ethics," *New Catholic Encyclopedia*. Vol XI, Detroit MI: 2003, 153.

[140] Alfred Marshall, *The RSV Interlinear Greek-English New Testament*, Grand Rapids MI: Zondervan 1968. The term *persona* is translated in the New American Bible as 'presence' which might be a bit vague.

This section concludes that Christ 'remade' the apostles. The new character of the apostles means that, in the apostles, "God is at work: he wants to gain possession of the whole person, and not only of the upper and visible layer, which is the person's activity."[141] Weaker theories of ordination—found in some ecclesial communities—aim for only the 'upper visible layers' of the individual being changed.

The latter part of the last sentence ties in with the reason for making the efficacy of the sacraments very clear. In the words of Johann Auer:

> The Reformers, starting from their conception of God's grace (God's own good pleasure) and justification (the overlooking or concealing of sin by grace of human guilt, explained the effect of the sacraments in a more largely subjective manner, on the basis of God's Word (the promises) and the human being's faith.[142]

So, starting from a particular anthropology, the Reformers remained in the subjective realm which the Catholic Church, at the Council of Trent (1545-1563), explained its doctrines on the sacraments through the relationship between the Creator who is all in all, and the human creature who only has the potentiality for grace. It is God who "brings about grace in human beings and gives to the sacrament that he has bestowed in Christ, the power to contain, effect and communicate this grace."[143] So, even though there are specific conditions for the recipient to receive the sacrament, it is God who gives the grace and the recipient merely receives but does not merit it or earn it. This is important for appreciating the drama of what happens at ordination. The treatment above explains that the candidate is remade to the depths of his being—hence the character that is received.

The priest's being in Christ means that . . .

(6) Participation in the Offices of Christ

The theology of the life of the priest *in persona Christi* can be developed from the scriptural data. But what does this mean? The Old Testament mediators between God and his people were the prophets (some of them), priests (some of them) and the kings (some of them). Jesus Christ is described in the New Testament as The Prophet (John 6:14), The Priest (Hebrews 4:14) and The King (Matthew 27:37). He fulfills the meaning of each of these mediatory roles superlatively. In the process, they also completely describe him! Through his fulfillment of these roles, he constituted the New People of God:

---

[141] Jean Galot, 202.
[142] Johann Auer, Joseph Ratzinger, *Dogmatic Theology 6: A General Doctrine of the Sacraments and the Mystery of the Eucharist*, Washington DC: CUA Press, 1995, 74.
[143] *A General Doctrine*, 75.

He has bought it for himself with his blood, has filled it with his Spirit and provided it with those means which befit it as a visible and social union. God gathered together as one all those who in faith look upon Jesus as the author of salvation and the source of unity and peace and established them as the Church that for each and all it may be the visible sacrament of this saving unity. (LG 9)

So, in terms of these mediatory roles, in the words of the council, "Christ the Lord, High Priest taken from among men, made the new people 'a kingdom and priests to God the Father'." (Cf. Rev. 6:1; cf. 5:9-10) It is also worth noting that the roles of priest, king and prophet parallel the words that John Paul II used earlier, namely, mystery, communion, mission.

The council's next sentence develops what this means by laying out the main elements of the structure of the People of God:

The baptized, by regeneration and the anointing of the Holy Spirit, are consecrated as a spiritual house and a holy priesthood, in order that through all those works which are those of the Christian man they may offer spiritual sacrifices and proclaim the power of him who has called them out of darkness into his marvelous light. (LG 9)

In the text, the council begins by describing the communion of the faithful in the Holy Spirit. The faithful are formed into a 'spiritual house' with all of the spiritual integrity and interrelationship that participating in the Holy Spirit brings.

Next, the council spoke of the 'holy priesthood'. There are two kinds of priesthood in the Church because there are two modes of participation in the priesthood of Christ—ordained and baptized. This set of concepts is based on the capacity of the word 'sacrifice' to totally describe the life of Christ. Traditionally, there have long been two complementary ways to offer sacrifice and then in Christianity "each of them in its own special way is a participation in the one priesthood of Christ" (LG 10) The two ways are the concrete visible sacrifice and the interior spiritual sacrifice corresponding to our participation in the two divine missions, that of the Son and that of the Spirit..

The public concrete and visible sacrifice results from the public sacrificial action of the priest. The spiritual complement to this public manifestation of sacrifice is the interior spiritual sacrifice that is the layperson's response to the sacrifice. Laypeople respond to the Eucharist both individually and as part of the believing, worshipping and serving community.

The council more generally described the life of offering spiritual sacrifices as follows: "all the disciples of Christ, persevering in prayer and praising God, should present themselves as a living sacrifice, holy and pleasing to God." (LG 10) Then they went on to list some others: "They likewise exercise that [common] priesthood in receiving the sacraments, in prayer and thanksgiving, in the witness of a holy life, and by self-denial and active charity." (LG 10)

The acts of the interior, receptive, spiritual priesthood of the lay person are in response to the actions of the external, expressive ordained priesthood in the Bishop who has the fullness of the priesthood (LG 21) or to the actions of the priest who shares in that priesthood. (LG 28) According to the council: "The ministerial priest, by the sacred power he enjoys, teaches and rules the priestly people; acting in the person of Christ, he makes present the Eucharistic sacrifice, and offers it to God in the name of all the people." (LG 10) This sentence applies to both the Bishop and the priest.

Sacrifice is also the key to much of the priest's life. Paul himself said: "Now I rejoice in my sufferings for your sake, and in my flesh I am filling up what is lacking⁻ in the afflictions of Christ on behalf of his body, which is the church." (Colossians 1:24) Thus the priest/Bishop aids in carrying on Christ's mission of reparation and atonement for sin daily. This is even outside of his Eucharistic duties.

Also. there is the same complementary structure in the way that the ordained and the faithful participate in the Prophetic Office of Christ. In the words of the council, the ordained "proclaim the power of him who has called them out of darkness into his marvelous light." (LG 12) For the faithful, their common prophetic office involves a first moment of hearing the proclamation and then a second moment of going out and "spread[ing] abroad a living witness to him, especially by means of a life of faith and charity and by offering to God a sacrifice of praise, the tribute of lips which give praise to his name." (LG 12)

Lastly, there is the Kingly Office of Christ. As far as the hierarchy are concerned, the Bishops are the "heads of the people whom they govern." (LG 27) Correspondingly priests "sanctify and govern under the Bishop's authority, that part of the Lord's flock entrusted to them they make the universal Church visible in their own locality and bring an efficacious assistance to the building up of the whole body of Christ." (LG 28) 'Governing' is just another term for the exercise of the kingly office.

The lay participation in the Kingly Office, involves the first moment of being obedient to the governing of the Clergy in order to come under the will of God and then in a second moment, the layperson develops kingship over himself first of all, by learning to live the virtues him/her self. Then subsequently: "They should raise all of society, and even creation itself, to a better mode of existence." (LG 41) And at a more elevated level: "In the word, in the works, and in the presence of Christ, the kingdom [becomes] clearly open to the view of men." (LG 5)

The priestly mode of each of the three offices becomes visible again and again in the words and deeds of the priest himself and of the Laity in the course of the priest's pastoral work and often when they act on their own.

However, the description of the lay participation in the offices of Christ does not stop with what was laid out above. Clearly, each of these participations in the common priesthood, common prophetic role and the common kingly role involves a second moment, a movement outward from the individual. That moment is beautifully creative and expressive. So, for example, the lay participation in the Office of the Priest not only involves the receptive spiritual response to the Eucharist but also the expression of sacrifice in what the individual does and says in the world. Essentially, he/she generates a sacrificial culture around himself. He/she brings it about "in the witness of a holy life, and by self-denial and active charity." (LG 10) Some people in society will see the example of the Laity and learn to live this kind of life themselves, seeing sacrifice as the authentic kind of human life, as exemplified by Christ himself.

Similarly, not only does the lay participation in the Office of the Prophet have the first moment of receptivity to the truth, it also has the second moment of expressing that truth in the world in everything that the individual does and says. The council described it as follows: he/she "spreads abroad a living witness to him, especially by means of a life of faith and charity and by offering to God a sacrifice of praise, the tribute of lips which give praise to his name." (LG 12) This is a uniquely personal moment expressing as it does the love and talents if this particular individual.

Lastly, the participation in the Office of King involves a first moment of responding to the authority of Christ in his Church. In the council's words: "In all of Christ's disciples the Spirit arouses the desire to be peacefully united, in the manner determined by Christ, as one flock under one shepherd." (LG 15) Then there is a second moment of bringing oneself under the kingship of Christ in heart, mind and body but also of bringing the whole world under the kingship of Christ.

The second moments of each of these are beautifully creative. The ingenuity of the individual and the uniqueness of the individual's situation mean that each layperson is distinctive in making Christ present. Now there is still one issue about the priesthood to be dealt with.

(7) The Gender of the Priest[144]

The ontological description of the Catholic priesthood involves unfolding the complete appropriation of the ordained man by Christ so that the priest is called and empowered to be part of a spousal physical-spiritual organism who is the presence of Christ in the world. His presence grounds the spousal relationship between the priest and his people participating in the spousal relationship between Christ and his people. This conception of priesthood fits what is known from the Scriptures and Tradition. Pointing to the new physical-spiritual existence in Christ that comes about, at ordination, is the only way to completely describe the reality of the priesthood and it means that the Catholic priesthood cannot be accurately reduced to a job or to employment in an organization called the Church. There is no list of tasks that can simply be transferred to someone else at will— 'these are the ten things that you need to be able to do. If you can do them then you can be a priest.'

The priesthood is one particular ontological state of an embodied person. This was mentioned in section (5) above. A consequence of embodiedness is that "the human body carries within itself the signs of sex and is by its nature male or female."[145] But John Paul II explained that:

> The theology of the body, which is linked from the beginning with the creation of man in the image of God, becomes in some way also a theology of sex, or rather a theology of masculinity and femininity, which has its point of departure here, in Genesis.[146]

So, the maleness of the priest and masculinity, specifically as regards his maleness and masculinity are concerned, are not based on some cultural bias but rather lie in the Book of Genesis itself.

This had to be established before moving on to the taking over of the whole person of the male ordinand by Christ at ordination. This was treated in Section 5 (above).

Now, things get complicated: the priesthood, specifically the episcopate, is the product of the two divine missions, the mission of the Divine Son and the mission of the Divine Spirit. They cooperate in a way that means that "the social structure of the Church is not primarily juridical but sacramental" according to Vatican II— visible form, supernatural grace and truth.[147] Then in Yves Congar's words: "I

---

[144] In this book, 'gender' refers to the nature of the spiritual biological human entity theologically considered.

[145] John Paul II, *Man and Woman He created them - A Theology of the Body*, ed. Michael Waldstein, Boston: Pauline Books, 2006, 157.

[146] *Man and Woman*, 165.

[147] Yves Congar, *The Word and the Spirit*, London: Harper & Row, 1986, 81.

would connect this [fact] with the relative duality on the one hand of the institution of the Church by the Incarnate Word during his presence in the flesh and, on the other, of the permanent activity here and now of the glorified Lord, who is Spirit."[148] There, in as neat a sentence as you could ever hope for, Congar has shown the concordance of the two divine missions, the one visible (from the Incarnate Word in history) and the one invisible (from the Holy Spirit in the interior of the faithful). They produce the form of Jesus Christ, the man in the world. They collaborate to produce the institution of the Church in the episcopate. What is important is that the glorified Lord is continuing what the Incarnate Word did during his time on earth.

Now, let's examine the masculinity of the priest more deeply.

A key text in helping to understand things is Jesus' words that "he who has seen me has seen the Father." (John 14:9) Similarly, Jesus "is the refulgence of [God's] glory, the very imprint of his being." (Hebrews 1:3) Jesus has received the imprint (character) of the Father and "ultimately, his character and his activity emerge from the very mystery of the Son's engendering by the Father."[149] The Son appears in the world as a male human being—a being capable of generating, although celibate in the Latin Rite.

Positively speaking then, the *male* priesthood manifests the fact that Jesus Christ is engendered in time as a man. When a male human being is spoken of, it must be understood that "the human body is the expression of the human person; the body participates in the dignity of the person. It is not some tool or instrument of the person. It is thus a good of the person, not merely a good for the person."[150] So the body is not a kind of puppet for a neutral spirit. This materialist notion is unscriptural to say the least. Importing it into a discussion of the gender of a Catholic priest is not rational.

Taking a step back: John Paul II does remind us: "Although it is not possible to attribute human qualities to the eternal generation of the Word of God, and although the divine fatherhood does not possess 'masculine' characteristics in a physical sense, we must nevertheless seek in God the absolute *model* of all '*generation*' among human beings." (MD 8)[151] This is so that we cannot be accused of anthropomorphism. At the same time, the reasoning shown here is reasoning that

---

[148] *The Word and the Spirit*, 81.
[149] Jean Galot, 204.
[150] W.E. May, 153.
[151] Based on Ephesians 3:14, 15.

follows the Scriptures rather than being objected to because it is not moving towards the ideology required by a particular power group.

A second reason that this is not simply an accidental feature of the priesthood is because "sexuality affects all aspects of the human person in the unity of his body and soul. It especially concerns affectivity, the capacity to love and to procreate, and in a more general way the attitude for forming bonds of communion with others." (CCC 2332) So gender is not a minor issue in the theology of the priesthood. It affects everything that the priest does, so apparently, the priesthood is not merely a job or an employment.

This means that each of the above capacities listed by the *Catechism* is to be sought in the male priest as he operates affectively, as he loves God and neighbor and as he forms community in the male way. Among other things, this approach avoids the seduction of recasting (and thus minimizing) the priesthood into purely social or political terms, ways of thinking that were never ultimately significant even in the Old Testament and certainly not in the New. Very significantly, when Christ was incarnated and acted the way that he acted, he acted with the sovereign freedom of God.[152] Nothing in his life was by accident. He was never bound by his culture. So, Christ's being a male and extending his presence through a male priesthood was not an accident either.

The gendered nature of the theology of priesthood is also evident in the physical-spiritual relation between Christ and his Church. The relation between Christ and his Church is an I-Thou relation and a spousal relation. It grounds the relation between the priest and the people and also describes it explicitly. The relationship has frequently been described in terms of marriage and covenant, for example in the *Letter to the Ephesians.* For example: "As the church is subordinate to Christ, so wives should be subordinate to their husbands in everything. Husbands love your wives, even as Christ loved the church and handed himself over for her" (Ephesians 5: 24, 25) The language of human gender is essential to this description.

Among other things, 'gender' refers to the biological nature of the human being, specifically regarding the genetics and the anatomy of the reproductive system of the individual. Priests are biologically male, not because of a social construct but according to the presence of male anatomy. To use other terms, the involvement of the maleness of the priest is due to the way *he* participates in the divine plan of

---

[152] The term 'political' recalls the fact that there are many different ways and degrees of thinking. Some handle reality more accurately than others. Political thinking simply works in terms of power—who gets which power by doing what. Such thinking has no connection to what exactly is being thought about. This incomplete way of thinking is not capable of describing the phenomenon of priesthood, for example.

salvation. He is a participant in the gendered structure of the unfolding of salvation throughout the Old and the New Testaments—most particularly in the male Christ—and it requires gendered metaphors to present the spiritual dimension of that reality. The language follows the reality!

To illustrate this point: The *Constitution on the Church in the Modern World* makes a general statement that in the theology of salvation: the "God of old made Himself present to His people through a covenant of love and fidelity." (GS 48) The constitution then refers to scriptural texts such as Hosea 2; Jeremiah 3:6-13; Ezekiel 16 and 23; Isaiah 54. All of these use gendered descriptions of God's relation to his people in the unfolding of salvation. In these texts, God is 'male' in some sense and the believing community is 'female' in some sense. Now, God is Spirit, so he does not have a gender in the biological sense. However, God the Father is generative in himself, in a divine and spiritual way, and so all being images this generativity in some way: "all 'generating' in the created world is to be likened to this absolute and uncreated model." (MD 8)[153] This is one of the consequences of the creation of man/woman in the image and likeness of God.

Developing the notion of generativity further: in the divine itself, there are the eternal divine "characteristics of 'action' and 'letting-be' in God . . . These actions are complimentary in divine love."[154] In other words, 'action' corresponds to the divine relations of generation and active spiration in the Godhead. And 'letting be' corresponds to the eternal divine relations of filiation and passive spiration in the Godhead. (Cf. ST I, q. 28, art. 4)

When considered 'acting' and 'letting-be' in the nature of love itself: 'Action' can be seen as acting in a masculine sense, something that Robert E. Joyce would describe as "giving in a receiving sense" and conversely then, the community of the faithful "receives in a giving way" which is acting in a feminine sense.[155] Importantly, describing one vital element of the unfolding of salvation, namely Marriage, the council described the union of male and female as "by that human act whereby spouses mutually bestow and accept each other a relationship arises which by divine will and in the eyes of society too is a lasting one." (GS 48) There is a definite parallel between the marriage between God and his people and the marriage of a man and a woman in the People of God. In other words, this is the Old Testament parallel to

---

[153] John Paul II also explains the analogous nature of language when it is applied to God and human beings.

[154] Bevil Bramwell OMI, *Laity: Beautiful, Good and True*, (Amazon: 2012), 242.

[155] Robert E. Joyce, *Human Sexual Ecology: A Philosophy and Ethics of Man and Woman*, cited by William E. May "Marriage and the Complementarity of Male and Female." *Anthropotes* VIII (1) June 1992.

the New Testament marriage between Christ and the Church. This is what the council called "the loving covenant uniting Christ with the Church." (GS 48)

In short, there is a gendered relationship between Christ and his Church, and hence between the male priest and his spiritually 'female' community. This is because the male priest acts and is giving in a receiving way to his 'female' community that receives in a giving way. The gendered language sums up the nature of the complementarity between the ordained minister's priesthood, prophecy and kingship that is carried out in loving relation to the letting-be of the community who receive the sacraments, teaching and leadership of Christ that the priest offers in a giving way. By being male, the priest has the initial components of the physical-spiritual giving in a receiving way that relies on his maleness. This will be elevated to the Christlike sacramental mode of being Christ's masculine presence through episcopal and priestly ordination.

(8) Spiritual Fatherhood

Lastly, the concept of spiritual fatherhood can be said to sum up the features of the manifestation of the Bishop and the priest in the world. The Bishop or priest teaches, sanctifies and governs as the spiritual father to the faithful and everyone else as well, by following the personalist principles enumerated above.

When the notion of fatherhood has been so sorely diminished in the culture wars of the past century, authentic fathering has to be manifested more emphatically. Many biological fathers are doing it but as with so many other things, the authentic embodiment of masculinity and fatherhood resides in the Church. In fact, all of the major concepts of the full realization of humanity reside with the Church. Despite some weak and incompetent Clergy and Laity, there are always enough good and faithful Clergy and Laity to keep the grace and the truth of the salvific Christ embodied in the world. There is no way to get to these concepts in the abstract "to what [people] as sinners would like to understand by love and mercy."[156] Concepts like motherhood, fatherhood, being a man and being a woman, proper human communication, being a community, being a business, being a citizen, being a nation, all are ultimately only understood in the truth held by the Church. These are spiritual-physical concepts that are only completely seen and understood in in the light of revelation and grasped in faith. Hence the problem with trying to import ideologies from cultures riddled with concupiscence and sin. Demonic elements are included in any culture that has not yet been evangelized.

One such concept is fatherhood. Fatherhood is creating the conditions for others to learn the meaning of love in a generative way where love is authentic love rather than

---

[156] Hans Urs von Balthasar, "Spirit and Institution," *Explorations in Theology IV*, 237.

lust. Love as wishing for and working for the authentic good of every other person. This is far more than an intellectual exercise, as important as the intellect has been shown to be. There is an essential concrete physical dimension too—of meeting a man who stands as the presence of Christ. The male priest is the spiritual-physical man as he participates in the missions of the Son and the Spirit in his time and place and acts as a spiritual father in good times and in bad.

Chapter Five The Priest and the Liturgy

In the Church's liturgy the divine blessing is fully revealed and communicated. the Father is acknowledged and adored as the source and the end of all the blessings of creation and salvation. *Catechism*

(1) Introduction

The nature of Catholic liturgy was introduced in the chapter on Jesus Christ because of its resting in the history of salvation, more specifically in the life of Christ.

(2) The Spirit of the Liturgy

A fine recent work on the liturgy is *The Spirit of the Liturgy* by Joseph Ratzinger (Benedict XVI).[157] He took the title from a volume written by his hero, the theologian Romano Guardini who wrote at the end of the First World War. Ratzinger acknowledged that he was producing his volume in response to the entirely new historical situation of the 1990's.

For Joseph Ratzinger, (Benedict XVI), the essence of the Catholic liturgy is that it is, at the same time, both the worship of God and the ordering of the world. Because the Church is the treasure-house of the understanding of all of the main ideas about humanity, the basic principle is that "when human affairs are so ordered that there is no recognition of God, there is a belittling of man."[158] Expressed positively, the same principle can be found in the teaching of Vatican II: "Really partaking of the body of the Lord in the breaking of the Eucharistic bread, we are taken up into communion with him and with one another.(LG 7) The eucharistic ordering of the world then leads to exercising the cult of the living God and the fuller realization of true humanity at the same time.

This general principle suggests a couple of important things for the priest. Some very practical things are: The priest needs to work to have a church building that praises the divinity of God (art, atmosphere, shape). Most Clergy know very little about Catholic architecture and that includes most Bishops. However, there is a growing group of Catholic architects and artists who really understand Catholic liturgy in the light of the tradition of the Church. These people together with properly trained liturgists—this group rarely includes Clergy—who know the liturgical tradition and usually produce a building for worship and learning the ordering of the world.

The priest can still organize and train a warm receptive group who will meet those entering the building. He can hire an organist who actually knows liturgical music and how to use it. Also, a priest is needed who preaches on the plan of salvation, show the faithful their place in it and who emphasizes their mission to the rest of

---

[157] Joseph Ratzinger, *The Spirit of the Liturgy*, San Francisco: Ignatius Press, 2000.
[158] Ibid. 19.

the world once they leave the building. He can also work to develop his parish as a Christian community, a community who want to spend time before the Holy Eucharist and as a place where they come to learn about the faith and how to be Christian families.

Another theological point that Ratzinger makes is that there is a recognizable difference between what are called replacement sacrifices and what are called representative sacrifices. This was already apparent in the Old Testament where the Jews learned that replacement sacrifices with fruits and animals were really replacements for true worship. In fact, these sacrifices were "aimed at 'principalities' and 'powers' with which man has to deal with on a daily basis."[159] In the modern period, there are still many who defer to the spirits of this world. They can be manifest in preoccupations with technologies like cell phones, with certain websites or with corporations and political parties.

Liturgically, the difference between replacement and representative sacrifices can show up when people use sacred spaces for secular activities. Of course, in an emergency, like a flood, one gives any shelter one can. However, deferring to the spirits of this world in normal everyday circumstances is simply unnecessary and worse it confuses the sacred reality manifested in that building. Other examples of such deference would be using secular music in liturgy, attempts to make liturgies 'relevant' by having a priest on a hoverboard and so on. The Tradition will inform the priest about what relevancy really entails.

Furthermore, priests might insert political or social elements into the Church space. In emergencies, church buildings have occasionally been used for political meetings but again this is usually when people are forbidden to gather anywhere else under pain of imprisonment. (South Africa under apartheid, for example.)

On the other hand, regarding representative sacrifices: Participating in a representative sacrifice offers a way of acknowledging that "adoration is due to God alone [which is] the first commandment."[160] In Catholicism, the ultimate representative sacrifice is the sacrifice of Jesus himself, something that continues to be present in the world, through the power of the Spirit, at the will of the Father. Thus, the sole authentic worship of God already lies in the sacrifice of the Son in this world.[161] Ratzinger could then define liturgy as follows: "Christian liturgy is a liturgy of promise fulfilled, of a quest, the religious quest of human history, reaching its goal."[162] A priest or the liturgical committee, cannot improve on this

---

[159] *The Spirit of the Liturgy*, 36.
[160] *Spirit*, 37.
[161] Cf. *Spirit*, 44.
[162] *Spirit*, 50.

starting point. As a result, the flaw in 'making the liturgy relevant,' is shown in its true colors. In effect, the 'relevance' movement puts the focus on the wrong issue. It often focusses on changing the ritual—basically because changing something is easier—rather than demonstrating to people the fact that *this* is how their salvation has been worked out in history in real historical events and how it is to be understood.

Ratzinger also pointed to the roles of space and time in the liturgy. Just as liturgy's role is apparent in manifesting the completion of human history, so too the simple considerations of time and space point to "something essential about the permanent limits of human existence [which is] the 'not-yet' that is part of Christian existence."[163] By this, he means that the other ever-present dimension of the liturgy is that the New Heaven and the New Earth have not yet come. Presuming to manage[164] the liturgy, in the way spoken about above, really assumes that for the parish or the group, having the liturgy, the New Heaven and the New Earth have already arrived and so the liturgy lies firmly in their hands—which it will not be even in Heaven.

The claim to be managing the liturgy conceals the meaning of time in the liturgy. Such a liturgy treats the past events of the death and resurrection of Jesus as being merely past. But, in fact, there is a transcendent dimension to his death and resurrection because "the obedience of Jesus' human will is inserted into the everlasting yes of the Son to the Father."[165] In other words, the inner Trinitarian life reaches into human history: "Just as the pain of the body is drawn into the pathos of the mind and becomes the Yes of obedience, so time is drawn into what reaches beyond time."[166] Saint Bernard of Clairvaux explained this complex situation in the following terms: "the true *semel* ('once') bears within itself the *semper* ('always')."[167] (Ratzinger's formulation) The principle is that something that is really true contains permanence within it. Truth is always true. As regards the liturgy, "we not only receive something from the past but become contemporaries with what lies at the foundation of that liturgy."[168] Going back to the earlier point about representation and replacement: The relation between the past and contemporaneity with us gives the

---

[163] *Spirit*, 53.

[164] This is not to say that there should not be someone who organizes the liturgy, but he/she does not originate the liturgy. Hence it is usually the priest who does this because he hopefully has had the training.

[165] *Spirit*, 56.

[166] Ibid.

[167] *Spirit*, 56.

[168] *Spirit*, 57.

basis for the understanding of the liturgy as being about representation rather than replacement. In the liturgy, representation brings contemporaneity.

Our salvation took place through the crucifixion of the physical body of Christ. Now that that event is made contemporaneous with us then "our bodies (that is our bodily existence on earth) become 'a living sacrifice', united to the sacrifice of Christ." (cf. Romans 12:1)[169] This sacrifice continues until the world has become loving and then, and only then, will true worship be offered to God by the world.

The way that the eternal becomes contemporary with our existence, the hope is that it takes hold of the life of the worshipper. This is the third dimension of the liturgy. In this case, the future dimension of the worshipper is accentuated. Interestingly, this feature of the liturgy, in this case the Eucharist, is relevant to the architecture of the Church building. Images of the saints—assuming that they have actually been explained—are one way that the architecture indicates this future dimension of the liturgy. One could go into the lines of the building itself, as well, but that will be for another time.

Preaching clearly reaches into each of these three areas. As regards eternity breaking into time, Clergy have the obligation to explain this feature of Christian life in as many ways as possible. They need the language and they need analogies and they need the specifically biblical language. This is the responsibility of the Clergy because the prevailing culture has no comparable resources for real hope.

The concrete bodiliness of the crucifixion, death and resurrection of Jesus Christ indicates many themes that the Clergy should know and obey. Just to pick one illustration of the problem: Sometimes Clergy concelebrate Mass without vestments, forgetting the requirement of the *ordo* that they vest. This requirement is based on the bodily nature of the liturgy. Attire is a vital way of disposing oneself spiritually to what is going on. Religious have the maxim: 'the man wears the habit and the habit wears the man,' for a reason. Vesting also indicates one's participation in *the liturgy of the Church* and not in someone's private construct. The liturgy is not a solitary activity. It is participation in the Church's worship as it joins the Liturgy of Heaven.

This is a profound conclusion in the face of modern materialism and rationalism which does not accept the notion of mediation. For a rationalist, there is nothing beyond what can be seen. Similarly, assuming that one is disposed to participate in liturgy does not mean that this is so. Much of the real world is outside of the immediate awareness of the individual. Hence, for rationalists, the proper idea of the symbol being "the openness of heaven," just is not possible.[170]

---

[169] *Spirit*, 58.

[170] *Spirit*, 61.

Thus, Ratzinger's stunning conclusion about liturgy: "the theology of the liturgy is in a special way 'symbolic theology'."[171] For him, and for a theologian like Karl Rahner, symbolic theology is "a theology of symbols, which connects us to what is present."[172] What is present is much more than what is visible. This is nothing like the modern idea of symbol which is a human construct. This conclusion implies that the Church still needs sacred space, sacred time and symbols that mediate. Taken together these dimensions mediate between our time and the liturgy of Heaven.

It is important to appreciate the essential nature of mediating realities. They "give us the capacity to know the mystery of God in the pierced heart of the crucified."[173] Thus, the priest had better be careful with how he handles mediating realities, how he respects them and how he describes them.

These considerations lead into the major feature of the priest's year.

(3) The Liturgical Year

One surprising thing that happens if a priest gets 'into' the priesthood more and more seriously, is that his life takes on the contours of the Liturgical Year. As you know the term refers to the calendar for the Church's celebration of the feasts during the year. The Second Vatican Council taught that:

> For the liturgy, 'through which the work of our redemption is accomplished,' most of all in the divine sacrifice of the Eucharist, is the outstanding means whereby the faithful may express in their lives, and manifest to others, the mystery of Christ and the real nature of the true Church. (SC 1)[174]

Theologically, the cycles of the liturgy are all connected because they celebrate the sequence of the sacred mysteries in history. These are brought about in history through the missions of the Missions of the Divine Son and the Holy Spirit. So the liturgy follows the life, death and resurrection of Christ, Pentecost and other feasts, such as the feasts of the saints (the successful followers of Christ), as well as the feasts of Corpus Christi and the Holy Trinity.

The way that God has worked with human beings for millennia is to reach specific human beings in history and then use them as messengers. The repeated use of the word 'history' here should make it clear that history is an important category in our understanding. Belabouring this point is necessary when facing a largely sentimental culture formed by eruptions of emotion, the commercial structuring of social values and the latest fads. This means that life is not often appreciated for its historicity. But for the faithful, in the words of Walter Kasper: "History is one of the basic categories

---

[171] *Spirit*, 60.
[172] Ibidem.
[173] *Spirit*, 61.
[174] Quoting the of the Secret of the Ninth Sunday of the Year.

of biblical revelation. Revelation does not merely throw light on history; it also gives rise to it."[175] It is the 'giving rise' part that is of interest here because one way of describing the situation of the faithful is that, during the liturgy, they step into the history of God and his people during. The faithful encounter God's revelation in the Liturgy of the Word and the Liturgy of the Eucharist that are continuous sources of revelation into people's lives in the present moment of history.

The Liturgical Calendar itself starts with the four weeks of Advent. These prepare the Church for the great celebration of Christmas. Now obviously, when we celebrate liturgy, Jesus has already been born so that the Church's celebration of Advent's various liturgical celebrations, reminds everyone again and again of Jesus' Second Coming as well as his first coming. This motif recalls that the Church lives between the First and the Second Coming of the Lord. In the Age of the Spirit, in which we live now, the Church is kept immersed in the events of the life of Christ by the Holy Spirit. The First Coming and the Second Coming of Christ are like bookends, or better, a frame (context again!) within which the faithful can understand their lives in relation to God and the world. This frame has priority over the purely worldly frames of meaning that the media and secular society try to convince us are really the important reference points for meaning, namely the lead-ups to the 'big' games, to the next election, to the next step in career advancement and so on. The real context for the meaning of the whole universe is salvation in Christ.

In Advent, the priest aids the parish's penitential dimension of Advent. His own personal spirituality becomes more Christological. The priest is the presence of Christ in all kinds of ways, but he is also tracing a future hope, for the world, the Church, his people and himself. This will be the hope of the New Jerusalem come down from Heaven. (Revelation 21:2) There will have to be a lot of catechesis on the nature of hope itself. According to Thomas Aquinas: "hope makes us adhere to God, as the source whence we derive perfect goodness, i.e. in so far as, by hope, we trust to the Divine assistance for obtaining happiness. (ST II-II q.17 a.6) People have to be clear why hope is a theological virtue. They also need to have a large enough hope, one that is not narrowed down to merely what I can get tomorrow.

Now, Pope Benedict XVI wrote an encyclical *Spe salvi*, that deals with the many dimensions of hope. The key aspect of hope is that

> we see as a distinguishing mark of Christians the fact that they have a future: it is not that they know the details of what awaits them, but they know in general terms that their life will not end in emptiness. Only when the future is certain as a positive reality does it become possible to live the present as well. So, now

---

[175] Walter Kasper, "III. The Theology of History," *Encyclopedia of Theology - A Concise Sacramentum Mundi*, Karl Rahner S.J. ed., Burns and Oates: London, 1975, 632.

we can say: Christianity was not only 'good news'—the communication of a hitherto unknown content. In our language we would say: the Christian message was not only 'informative' but 'performative'. (SS 2)

By performative, Benedict XVI means that hope enables the faithful to function properly in the present. It gives people the spiritual context in which to live.

Christmas and the Christmas Season follow Advent. During the season, the Church celebrates the first day of the secular calendar year. The first of January has been made the Feast of Mary the Mother of God. She is the Mother of God because she is the epitome of faithfulness, not in some abstract sense but as the one who believes in God's history with his people up to the moment of her Magnificat and beyond. The Church begins the secular year not so much with a secular celebration but by specifically reminding the whole Church community to the mystery of Mary, the faithful one, the powerful model of faith as it is lived positively. (Mary, the Mother of God) Her commitment is: "I am the handmaid of the Lord," (Luke 1:38) and it models the complete disponibility of the Christian. (Cf. LG 52-54) But it is the Church who is celebrating the feast, showing the world the right posture for entering what would otherwise be a pagan New Year. Christ has already come and established his Church. Mary shows what membership of the Church looks like. The Church shows the world the spiritual posture for living in time.

The Christmas Season is followed by a period of Ordinary Time before the season of Lent. Ordinary Time is simply when there are no major feasts. The word Lent is from the Old English *lencten*, literally referring to the lengthening of days in spring. It is a penitential time, in a period in history when penitence is far from most people's minds. Since penitence is a major part of Christian life due to its acknowledgement of God, this time is one occasion to advocate for penitential practices. It is also time to teach what Confession means and underlying everything should be a proper understanding of conversion. (Cf. Chapter One The Mystery of Iniquity.)

The high feasts of Holy Week, at the end of Lent, help the whole Church to experience the great mysteries of Christ's life, his death and resurrection liturgically. The faithful work on becoming more and more like Christ and these feasts are the key moments in their spiritual growth through union with Christ.

The feasts of Pentecost, Holy Trinity and The Body of Christ lead the Church into another period of Ordinary Time that will end with the beginning of Advent, once again.

Chapter Six The Bishop and his Priests

Bishops should always embrace priests with a special love since the latter to the best of their ability assume the Bishops' anxieties and carry them on day by day so zealously. (CD 15)

(1) Introduction

Among other things, the wave of scandals in the Church in the US and other countries, highlights the relationship between the Bishop and his priests. The theology of the relationship between the priest and the Bishop is generally well known but there is still the matter of living it out in practice.

Half in jest, one priest described the *actual* relationship between the priest and the Bishop as 'indentured servitude'.[176] This is not to discourage new candidates for the priesthood or to denigrate Bishops. This situation is however one face of the "easy yoke" of Jesus. (Matthew 11:30) One *is* responsible to the Bishop. The relation is no mere secular connection, although it has some similarities. It is rather the different degrees of participation in the priesthood of Christ that is the key. The one who completed the *Summa* after Thomas Aquinas' death explained:[177]

> [the Bishop] is the higher who represents Christ according to a greater perfection. Now a priest represents Christ in that he fulfilled a certain ministry by himself, whereas a Bishop represents him in that he instituted other ministers and founded the Church. Hence it belongs to a Bishop to dedicate a thing to the Divine Offices, as establishing the divine worship after the manner of Christ. For this reason also a Bishop is especially called the bridegroom of the Church even as Christ is. (ST Supp. Q. 40 a. 4)

The Bishop manifests Christ in a certain way that is far superior to that of the priest hence the priest's subservience to the Bishop. Vatican II: "In the Bishops, therefore, for whom priests are assistants, Our Lord Jesus Christ, the Supreme High Priest, is present in the midst of those who believe." (LG 21) In the present crises of child abuse, the pandemic and the cultural revolution, the personal maturity of the priest and the Bishop, and their understanding of their relationship are going to be sorely tested. The scandals do mean that the time for naivete has long passed.[178] The research of Mc'Shea has shown that the authority of the Bishop is free of many of the lay social claims on the Bishop that existed a century ago. In earlier times, the power

---

[176] Fr. Dwight Longenecker, "Why was the McCarrick abuse hushed up?", https://dwightlongenecker.com/why-was-the-mccarrick-abuse-hushed-up/

[177] Probably Fra Rainaldo da Piperno using propositions from Aquinas' *Commentary on the Sentences of Peter Lombard, Book IV.*

[178] Cf. Bronwen Catherine McShea, "Bishops Unbound-The History behind today's Crisis of Church Leadership," *First Things*, January 2019.

of the Bishop was restrained by legitimate obligations to other figures in society. Now, they only exist in a much weaker form in the bodies such as the diocese's pastoral council and other consultative groups. The claims on the Bishop, such as the obligations to consult others and to take their needs into account are not going to be rapidly restored in the short term, but the research does show that the present high degree of episcopal authority was not always the case.

The image of indentured servitude does have some use because it captures the quiet uncomplaining cooperation of Clergy, yet it is sometimes accompanied by the resentment that some men carry around with them. This resentment might be due to family issues, personal immaturities or to dissatisfaction with the decisions of the Bishop. On occasion, this situation might be further helped or complicated by the activities of the chancery staff who act in the name of the Bishop.[179] Much the same kinds of aggravations can be found in the situations of personnel in many big organizations and businesses. The fact is that they should be much tempered by the Catholic ethic which might have to be learned insofar as it applies to ecclesiastical leadership.

The relation between Clergy and Bishops involves many factors. Some come from the theology of the Church because a diocese is a communion in the spiritually constituted Body of Christ and some dynamics come from how men, of comparable age and status, in the secular world behave when dealing with someone having near total power over their situations and their futures. One similarly finds 'going along to get along' in some marriages, in some military offices, in businesses, and in government offices. There is also a possible dynamic on the part of the Bishop, who might be politically inclined or might have a problem as simple as being scared of his diocesan departments. The problem is that these dynamics are a caricature of what would happen if the spiritual structure instituted by Christ and his apostles were followed rigorously. It may sound very trite but in fact when priests and Bishops are acting like Christians all day every day the appearance of the Church changes dramatically. However, just retraining angry, arbitrary or snobbish Clergy would be a great start. Laypeople do have some very valid complaints about the leadership.

The terrible thing that the present scandals have revealed is that at least some Clergy—and these are Clergy who were originally trained to know what Christian behavior is—choose *not* to live by what they know and instead they have reverted to sinful secular cultural modes of behavior. After all, these behaviors are not so rare in US culture. Apparently, the malefactors do not have faith in the validity—and more

---

[179] The Chancery is the Bishop's staff. They handle everything from the financial management of the diocese to the diocesan law court and charitable wings of the diocese. They will be both Clergy and Laity.

than that, the wholesomeness—of the Christian revelation on which the moral doctrine is based. For them, cultural and selfish considerations such as getting what I want, putting on a good face, concealing bad things and so on rule the day. This is extremely embarrassing for those Clergy who *do* live the faith as well as teach it. Having priests who do not believe that Christ's teaching is true interferes with the public presence of the Church. Moreover, many lay people are also rightfully disgusted and confused.

If one has faith, then Christian moral teaching is true. Moreover, Christianity does have all of the elements needed to shape healthy and productive relationships and make them spiritually fulfilling, even though it is much quicker and easier not to follow the moral teaching. The alternative to believing is to simply deviate from God's will. This is sinful and it may well have serious civil legal repercussions as well. Such choices on the part of a few make a joke out of the mission of the Church to spread the values of Christ to the world. In many cases, the recent scandals show that the morals of the pagan culture and its preoccupation with self-indulgence and survival dominate how some Clergy behave.

With regard to the Bishop, religious Clergy are not in exactly the same situation as diocesan Clergy. Religious Clergy usually work in dioceses by a contract between their order and the diocese. Nevertheless, anecdotally at least, secular patterns of behavior seem to intrude just as much among religious Clergy as among their diocesan counterparts. Historically, there seems to have been a general slackening of trust in the value of orthodoxy in the last century. In a Protestant culture such as in the US, this is not surprising even though it is disappointing. The answer as to why it happens is more complex. I suspect that it has to do with illusions about the superiority of the US Enlightenment secular culture over Catholic teaching but that needs research.

Now, of course, *some* diocesan structures do work admirably but, as the scandals indicate, sometimes there is a lack of Christianity not just in the normal relations between some Clergy but also in Clergy-lay relations, in the arena of child abuse, adult homosexual abuse of adults, and abuse of religious[180]—absolutely the last things that ought to be associated with Catholic Clergy. From a practical existential point of view, every priest has to learn very quickly that Paul's dilemma was that "I myself, with the mind, serve the law of God, but with the flesh, the law of sin." (Romans 7:25) Paul's experience is typical for the rest of us. Aquinas quoted the problem as well. (ST II-I q.109 a. 8)

---

[180] Fr. Paul Sullins, "Is Catholic Clergy sex abuse related to homosexual priests?" Ruth Institute, 4845 Lake Street Suite 217, Lake Charles, Louisiana 70605, 2018-11-06.

Paul's mention of the mind was crucial as Aquinas went on to explain: Paul could hold on to God's law with his mind and thus "in this state man can abstain from all mortal sin, which takes its stand in his reason; but man cannot abstain from all venial sin on account of the corruption of his lower appetite of sensuality." (ST II-I q.109 a.8) The reason that man cannot avoid all sin is because: "For [although] man can, indeed, repress each of its movements (and hence they are sinful and voluntary), but not all, because whilst he is resisting one, another may arise." (ST II-I q.109 a.8) So, in crude terms, we come back to the twenty minute-a-day Catholic. (Chapter One)

When such a person chooses to cooperate with grace, then he/she gradually learns to love God and neighbour for longer and longer each day. The tricky thing is that this is an anthropological issue and so priests and Bishops have exactly the same problem, despite their ordinations.

However, being loving is only part of the equation. Loving is an act of the will and to love involves knowing what is good and then choosing it. That is the one way that the intellect is involved but there is another way too. When Peter and John encounter authorities who are trying to suppress the message of Jesus, they ask quite straight-forwardly: "Judge for yourselves whether it is right in God's sight for us to obey you rather than God. Surely, we cannot help speaking of what we have heard and seen." (Acts 4:19-20) Clergy have heard and seen the Lord speaking in liturgy, in community and in their classes. So even intellectually, provided that they are fully devoted to Christ, they "cannot help speaking of what they have heard and seen." There is no mention here of also passing on the messages of one's political party or one's social class. This point will arise again and again because we live and die "in God's sight."

This book was written before the recovery of the Catholic structure and relationships in dioceses has been fully attempted.[181] What is involved here is not so much restructuring—an American obsession—but rather the consistent application of

---

[181] The Dallas Charter, The Charter for the Protection of Children and Young People was passed by the USCCB in June 2002. And Pope Francis motu proprio, *Vos estis lux mundi*, came out 7 May 2019. There has not been sufficient time for the *motu proprio* to be implemented but it is apparent that the Charter has had many positive effects. Beyond dealing with extremely egregious cases, there has to be the more general implementation of Christianity itself. This involves teaching basic pictures of authentic Christian male and female behavior, that are more finely grained than simply speaking about love. Most people do not know how to be loving all day and every day. For example: what are the components of a priest's behavior when dealing with the poor? How does a Catholic layperson operate in the Chancery office? Just to cite a few examples.

Christian principles to relationships between Clergy and with chancery and the evaluation of results. What structural development that was needed seems to have been dealt with by empowering metropolitan Bishops to investigate Bishops and by the procedural rules laid out in *Vos estis lux*, from Pope Francis, 7 May 2019. The real issue is taking Catholicism seriously. It is a highly successful and very satisfying rule of life.

Recovery of Catholic practice in structures, for example, aids the credibility of the Church. When the scandals started to surface, Archbishop Chaput OFM of Philadelphia pointed out that: "We have lost credibility." This applies to the priest-Bishop relation just as much as it applies to the relation between Clergy and laypeople. Faith is the issue once again. The relationship between priests and Bishops only works when the priest, the Bishop and the Laity all grasp the theology involved and then enter it in complete faith. Everyone needs to believe that theologically directed behaviour is part of the plan of salvation, so it is graced and develops the holiness of both parties. This behaviour includes the other two theological virtues, hope in this theological structure and expressing charity in all relationships. Given the egregious behaviour of some authorities, rebuilding the trust that is also a part of faith will take some time.

For priests, what is involved is not merely the relationship to a boss who is absent most of the time but the relationship to authorities as well as with brothers and sisters in Christ. This takes a lot of maturity all round. This point highlights a major difficulty in the Church in many places and that is that most Clergy only learn enough and grow enough to get ordained. Do they learn more and grow more after ordination? Who asks them to?

One final point: the hypocrisy in the US Catholic Church has yet to be fully documented, but from what is known already, it can be said that in many respects, a new priest is joining an organization with a number of Pharisees and yet he still hopes to serve and live with integrity, to grow to sanctity, as a Catholic priest among them. (At the time of writing, about 26 Bishops have had to step down in the US as a result of the abuse controversy.) The posturing and the fraudulent presence of some priests and Bishops means that the new priest should spend time reading the Gospel and the Pauline texts on hypocrisy. He will often meet the modern Pharisees and will have to reflect on how to work with them and sometimes against them.

(2) The Theology

The relationship between the Bishop and the priest is, first and foremost, a theological issue and not just a social or managerial one. Also, the theology is not just an ideal. The theology of an institution describes the nature of a spiritual sacramental reality *that God's Spirit brings about* to the extent that we cooperate with it. The real issue is how to extend the spiritual sacramental aspects into practice and to keep doing it, through the continued conversion of the priest and the Bishop.

The New Testament says a great deal about Catholic leadership. For example, when Jesus washed the feet of the disciples, he said

> You call me 'teacher' and 'master,' and rightly so, for indeed I am. If I, therefore, the master and teacher, have washed your feet, you ought to wash one another's feet. I have given you a model to follow, so that as I have done for you, you should also do. Amen, amen, I say to you, no slave is greater than his master nor any messenger greater than the one who sent him. If you understand this, blessed are you if you do it. (John 13:13-17)

One would think that the image of a priest as an aristocrat would not survive in the face of this teaching. Nevertheless, in some people it has for 1500 years! This illustrates how Clergy can fool themselves that almost anything that they do is automatically Catholic. Unfortunately, Laity do no better! We are all bound by the 20-minute rule.

Then, there are the extensive teachings from Saint Paul, in his letters. He wrote to Titus, for example,

> For a Bishop as God's steward must be blameless, not arrogant, not irritable, not a drunkard, not aggressive, not greedy for sordid gain, but hospitable, a lover of goodness, temperate, just, holy, and self-controlled, holding fast to the true message as taught so that he will be able both to exhort with sound doctrine and to refute opponents. (Titus 1:7-9)

Then, further into the letter, he explained the characteristic *steadiness* of Christian life: "As for yourself, you must say what is consistent with sound doctrine, namely, that older men should be temperate, dignified, self-controlled, sound in faith, love, and endurance." (Titus 2:1, 2) The 'older men' are the presbyters, who soon came to be called priests. Then too: act in such a way as to "show yourself as a model of good deeds in every respect, with integrity in your teaching, dignity, and sound speech." (Titus 2: 7, 8) Of course, all of this applies equally to priests and Laity.

Celebrity worship in the US causes a bizarre separation between what people do and who they are. Everyone knows a 'talented musician' whose personal life is a swirl of drugs, and sex, for example. However, demonstrating Catholic teaching consistently in one's life relies on the integrated nature of one's being where what one does and who one is are of a piece. Christ does what he does *because* of who he is. For example, he says: "if it is by the Spirit of God that I drive out demons, then the kingdom of God has come upon you." (Matthew 12:28) He is still the power of God present in the world through the Spirit of God. Clergy today have received the same Spirit. Laity too!

(3) Charitable Service

In presenting the theology of the episcopate, the Second Vatican Council started with the spiritual status of the Bishop. The quote from St. Thomas (above) already indicated what the spiritual state of being of the Bishop is.

In the same vein, the council taught "that Bishops by divine institution have succeeded to the place of the apostles,[182] as shepherds of the Church, and he who hears them, hears Christ, and he who rejects them, rejects Christ and Him who sent Christ."[183](LG 20)[184] They led up to this statement by describing Jesus' authoritative selection of the Twelve in history. (Luke 10:16) So Jesus' making of the apostles is ontologically grounded! Then the Bishops succeeded the apostles, so that "by a succession running from the beginning, [they] are passers-on of the apostolic seed." (LG 20) In practice this means that "as sharers in [Jesus'] power [Bishops] might make all peoples his disciples, and sanctify and govern them, and thus spread his Church, and by ministering to it under the guidance of the Lord." (LG 19)

The last proposition is based on the Bishop's complete participation in the Offices of Christ, as prophet, priest and king. Consequently, there is simply no way to avoid episcopal authority and his authoritative decisions. This is what the Office of Christ as King is all about.[185] But the authority in the Church is more differentiated still: Jesus "placed Blessed Peter over the other apostles and instituted in him a permanent and visible source and foundation of unity of faith and communion." (LG 18) There is the Supreme Pontiff and the essential relationship of the valid episcopate with him.

Then having dealt with the authority and power questions, the council got to the issue of the Bishop's service. The gifts of Christ that Bishops receive at ordination mean that:

> Bishops, therefore, with their helpers, the priests and deacons, have taken up the *service* of the community, presiding in place of God over the flock, whose

---

[182] This statement has the accompanying note: Cf. Council of Trent, Sess. 23, ecr. de sacr. Ordinis, cap. 4; enz. 960 (1768); Conc. Vat. I, ess. 4 Const. Dogm. I *De Ecclesia Christi*, cap. 3: Denz. 1828 (3061). Pius XII, Encyclical. *Mystici Corporis*, 29 iun. 1943: ASS 35 (1943) p. 209 et 212. Codex Iuris Canonici, c. 29 1.

[183] Accompanying note: Cf. Leo XIII, Letter. *Et sane*, 17 dec. 1888: ASS 21 (1888) p. 321 s.

[184] Cf. Luke 10:16.

[185] But do see the history: Bronwyn Catherine McShea, "Bishops unbound." *First Things*, January 2019.

shepherds they are, as teachers for doctrine, priests for sacred worship, and ministers for governing. (LG 20)[186] (Emphasis added.)

Note how the statements that *could* have been interpreted in a merely authoritarian fashion have deliberately been transposed into a Christological key through the insertion of the word 'service'. (Referring to the 'authoritarian' role recalls the sixties horror of having people use their legitimate authority.) The whole clerical structure, which for good reasons is a hierarchy[187], is at the service of the community precisely *because* of the special notion of presence-in-service demonstrated by Christ. *He* is the one who speaks with authority (Matthew 7:29) so authority cannot be all bad. Then, further, in Jesus' words: "the Son of Man did not come to be served but to serve and to give his life as a ransom for many." (Matthew 20:28) Authority and service are not contradictory. (Earlier the council had explained the participation of the hierarchy in the Offices of Christ.)

Understanding what 'service' means involves the interrelationships of the Clergy with each other and with the Laity. At a supreme level, their service is an *intellectual* service based on the highest power of the soul, the power of reason. The Clergy's proclamation should be true. This is not a trivial issue. The identity and unity of the Church as the Body of the Divine Word of God is at stake. A common mind is the basis of this unity. "Be transformed by the renewal of your mind." (Romans 12:2) On another level, at the level of the will, service is a personal working to love the other to bring them to greater and more true humanity. First of all, the individual has to learn what the good of the other person is. They can only learn this from the Church. In other words, Bishops and priests are to love people the way that Christ does.

However, there is a problem, a tendency that disrupts the purity of the service: the hierarchy in the US is seriously divided along ideological lines, as it is in many countries, much to the shame of the episcopate because it demonstrates that they are not clear about why they are there in the first place! They do not see the problem in its true seriousness. The division also interferes with the service that they are called to offer to the People of God.

The most problematic feature of the theological landscape today is the willing self-division of the Bishops into so-called liberal and conservative camps. The labels

---

[186] In the document, the article has a note attached: S. Ign. M., Philad., Praef.; ed. Funk, I, 264. Also, according to Pope Benedict XVI: "At this point, simultaneously, a new concept of power and a new concept of lordship and dominion is born." *Introduction to Christianity*, San Francisco: 1990, 104.

[187] The term comes from the ancient Greek word for 'sacred ruler'. There is a structured authority in the Church due to the need for spiritual leadership where everyone in carrying out the mission of the Church.

themselves are borrowed from political discourse and are completely unsuited to describing the nature of the *theological* obligations that are part of the Church's mission. Historically these labels have a complex history that is not of interest here. The trick of the Left has been to have everyone calmly buying into the use of these labels with the implication that the liberals and the conservatives are just two different groups of opinions. The opinions do not relate to reality, they just indicate different tastes. In fact they represent two completely different kinds of thinking!

My point is that theology is based on ontology. Clergy should know that. But some Clergy are poorly trained and so these political labels are simply adopted instead of reinstating the proper analytical terms, which are 'orthodox' and 'heterodox'. These relate to reality and the political terms do not. Yet many Bishops, Clergy and Laity just go along with it.

The result of going along with the political terms is that the truth questions are reduced to mere opinions—'you can believe what you want, and I will believe what I want' and that is not Catholicism. Catholicism teaches the truth then the truth applies to everyone at all times because it is the universal truth of existence. Apparently, the lack of precision suits everyone even though it has allowed pockets of seriously heterodox thinking to exist and to thrive. This means that the true Christ is not being preached, and the true nature of man, community etc. is not presented consistently everywhere by the Church.

Misunderstanding what Catholicism is, allows and promotes intellectual divisions in dioceses, seminaries, colleges and parishes—which is apparently not a problem for some Bishops and religious superiors! Yet their participation in Christ's Office of Prophet requires that they teach *the* truth. A large part of their job resides in passing on accurate information about humanity, community and Christ. The intellectual dimension of Catholicism is not just something that would be nice to attend to. It is essential to accurate evangelization. It is essential for the unity of the Church, which is one of the signs of the true Church, after all. It is neglected at humanity's peril.

In total contrast to the weak-kneed acceptance of division, as far as the unity of priests is concerned, the council taught that:

> In virtue of their common sacred ordination and mission, *all priests are bound together in intimate brotherhood*, which naturally and freely manifests itself in mutual aid, spiritual as well as material, pastoral as well as personal, in their meetings and in communion of life, of labor and charity. (LG 28) (Emphasis added,)

There is a spiritual brotherhood that bonds the Clergy together, all of them—no boys clubs. It is driven by the Spirit of God and not by considerations of psychological maturity or political affiliation. One should validly expect this behavior from religious and Laity as well. The 20-minute rule means that priests, most of whom are nowhere near living Catholicism twenty-four hours a day, have a lot of work to do.

With many chanceries just doing what the previous administration did, to implement this deepened Christian vision of what Church government and community relations could be would be a monumental task. The deepened vision of Christianity is founded on love of neighbor and love of God. Unfortunately, the 20-minute rule (explained in Chapter One) applies here as well. The Christian vision applies to using doctrine too. After all the truth is intimately connected with being loving. So, perhaps Christian rules and Christian truth should control the way that chanceries function? And the ways that dioceses and parishes function too?

The common deficiencies in love and truth have caused serious problems, as is being found out at the time of writing. The way that Clergy are disconnected from each other might be one of the contributing causes to the abuse crisis. Perhaps Clergy have slipped into drifting in and out of Christian behavior and so some have avoided the issues or covered them up or done disgusting things. Regarding the latter: another possible cause could be that abusive priests come from a culture that already has a high rate of abuse so that inevitably some abused men will become priests and then abuse further.

The brotherhood of the Clergy requires that the Clergy (including Bishops) be the grown-ups in the room. Only adults can make the spiritual communion function fully! Otherwise it just becomes a boys' club. One of the spiritual communion's dimensions is sharing in a common truth. Part of this truth is that: "Christians should be taught that they live not only for themselves, but, according to the demands of the new law of charity; as every man has received grace, he must administer the same to others." (PO 6) Logically, this applies to everyone in the Church including the hierarchy. The mention of grace and charity shifts the concept of service into its proper spiritual frame, one from which all Clergy and Laity should be working.

After my initial writing, someone reminded me that frequently the Laity are the adults in the room. It was suggested that this is because most Laity have phenomenal responsibilities such holding down jobs where they can get fired. Laity have to bring up families and so are very conscious of the value of real relationships and of money. The implication was that parishes and dioceses are not always the most responsible sustainers of relationships or responsible consumers of money. As noted elsewhere, the US dioceses and religious orders did find four billion dollars to pay for legal penalties in judgements against individual Clergy and organizations. This money was never intended for such uses. It was given to serve the poor.

Going back to the Vatican II document on priests: "Bishops regard [priests] as necessary helpers and counselors in the ministry and in their role of teaching, sanctifying and nourishing the People of God." (PO 7) Bishops and priests have a collaborative job to do! That is why they are there at all. Consequently, the council went on:

> on account of this communion in the same priesthood and ministry, Bishops should regard priests as their brothers and friends and be concerned as far as they are able for their material and especially for their spiritual well-being." (PO 7)

This fraternal relationship is often affected by suspicions and immaturities. It can get frayed by the ambitions of some of the Bishops, priests and Laity. It is also diminished by historical events. For example, it has been seriously damaged by the revelations about Clergy child abuse and the cover-ups.

A further implication of the Bishop-priest relationship appears in the next sentence in the document: "For above all upon the Bishops rests the heavy responsibility for the sanctity of their priests. Therefore, they should exercise the greatest care in the continual formation of their priests." (PO 7) The power of the term 'sanctity', lies in the fact that it shifts the weight of the relationship out of the boy's club into its proper context, that of a holy priesthood serving the Bishop and worthy of serving a holy people.

Sanctity is a vast topic, but something needs to be said because it is what is expected of all Christians, ordained or not.

(4) Holiness

The sanctity of human beings comes about as they participate in the holiness of God starting with the sanctity of human life itself, because life is conferred by the living God. As Paul reminds: "Do you not know that you are the temple of God, and that the Spirit of God dwells in you? If anyone destroys God's temple,
God will destroy that person; for the temple of God, which you are, is holy." (I Corinthians 3:16-17) This is done by the God who is the God of life. (Cf. Luke 20:38)

Now, growing in holiness involves developing the virtues. It involves suffering in love. It involves obeying the Natural Law. These are the signs of the holiness of those who follow Christ. In the process, they are becoming conformed by degrees to Christ. If priests are growing in this way then they will know what to tell their people.

Article seven (above) of *Presbyterorum ordinis* relies on the character of the *interpersonal* relationship between the Bishop and his priests. First, one can conclude that a significant part of the relationship's success rests on the shoulders of the Bishop. At this point, the cultural fascination with secular management techniques[188] intervenes because most Bishops staff out the work of their interpersonal relationship to liaison officials of some kind. Viewing this set of interpersonal relationships as *sacramental* might transpose the focus of the Bishop's view of his work enormously.

Secondly, the view of the council was that the relationship between Bishops and their priests relies on personal knowledge. This is how persons relate and affirm each other. Such knowledge has a *theological* role because the community of the Bishop and his priests is a spiritually driven entity. They are bonded spiritually as persons and not merely as good-old-boys. The spiritual dimension is the concern. Promoting the interpersonal relationships of this apostolic community is essential for the presence of the Church in the world. How this happens in a large diocese is an open question. Inevitably where a Bishop has a large number of responsibilities, he can choose—and has to, to stay sane—which ones he will spend his time on. He still has to care for his own spiritual growth. The spiritual community's development here is also open for discussion, but the sense of a corps of Clergy, men united by a spiritual bond, pastoring the diocese together for the glory of God, the care of the Church community and service to the world, gets weakened if it is not one of the primary attentions of the Bishop.

Sometimes, it is very unsettling to find that the body of Clergy is not homogenous as far as their training or their take on Catholicism is concerned. Many were trained in the sixties and seventies, and smaller groups were trained later. Inevitably, some of each group imagine that they are called to be aristocrats. In their minds, status and an independence are attached to their 'job', so they do not work beyond certain hours, or with certain people, or do certain tasks ("I don't do windows.") etc. etc. They do not take instruction from the Bishop ("You can't touch me.") and so on. Historically, they are holdovers from an age long past and manifest it in their giving in to their own inadequacies.

With such people, their expectations are clashing with the theological requirements of their role. Frequently. the aristocrats behave differently from those who were trained later and especially from those who have taken on the priesthood despite all the distrust of Clergy. Those with aristocratic dreams ought really to be weeded out in the seminary. All Clergy now have to contend with the fact that Clergy, even the aristocrats, have lost the trust of the people! Lay people are not so easily fooled any more. In fact, it may well be that pressure from Laity will drive some of the needed improvements in the diocese.

---

[188] This is a force that should not be underestimated! Concupiscent people will seek any behavior rather than that of developing their own spiritual lives.

The majority of abuse cases occurred early in the last seventy-years, the time frame chosen for the data collection of the Pennsylvania report, for example.[189] Fortunately, religious psychology, the evaluation of candidates and the formation process in the seminary have all improved over the last decades. Hopefully, promoting the imperial mindset in seminaries has diminished as well. Perhaps the spiritual dimension of the priesthood and the role of service now receive more emphasis. Certainly, there is much more focus on the psychology of the priest in formation for the priesthood and a lot more teaching about psychological boundaries in interpersonal relationships. Interestingly, mature men with integrity know these things already! These developments have not yet made much change in the composition of the dioceses and orders because right now men are not being ordained in large numbers.

Back to the Bishop: allied to maintaining the spiritual community of the Clergy in Christ is the Bishop's responsibility for the ongoing formation of his Clergy. Once again this is something that usually gets staffed out. Also Clergy, particularly pastors, are usually swamped with work so how much free time do they have for additional formation?[190] It is still part of one's pastoral responsibilities. In fact, everything in *Presbyterorum ordinis* and in the formation of a spiritual pastoral communion rests on the centrality of communing in the truth, communing in the Word. So, apparently some kind of input has to happen. Everything turns on how seriously Clergy take the idea of consciously belonging to a spiritual communion in grace and truth and that is their responsibility to consciously make it happen day-by-day.

(5) Reciprocal responsibilities

Presbyterorum ordinis also notes the reciprocal responsibility of the priest vis-a-vis the Bishop:

> Priests, never losing sight of the fullness of the priesthood which the Bishops enjoy, must respect in them the authority of Christ, the Supreme Shepherd. They must therefore stand by their Bishops in sincere charity and obedience. This priestly obedience imbued with a spirit of cooperation is based on the very sharing in the episcopal ministry which is conferred on priests both through the Sacrament of Orders and the canonical mission. (PO 7)

---

[189] Cf. Kevin Jones, "Pennsylvania Grand Jury's Catholic Sex-Abuse Report Gets a Fact-Check", NCR, January 14, 2019.

[190] Sometimes lay people are not aware of what a pastor does. Obviously, there are pastors who do nothing and parishioners who know that. A fully functioning pastor, on the other hand, is responsible for maintenance of the physical plant of the parish church, the celebration of the sacraments, the maintaining of records, management of finances. This is even before he gets into the massive task of building the parish into a place where people come to become holy.

The theological point on which everything turns is that priests and Bishops participate in the priesthood of Christ to a different degree. The Bishop has the fullness of orders because "by episcopal consecration the fullness of the sacrament of Orders is conferred, that fullness of power, namely, which both in the Church's liturgical practice and in the language of the Fathers of the Church is called the high priesthood, the supreme power of the sacred ministry." (LG 21) Having the fullness of the priesthood means that the Bishop has the powers necessary to constitute all of the elements of the local Church (diocese).

The council explained that the high priestly power means that Bishops in "an eminent and visible way sustains the roles of Christ himself as Teacher, Shepherd and High Priest, and that they act in his person." (LG 21) With the licit ordination of the Bishop, his participation in the communion (or college) of Bishops, and his unity with the Holy Father is established. Then, the Bishop participates in the roles of Christ and "acts as his representative." (LG 21) This could not be a more superlative kind of power. The council meant that the Bishop can act *in persona Christi*—in the person of Christ, in terms of teaching, sanctifying and governing. However, there is still "only one mediator between God and man, Jesus Christ." (I Timothy 2:5) There is a oneness of Christ and his Church and in that Church, Christ acts in his Church '*ex persona caput*' i.e. as the Head, as the Bridegroom. Further, Christ also acts '*ex persona corporis*' as the body, that is as Bride. (cf. CCC 796) (Explained in Chapter Four.)

Now, the priest participates in the ministry of the Bishop. That is the only reason that he is ordained. The priest's obedience, respect and charity are part of responding authentically to the high-priestly status of the Bishop, for the theological good of the Church, the Bishop and the priest himself. The priest extends the teaching of the Bishop because he teaches on the Bishop's behalf. He extends the ministry of sanctification of the Bishop. Finally, he extends the governance of the Bishop. How this actually works in practice will depend on the degree of Christian maturity of the two parties. The comment in the first chapter about '20-minutes-a-day Christians' applies here too.

One of the more surprising things that becomes apparent very quickly is that it is not uncommon to find Clergy and Laity who work in the chancery or the Bishop's conference and who have a heterodox concept of Church that they are trying to insert in the operations of the diocese or the conference or the religious order. To have vicar-generals who want women's ordinations etc. is just one example. It is part of the Bishop's good stewardship of the diocese that he weeds out such people as unpleasant as that is to do. Of course, this presumes that the Bishop is orthodox himself.

Several times a day, Bishops and priests face the question: how am I going to handle this issue—as a Christian or in the way that a man of my status, culture or political party with no faith would handle it—as a boss (Bishop) or in reaction to my indentured servitude (priest)?

Lastly, for completeness' sake, the responsibilities of other ordinaries should be mentioned. Male religious major superiors, for example, although only for the length of their tenure, are ordinaries much like Bishops, although they cannot ordain. They have exactly the same responsibilities with regard to their priests in all of the senses mentioned above.

(6) Personal Sin

The power of ordination does not guarantee that priests and Bishops are free from sin so, according to the *Catechism*:

> This presence of Christ in the minister is not to be understood as if the latter were preserved from all human weaknesses, the spirit of domination, error, even sin. The power of the Holy Spirit does not guarantee all acts of ministers in the same way. While this guarantee extends to the sacraments, so that even the minister's sin cannot impede the fruit of grace, in many other acts the minister leaves human traces that are not always signs of fidelity to the Gospel and consequently can harm the apostolic fruitfulness of the Church. (CCC 1550)

Here the *Catechism* points to the ways in which priestly actions are guaranteed to be grace-filled and also the ways that the efficacy of some priestly actions is limited by the sins of the priest. The reason for starting this book with a chapter on iniquity is precisely the need to offer a complete anthropology of the priest with all his powers and limitations. The complete anthropology greatly helps in the understanding the priest's own growth in sanctity but also in showing how he contributes to the spiritual efficacy of organizations of Clergy and so that he may better help his parishioners.

(7) Chancery Personnel

Lastly, the personnel of the diocesan chancery and the personnel of the US Bishops' conference have not yet been mentioned but they are intimately involved in the practical exercise of the relationships between the Bishop, priest and the Laity. The problem is that chancery personnel are rarely if ever instructed in the theological meaning of what they do. Mostly, at best, they know the principles of their jobs, secretary, accountant, etc. The problem is that their training for their positions is often entirely secular and is based on secular and even unconsciously anti-Catholic thinking. So, in finance, in communications, or even simply evaluating diocesan projects, personnel can be far removed from the Catholic worldview. The Catholic world view is not optional. At the very least, it needs to involve staff's acquiescence with the Catholic world view. In fact, working for the advancement of that world view should be a professional requirement because everyone in chancery is hired to advance the work of the Bishop.

Chancery personnel are being asked to exercise a theological role in the diocese even though they are sometimes at one remove from the direct relation between the Bishop, his Clergy and his people. The theological structure provides context for everything from how they answer the telephone to what they pass on to the Bishop or from the Bishop, what they pass on to the Bishops in the conference and from them to the rest of the Church in the US. All kinds of pitfalls open up here if they do not have theological training and loyalty to the Church. Personnel in the right positions can completely undermine valid elements of the operation of diocese or the Bishops conference. Pro-abortion personnel can get in the way of pro-life initiatives simply by changing the emphases in communications, for example.

(8) Contradictory Witnesses

One of many great surprises for a newly ordained priest is that, some Clergy do not consistently follow Catholic teaching. The Clergy may know the words but sometimes what they think they mean relies a lot on personal opinion and which political party they belong to. The same is often true of the Laity. Knowing the correct meaning of something is crucial especially when people's salvation depends on it. It is worth noting, for example, that Catholic marriages fail at the same rate as non-Catholic Marriages, because people will sometimes get married without the vaguest idea of what the sacrament really means. The International Theological Commission has extensively treated the cases of baptized non-believers in Marriage.[191] The problem is that the heterodox Clergy do not know what they do not know. With that intellectual flaw and with pride they comfortably spoil everything they touch. They undermine the good work of their predecessors, for example.

Experiences like this are the reason why the priest cannot be too brittle when he joins his brother Clergy in the diocese or in a religious order. He is going to encounter a lot of almost inexplicable ignorance, obtuseness or just plain nastiness in the community of Jesus Christ and yet he continues to serve Christ and his Church.

One shattering example is that some Clergy support abortion, some Bishops do too.[192] When asked they will say that they do not, yet they vote for politicians who

---

[191] International Theological Commission, *The Reciprocity between Faith and Sacraments in the Sacramental Economy*, December 19, 2019.
[192] For example, "US Bishops' Catholic Campaign for Human Development continues to fund pro-abortion, pro-LGBT groups," https://www.lifesitenews.com/news/us-Bishops-catholic-campaign-for-human-development-continues-to-fund-pro-ab

lavishly fund abortions. What they do not acknowledge is that there is no constitutional mechanism for the voter who votes for pro-death politicians because he likes some of their policies, to subsequently take back the abortion part of his vote. In their pride they can imagine that there is. One quickly finds the limits to their dedication to the Church!

Then, there are Clergy who don't believe the Church's teaching on sin. There are certain sins that they do not listen to when they are mentioned in Penance—if indeed they ever celebrate the Sacrament of Penance.

These are signs of the presence of modern agnostic liberalism in the Church and some of the Clergy have gotten away with this for decades. Some Bishops have lost sight of the importance of the integrity of the intellectual side of Catholicism or better, of their responsibility to take the steps to ensure that the truth is proclaimed everywhere and always in their dioceses. They might censure individual Clergy on occasion but as regards getting the whole diocese to teach the same thing about Catholic truth and practice, they often do not act. Rebel Clergy also miss the fact that there are more and more very well-informed Laity. Bishops and papal nuncios need to take them very seriously. I have heard the complaint "I never heard anything back" when people write to their Bishop about a concern, more times that I can count.

Fortunately, there are also many good and faithful priests. It takes a while to identify them, but they are there. These are men to associate with.

Chapter Seven The Priest and Laity

The People of God and the human race in whose midst it lives render service to each other. Thus, the mission of the Church will show its religious, and by that very fact, its supremely human character. *Gaudium et Spes*

(1) Introduction

The 1987 Synod on the Laity taught that the Church

is a mystery because the very life and love of the Father, Son and Holy Spirit are the gift gratuitously offered to all those who are born of water and the Holy Spirit (cf. John 3:5) and called to relive the very communion of God and to manifest it and communicate it in history (mission). (CL 8)

By their baptism with water and the Holy Spirit, the Laity have a massive share in the presence of the Church in the world and its mission in the world because they are charged with exemplifying the life and love of the Divine Trinity and doing it in the marketplace. The two other foundational groups in the Church are the Clergy and religious. The lives of the three groups are not reducible to attendance at the sacraments. The real interpersonal spiritual dynamics of the Church are far more complex.

Regarding the Laity itself: the canvas of lay life is very large. John Paul II explained that:

The gospel parable [Matthew 20] sets before our eyes the Lord's vast vineyard and the multitude of persons, both women and men, who are called and sent forth by him to labor in it. The vineyard is the whole world (cf. Matthew 13:38), which is to be transformed according to the plan of God in view of the final coming of the Kingdom of God.

The Church is not a way of life that only looks in on herself, but she is an outward looking one as well, an institution on a mission. In one of Vatican II's great constitutions on the Church, *Gaudium et Spes*, the Church in the Modern World, the council explained that there is an anthropological principle underlying all of salvation, namely:

As God did not create man for life in isolation, but for the formation of social unity, so also 'it has pleased God to make men holy and save them not merely as individuals, without bond or link between them, but by making them into a single people, a people which acknowledges Him in truth and serves him in holiness.'(GS 32)

This Spirit-filled people who form a unity is a visible public sign to the nation and to the nations. The People of God lives out the holy way of life, offers worship to God and calls others to the altar. As salvation unfolds, the Church community daily continues to be formed out of deepening the eucharistic experience of faithful individuals who are "summoned" (Eucharistic Prayer III) through baptism to share in the same spirit, the Spirit of Christ and to share in the same sacrifice. They are called into the Church community by the Spirit of God and are called ever afterwards to gather for the Eucharist, the other sacraments, and to do the dozens of other activities that make the holy community happen and expand.

The collective unity of human beings internally and externally fractured by sin is restored as God's work of salvation manifests itself and people's conversion advances. Salvation is concretized in the word "kingdom," the Kingdom of God, that exists here *in nuce* even now. The idea of God's kingdom first surfaces in the history of salvation in the Book of Exodus, where God says: "Now, if you obey me completely and keep my covenant, you will be my treasured possession among all peoples, though all the earth is mine. You will be to me a kingdom of priests, a holy nation." (Exodus 19:5, 6) The collective or corporate aspect of the relationship between God and humanity is essential in explaining the theology of the Catholic Church and its character as a priestly people.

(2) The Covenanted People

God made a number of covenants with his people. There were the covenants between God and Noah, God and Abraham, between God and Moses, and God and David, all as representatives of their people, just to cite a few. Each covenant still helps people comprehend something of the most superlative covenant of all, the covenant between God and man that takes place in the person of Jesus Christ (the hypostatic union) himself.

Several features of covenants do not change from the Old Testament to the New Testament.

First, they manifest the overwhelming love, dignity and power of the saving God. They speak of what would later come to be the wonder of the Church, or as Henri de Lubac would call it, the *splendor* of the Church. This wonder is caused and sustained by the power of God. It has nothing to do with human merit. As a result, the visible side of the Church as a human community has a wondrous spiritual dimension to it that acts as the higher principle of the operations of the visible community.

Second: the initiative and the moral authority in the relationships forming the People of God (Church) lie totally with God. Hence things like the moral teaching and the form of the liturgy of the Church come from God. They are revealed in Scripture and tradition. (cf. *Verbum dei.*) Moral principles are not generated by solipsistic individuals neither are the liturgies or many other things. The principles precede in time those who apply them or participate in them. Liturgies are not like spontaneous parties that people organize. They come from the history of salvation itself.

Third: the mystery is always God's. From the hassled priest rushing to give Holy Communion to as many hospital patients as possible to the most sublime moments of the exposition of the Blessed Sacrament, there is always an attendant depth to the moment that comes from somewhere and someone else and the priest just serves that mystery.

Vatican II describes the dynamic and fruitful mystery in this way:

> The Spirit dwells in the Church and in the hearts of the faithful, as in a temple. In them he prays on their behalf and bears witness to the fact that they are adopted sons. The Church, which the Spirit guides in the way of all truth and which he unified in communion and in works of ministry, he both equips and directs with hierarchical and charismatic gifts and adorns with his fruits. By the power of the Gospel he makes the Church keep the freshness of youth. Uninterruptedly he renews it and leads it to perfect union with its Spouse. The Spirit and the Bride both say to Jesus, the Lord, 'Come!'" (LG 4)

In this paragraph, the council gathered together some aspects of the mystery of the Church. The teaching draws on things such as Pauline ecclesiology where, for example, Paul asks: "Do you not know that you are the temple of God, and that the Spirit of God dwells in you?" (I Cor. 3:16) Paul himself drew on the results of the long history of God working with his people. God will continue to do this until the end of time, but his work even reaches back into the mists of antiquity.

As if it were not clear enough already, from the last statement in I Corinthians, Paul went on to say about the Spirit of God: "the holy Spirit [is] within you, whom you have from God, and you are not your own?" (I Cor 6:19) Very specifically, our bodies, our bodily behaviour, our minds and hearts form part of the presence of the Church. This text was also the biblical reference for the council's statement: "The Spirit dwells in the Church and in the hearts of the faithful, as in a temple" (LG 4) and it also points to the mysterious origin of the Church community in the 'community' of divine persons that is God himself.

The phrase that 'we are not our own' cuts right across western solipsism, western individualism and western pride. The faithful are at someone else's disposal, "so humble yourselves under the mighty hand of God." (I Peter 5:6) Humility is what makes the covenant work.

(3) Laity as Prophets, Priests and Kings

The wonder of the Church community is that it is the presence of Christ in the world by the power of the Holy Spirit. His presence is mediated through relationships where the faithful participate in Christ's Priesthood, Prophecy and Kingship. Thus, there is a priestly, prophetic and kingly people present in the midst of society, as a concrete daily sign of the presence of Jesus Christ. (See Chapter Four)

(4) The Parish

Laypeople probably have some of the most complicated roles in the Church and its mission. They must balance forming families, careers and extensive social responsibilities and they have to do all these in Christian terms—where the exercise of each responsibility can consciously be an expression of the priesthood, prophecy and kingship of Jesus Christ.[193] The social group where Laity learns much about these roles is the parish. Pope Paul VI described a parish:

> We believe simply that this old and venerable structure of the parish has an indispensable mission of great contemporary importance: to create the basic community of the Christian people; to initiate and gather the people in the accustomed expression of liturgical life; to conserve and renew the faith in the people of today; to serve as the school for teaching the salvific message of Christ; to put solidarity in practice and work the humble charity of good and brotherly works.[194]

At the same time, Paul VI included some of the difficult tasks of the pastor who accompanies the members of the parish on their spiritual journey.

The idea of the parish starts with the fact that the parish is a spiritual and physical community. 'Parish' is a profound term because not only is the human community a created image of the Divine Trinity, that primordial community. The parish also exercises a vital created dimension of being human, namely, the intersubjectivity of men and women in spiritual communion. One could do a whole treatise on helping Catholics to communicate with each other and develop their relationships as Christians. For example, Catholic marriages fail at the same rate as secular marriages, so some people do need to learn how to communicate as Christians! Perhaps they might ask themselves if God wants them to get married in the first place.

Most importantly, the Christian community is formed by the Holy Spirit himself. It is not merely a voluntary association like a golf club where one pays one's dues and gets certain benefits. In fact, Eucharistic Prayer III says that we are "summoned" by God to gather for the Eucharist, for example. Then further, Jesus himself explained: "God is Spirit, and those who worship him must worship in Spirit and truth." (John 4:24)

---

[193] Thomas More for example, was responsible for himself, his growth as a Christian, as a cultured man and as an able lawyer. He was also responsible for his family, the safety and happiness of his wife, the holiness and happiness of his children and the security of their futures. Then he was also a judge in various courts and a counsellor to the king. He owed good service to the plaintiffs and to the law. He sometimes imposed fines and then paid them himself. He worked on many international treaties. In London, he started charitable homes that he paid for himself. He also went into the poorest areas of the city to help the poor where he could.

[194] Paul VI, Discourse to the Roman Clergy (June 24, 1963): AAS 55 (1963), 674.

Through God's gift, everyone in the community participates in God's Spirit and they are formed into a community because of what they share in common the Spirit and the truth of God. Now, already as creatures, the Preface for Sundays VII says: "In him we live and move and have our being." These common factors are far more potent and active than what divides us, namely, ethnic history, social status, political interests etc. but, because we are human, this commonality has to be grasped again and again in faith which is a theological virtue.

Furthermore, parishes are only subdivisions of the diocese under the Bishop. They are not kingdoms on their own! The diocese is also known as the particular Church. Vatican II said: "The individual Bishops, however, are the visible principle and foundation of unity in their particular churches, fashioned after the model of the universal Church, in and from which churches come into being as the one and only Catholic Church." (LG 23) Moreover, the particular Church is a complete Church in the sense that it has all of the required elements of grace and truth that are necessary for salvation because of the presence of the Bishop. More of this theology was treated in the chapter on the priest and the Bishop.

(5) The Christian States of Life

The theology of the Catholic Church community is complex. One person who thought a great deal about the Church community was the Swiss theologian Hans Urs von Balthasar. He identified a set of basic theological relationships that give the community of faith its organic nature as a Catholic community. The Church is made up of the states of life of the Clergy, Religious and Laity and these interact with each other on several levels.[195] The participation of all three groups is required for the proper realization of all of the spirit-filled relationships in the Church so that the diocese is a sacrament in the world. There are six relationships in all.

(1) First of all, the states of life are interrelated in the communion of love with all that that entails. Love of God and love of neighbour are the core ethos of community. In practical terms, this is probably the most ignored dimension of the Church especially in individualistic cultures.[196] Acting out the dynamics of one's state of life in Christ is crucial to each person's authentic participation in the Church "so that they may be one, as we are one, I in them and you in me, that they may be brought to perfection as one, that the world may know that you sent me, and that you loved them even as you loved me." (John 17:22, 23) God's love of all brings everyone into being part

---

[195] Hans Urs von Balthasar, *The Christian States of Life*, San Francisco: Ignatius Press, 1983.
[196] Other cultures have their own ways of destroying love.

of a loving unity. On our own we cannot achieve this unity and do not really want to.

(2) Secondly, the Clergy and Religious have important functions vis-a-vis the Laity and each other. The Clergy make the concrete *objective* sacrifice of the Eucharist for the whole community. They achieve this successfully regardless of their personal failings. Those in the religious state exemplify the life of the interior spiritual (subjective[197]) sacrifice that is essential for both Clergy and Laity. This aligns with Vatican II's notion that: "The baptized, by regeneration and the anointing of the Holy Spirit, are consecrated as a spiritual house and a holy priesthood, in order that through all those works which are those of the Christian man, they may offer spiritual sacrifices." (LG 10)

(3) It has to be noted that the organizations of Religious are uniquely structured to allow them to conform themselves closely to Jesus Christ. This means that both Clergy and Laity can learn from their example how to conform their lives to Christ *interiorly and externally.* Through the Religious, Clergy and Laity can get some sense of what is more important in the hierarchy of values in human life, in the life of daily prayer, for example. Also, Clergy and Laity have other concerns in the world, so some of the parameters of their lives do shift because they are responsible for so many things that they have to do— such as owning property, participating in the political and economic community. Nevertheless, Religious can show that there is even a spiritual side to each of these relationships.

(4) As the ordained, the Clergy participate in the Offices of Christ objectively so that they lead, sanctify and teach themselves and the other two groups. The Clergy are the official side of the Church, not as the expression of someone's longing for control but as the responsible participation in the priestly leadership of the Church by Jesus Christ.

(5) The fifth interrelationship of the three states of life indicates that, in their personal commitment to their spiritual and physical sacrifices, the Clergy and the Religious serve the Laity in every way that they can, bringing the resources of their states of life into the lives of the Laity. Remember Saint

---

[197] Here 'subjective' does not mean 'what one *imagines* personally'. Instead, von Balthasar uses the term to refer to the interiorly held truth of the Church—and hence of people like the Religious founders whom the Church recognizes—that one appropriates into one's spirit so that he/she becomes docile to the Spirit working in the Church.

Paul's words: "I will most gladly spend and be utterly spent for your sakes." (II Corinthians 12:15) This obligation to service does not replace the additional individual missions of the people involved.

(6) Lastly, from the perspective of "the active participation in the reality and effectiveness of the Lord's redemptive mission," it is the Religious state that does this particular kind of participation in the most intense way, because Religious have the fewest ties to other things that, at the very least, take time from participating in the redemptive mission.[198] Theologically, the clerical state actively participates in the Lord's redemptive mission only indirectly, through the holding of an office, and so it lies in the medial position between religious and Laity regarding their degree of participation. In the hierarchy of the degrees of participation, the Laity's situation is lowermost when judged in terms of the intensity of being able to follow Christ because of the complex way that Laity are necessarily embedded in the world and worthily bound by the dynamics of the world.

(7) The Contemporary Mission of the Parish

Going back to Paul VI's statement: the pope noted that a parish has a *contemporary* mission. Its mission lies in the present moment to the present society and culture. The word 'contemporary' touches many aspects of the existence of the parish. It means that the priest and laypeople should not only be aware of their community but also of the world beyond its borders. The parish is contemporary in many senses besides this one: the parish lives in the present; the parish is where the twin resources of Scripture and Tradition are available to everyone to be studied and applied right now; the celebration of the sacraments brings God's grace to God's people *now*; and perhaps the most difficult—the parish actually addresses the present-day world prophetically, speaking the message of the love and truth of God to the world. It evangelizes the surrounding neighbourhood and by charity and prayer reaches out to communities on the other side of the world.

However, just as importantly, inside the community, there is a constant need "to create the basic community of the Christian people." (Paul VI) This is a daily ongoing project and involves a very complex set of activities. Listen to John Paul II's description of some of the spiritual process that takes place in the life of the community. In his encyclical *Veritatis splendor*, (which is about living in the truth), he wrote about

---

[198] CSOL, 366.

111

the dynamic aspect [of truth] which will elicit the response that man must give to the divine call which comes in the process of his growth in love, within a community of salvation. In this way, moral theology will acquire an inner spiritual dimension in response to the need to develop fully the *imago Dei* present in man, and in response to the laws of spiritual development described by Christian ascetical and mystical theology.[199] (VR 111)

John Paul II wrote in developmental terms: the truth of God has its own power to draw men and women into responding to the divine call to become more and more the community that God intended. They then move past getting stuck at the 20 minute barrier. (Chapter One)

His mention of moral theology is significant. Moral theology is the theology of the proper exercise of human freedom. In fact, moral theology is a recurring theme in this book. According to the *Catechism*: "Freedom makes man a moral subject. When he acts deliberately, man is, so to speak, the father of his acts. Human acts, that is, acts that are freely chosen in consequence of a judgment of conscience, can be morally evaluated. They are either good or evil." (CCC 1749) Here, of course, the word 'conscience' refers to a morally developed conscience that knows the moral truth of Christ. It is not a question of mere "feelings".

The underlying principle of development of conscience is that one is drawn into obedience to the truth (who is the Word of God) that one hears. One submits to this truth and entrusts oneself wholly to God. Remember Mary's: "I am the handmaid of the Lord." (Luke 1:38) Growing to this extent can and should be happening to many members of a parish.

Above, Paul VI also said that a parish is "to initiate and gather the people in the accustomed expression of liturgical life." The pope devoted a whole chapter to the liturgy, but here one should add that this means that Clergy themselves have to know how and why the liturgy unfolds in order to be able to explain it. Just 'presiding' is not enough. The liturgy is the formal expression of Christ's sacrifice on the Cross and so it sets the form of the Church's liturgy. It is not modifiable even in a country that is obsessed with theatricals, with change and with being modern or woke.[200]

The word "initiate" is interesting. People are baptized and confirmed *so that* they can worship fully but they need to know what that means. The priest is the one who

---

[199] He is quoting the Sacred Congregation for Catholic Education, "The Theological formation of Future Priests" (February 22, 1976), No.100. See Nos. 95-101, which present the prospects and conditions for a fruitful renewal of moral theology: loc. cit., 39-41. *Veritatis splendor* was a major step in the process.

[200] Cf. *Sacrosanctum concilium.*

is the example of how to worship fully but he also has to have the training and the personal style to encourage laypeople to participate more deeply. (Eg. How many Catholics will not sing?) Vatican II spoke about the need for the Laity to offer their personal "spiritual sacrifice" at the liturgy. The phrase describes the first moment of the Laity's' involvement body and soul in following Christ. They then move on to creatively expressing the grace and truth of the liturgy in the events of the rest of the day.

Continuing with Paul VI's statement (above), the parish is "to conserve and renew the faith in the people of today." Among other things, the activity of 'conserving and renewing' the faith involves the content of the faith. (The chapter on the priest's intellectual life treats this point in more detail.) Also, the word 'today' is central to what he means. Parish life is not about nostalgia for a lost past. Von Balthasar noted above that religious have an essential place in the life of faith of Clergy and Laity. Against the resentful attitude of some parish Clergy, perhaps some religious could be invited into the parish to collaborate in helping the Laity learn the faith.[201] The mention of faith 'today' suggests that Laity might need some help in analysing the frequently confusing trends in society—and very often in the Church as well— that owe more to the 'spirit of this world' than to the Spirit of God that the faithful ought to be following.

Paul VI also said that the parish is "to serve as the school for teaching the salvific message of Christ." Nevertheless, the family is still the primary 'school' for learning the faith. Many, many families still have to learn this skill from scratch because they may not have considered their family this way before. The Clergy might well be in the same boat! A powerful tool here could be the stories of faithful families. John Vianney's family comes to mind, as does that of Teresa of Lisieux. Theresa of Avila's family also. Again, the intellectual horizon of the priest or of able laypeople is going to be central to much of the work done with families in the parish.

One problematic mindset to work through is where someone 'has to live the same or better life than the neighbors.' This is meant from a material point of view. The faithful are frequently still hostage to this rule from the secular environment. Nevertheless, Christianity is a religion of courage. Speaking about the inevitable and necessary 'gap' between Catholicism and the local culture is absolutely crucial in the US. That Catholics both are and ought to be different from other people should be mentioned so often that it finally becomes accepted because: "We have not received

---

[201] Unfortunately, the US has done a great deal to design religious life to be dominated by the American middle-class way of life with all that that means in terms of being liberal. Of course, there are exceptions! So, the choice of which religious community is a complex one for a candidate.

the spirit of the world but the Spirit that is from God, so that we may understand the things freely given us by God." (I Corinthians 2:12) Paul's mention of the Spirit means that living in the world is a spiritual battle and one to be dealt on that level. The issue of how much people are tied to material things is not supposed to be decided by the degree of one's social acceptance. How material things serve us is an issue of salvation and of living a fully human life. Usually religious and secular Clergy can show people how to handle material things.

The notion of the parish as a school raises all kinds of bogeymen for Laity and Clergy. Some Clergy and Laity don't like teaching, some don't like learning, some don't like school, some don't like missing their TV shows and so on. Everything Paul VI has mentioned involves conversion of mind and heart and it is going to take faith, prayer and charm to develop the parish into a school of the faith. Programs go part way but really it is about 'Father' taking this issue seriously, so that *he* lives it out in practice and organizes each conversation in this direction. "How are you growing holiness today?"

Above, Paul VI spoke about "put[ting] solidarity into practice and [doing the] work of the humble charity of good and brotherly works." In the hyper-individualism and desperate class consciousness in the US, 'solidarity' is a profoundly difficult thing to initiate. Some parishes are communities of strangers. Secular society recognizes the problem, it spends a lot of time training people to be part of a team, say in the military or in a sport. This training does not reach everyone. People act together when there is a catastrophe, at least to some extent, but almost every aspect of the culture militates against forming a religious solidarity in a time when there is no threat. Moreover, solidarity is not politically correct because it cuts across the divisions that are needed to run a regime of identity politics.

These observations have been somewhat piecemeal, but one useful organizing term when considering the parish is "civilization". Thinking in terms of Catholic civilization has the beauty of offering an umbrella term for many of the parish roles. It also has the beauty of asserting that there *is* such a thing as Christian civilization, and it does this in the face of the ever-present Enlightenment conviction that there is no such thing.

Paul VI opened the door to describing Christian civilization by his own words. He spoke of a 'humble charity' and of 'good and brotherly works.' But at least as far back as Leo XIII (pope from 1878 – 1903), the word civilization has been part of the language of Catholic teaching, so for example: "the very notion of civilization is a fiction of the brain if it rest not on the abiding principles of truth and the unchanging laws of virtue and justice, and if unfeigned love knit not together the wills of men, and gently control the interchange and the character of their mutual service." (*Inscrutabili dei consilio* 5) Again truth is key! Furthermore, Leo XIII summarized the notion of civilization as the collaboration of wills for a higher purpose. This is not for the purpose of the socialist state but for the purpose of advancing the internal spiritual integrity of the People of God and adding to their number as well as serving humanity at large.

Pope John Paul II called this a civilization of love. (Letter to Families)[202] It is a civilization that follows the principle of 'love thy neighbor' as the foundation of every relationship: in families, in giving the elderly a place in society, in helping the sick and the downtrodden, particularly those who have no voice, like the unborn, the battered women and the homeless. This principle is also a measuring stick to judge which political principles one adopts! (See chapter of a priest's intellectual life.) This concept counters the community of social sin that John Paul II described in Chapter One. It also makes people more loving for longer periods!

There is however more to this notion of Christian civilization namely that the parish is what Pius XII called "the storehouse of Christian civilization." (*Miranda prorsus*)[203] He referred to the media and the qualities that they ought to promote, namely truth and virtue. This topic alone deserves a book. In today's world, truth and virtue would be highly desirable goals for both the reporting and broadcasting side of the media industry and well as on the side of the audience.

One list of the virtues would be Chastity, Temperance, Charity, Diligence, Patience, Kindness and Humility. Changing the direction of the flow of the information and values from 'bad stuff' (lies, deceptions, vices etc.) *into* the parish to 'good stuff' *out of* the parish would be a major service to the parishioners themselves and to the larger society. Parishioners could learn what the life of the virtues is all about and then practice how to carry that knowledge into the law courts, businesses, supermarkets and homes.

John Paul II specifically took this kind of thinking into the field of art and artists. Hence, "artists, the more conscious they are of their 'gift', are led all the more to see themselves and the whole of creation with eyes able to contemplate and give thanks, and to raise to God a hymn of praise. This is the only way for them to come to a full understanding of themselves, their vocation and their mission." (*Letter to Artists*, 1)[204] It is only the centuries of the Enlightenment's war on the Church that have airbrushed the achievements of the members of the Church out of history. Many of the institutions that are taken for granted today in society originated in Church initiatives. So much of the fields of science and art, law and manufacturing, originated

---

[202] February 2, 1994.
[203] November 8, 1957.
[204] April 4, 1999.

in the work of members of the Church. The list is endless. The parish can be and should be a center of virtuous and truthful civilization.

Finally, the works of truth and virtue do not end there. Hopefully, the parish will look for the people who need material and social help in their parish. There will be people who have no food, no jobs who could be helped. In this way, all of the different dimensions of human life under God can be developed. In fact, the parish puts 'cult' back into culture in all of its forms!

Ceremonies however beautiful, or associations however flourishing,
will be of little value if they are not directed toward the education of men to Christian
maturity. Paul VI

(1) Introduction

The Second Vatican Council was clear that: "Priests by sacred ordination and mission which they receive from the Bishops are promoted to the service of Christ the Teacher, Priest and King." (PO 1) The concept of "service" sets the tone for the priest's approach to Christ and to people in general. The whole purpose of a priest's pastoral work is to help parishioners worship and become saints.

The priest is responsible for a specific part of the local Church, a parish or a chaplaincy, for his Bishop. He confects the Eucharist and the other sacraments as well as leading the people in his part of the Church to a deeper faith and life of love. Regarding the Eucharist, Vatican II was clear: "the divine sacrifice of the Eucharist, is the outstanding means whereby the faithful may express in their lives, and manifest to others, the mystery of Christ and the real nature of the true Church." (SC 2) One part of the priest's work is training his people to approach the Eucharist in this way. The priest also organizes catechetics for the children, young people and adults. Hopefully he is also teaching people personally himself. Then there are special groups in the parish who require attention, couples preparing for Marriage, the bereaved, women's groups and men's groups, for example. Some groups are more complicated than others. These might be the ones who help immigrants, or the poor, or the abused. Fortunately, there will always be someone around who knows more than the priest does about a given issue. It may involve bringing in people from outside the parish.

(2) Reaching Everyone

A large project and one that is often ignored is the mission of reaching *everyone* within the bounds of the parish. 'Everyone' includes those who do not go to Church and those who do not even belong to the Church. Priestly pastoral work involves serving more than those who cross the threshold of the Church building. It will test the priest's ability to relate to his parishioners and to motivate them because this part of the parish mission will not happen without substantial assistance from parishioners. To my mind, the selection of candidates for the priesthood should center on two things: the faith of the candidate and the demonstrated ability of the candidate to lead and motivate people.

As soon as a priest arrives in a parish as a pastor, he needs to pick the brains of other Clergy and the parishioners. He would also gain much traction by communicating with the schools and agencies in the area. Then of course, there will be some remarkable Catholics in the parish who are doing all kinds of charitable activities anyway. The priest's first rule of thumb should be that he does not alienate them. The second rule may be that he affirms them and helps them in any way that he or the parish can. Odds are that they have not been supported or affirmed by some of the other Clergy. When such people get over their surprise, they will be very helpful go-to people when the pastor is put on the spot trying to help someone who comes to the door or who he finds in travelling around the parish.

The already active Catholics in the parish will help the new pastor start to uncover the numerous charitable streams of help in the local area, starting with the diocesan resources. Lay Catholics will respond if they are asked and if the priest shows any interest at all. There will be other organizations as well, and these should be approached systematically so that the pastor rapidly becomes an expert in the local area, the local government and with any links to federal agencies that can be helpful. It is a commonplace that people who are hurting most often do not know where to get help from. At the time, they may just be under too much pressure to think clearly.

The pastor obviously cannot do all of this himself. This is where women's and men's groups come into play. If they do not exist, then they will have to be started. People will have to be trained. They will have to be inspired and they will have to have their own spiritual needs cared for.

The notion that Laity were discovered by Vatican II is largely false because it is clear that Laity have been doing a lot for millennia and the real discovery has been to uncover the magnitude of the true focus of the Church.[205] The focus is to worship God and serve humanity.

Historically, there have always been some lay people in the Church who do charitable work with or without the support of the Clergy. But what was re-emphasized by Vatican II was the sheer magnitude of the presence of the Church in the world through the Laity. The visible structure of the Church has always been predominantly clerical with some notable Laity and some who are just going through the motions. Vatican II's emphasis on mission was one of the important consequences of the council. The lack of involvement of numerous of the faithful is still serious because it means that many families, many cities, many legislatures, courts etc. are *not* experiencing the new full quality of life that Christ brings. Because of the lack of involvement by some Clergy and some Laity, the Church's mission is not

---

[205] Historically, the claim of 'rediscovery' is the result of researchers not knowing the interlocking network of relationships that has actually existed in society since the beginning of the Church. If one goes back to the Middle Ages, for example, then the real surprise is the number of ways that people at all levels of society *were* involved with the Church. Cf. Andre Vauchez, *The Laity in the Middle Ages*, Notre Dame: University of Notre Dame, IN. 1993.

being done completely. Many faithful believe somewhat in Christ but not enough to have him change their lives and work.

Emphasizing the *presence* of the Laity in a way that involves them in the public presence of the Church and its service to the world still has not been fully integrated into the present-day still-clericalized Church. Fortunately, there has been a shift away from some of the all-pervasive clericalism in the past decades.[206] This has been due to the decreasing numbers of Clergy and the scandals. Hopefully the seminary mindset has developed in the 'new' direction of developing lay public presence in society. One glaring sign of a problem is the blind assumption that candidates for the priesthood are equipped pastorally if they have heard some information in class. This has been true for so long that it remains unchallenged to this day. In fact, it is complete nonsense. Anyone who has done any teaching knows that few students can make the transition from hearing something to competently applying it. Leadership in the Church should be working with this 'new' way of training.

The poor quality of some preaching is just one factor that explains why people are not learning what to do. Quality preaching is something that only comes with practice and prayer as well as a serious knowledge of scripture, tradition and liturgy. The problem is apparent too when the spiritual growth of seminarians is poor. Thankfully, great spiritual development is evident in how some priests do pastoral work, administration and recreation.

The best way that a new priest learns a lot of things quickly is through assisting a much more experienced priest. However, few get the opportunity to do this for any length of time. Simple things like how an experienced priest draws lay people into many of his tasks, or how he chooses his recreation so that it is priestly and not that of a secular bachelor can be learned quickly by just being around an authentic priest at work and play.

(3) Enactive Christianity

This complicated title has to do with helping people to begin acting like saints all day. (Remember the 20-minute rule in Chapter One.) The tough part is planning parish activities with this focus despite the constant avalanche of tasks and troubles that the priest deals with. Just telling someone something does not mean that they will act on it. Hearing the teaching of the Church does not mean people will even see how to apply it.

---

[206] Bronwen Catherine McShea, "Bishops Unbound: The History behind today's Crisis of Church Leadership," *First Things*, January 2019.

Obviously, liturgies and preaching have their place in lay life but even the virtues of sainthood might need to be explained again and again. The 'checking the boxes' kind of Catholicism does not necessarily lead to interior change. Just anecdotally, the 'check the box' Catholics often seem to revert to where the pagans in their demographic are, behaviourally speaking. They can return to being just as selfish as their peers.

Interior spiritual change comes from growing up around people who *are* working on their own conversion because then conversion comes to be the norm which it is, in fact, theologically. Seeing other people taking the risks of conversion makes it seem more possible. The fact is that people are responsible for their own spiritual development from the age of reason. Sadly, if Laity have only encountered Catholicism in a passive mode then they are never going to take the initiative. Conversion becomes a very useful concept in the priest's work. It becomes central in all of his interactions with laypeople.

Seminarians need to leave the seminary with the right training to help themselves and others to become holy. This is a big subject but at the very least, it means knowing some basic books that describe the lives of saints. Books on saintly families are important too. Then the priest has to have enough skill and know enough to be able to augment his judgements in confession with spiritual guidance and to hold group discussions on these things. These skills should be accompanied by the appropriate liturgical exercises because much of the help to the soul that is searching will not be from group activities but from the supernatural side of things, namely sacraments, prayer and meditation. Having said that, knowing how to organize some activities, such as helping in soup kitchens, helping people to get the government benefits that they are entitled to and so on are all things that show the interpersonal side of Catholicism where 'love thy neighbor' is put into action.

(4) Disappearing Catholics
It is pretty obvious by now that Catholics are leaving the Church, perhaps because of the scandals[207] but more likely because of the influence of modernity. Moderns do not need religion. They cannot handle it. Their souls are not big enough. Instead they make religions out of small things such as their cell phones, their own comfort, their possessions, their appearance and so on. These are devotions cut down to the spiritual size of the modern individual.

---

[207] According to the Pew Research Center: "Roughly a quarter of former Catholics who are now religiously unaffiliated say the *Clergy* sexual abuse scandals were a reason for their leaving the Church." March 10, 2010. Pew Research Center 1615 L Street NW, Suite 800, Washington DC, 20036.

In addition, families often have a serious generational problem with regard to religion. The older generation might perhaps be settled into a routine of observance but not so with the younger generation. The only possible approach seems to be the personal one and, of course, prayer for the younger people—á la Saint Monica. The fading of the faith of some of the younger generation causes a great deal of grief to many parents. Nevertheless, each individual has their own responsibility to honor God. Parents ought to do what they can but even watching their progeny drift is part of parenting, painful as it is. There is evidence that some young people come back to the Church after some years away.

Then, there are some things that parents can do when their kids are growing up. First, parents need to show how precious their faith is to themselves and to behave like Catholics, in good times and bad. It would help parents to read about other faithful parents, particularly about the parents of saints. The parents of Therese of Lisieux, and the parents of John Vianney, would be great examples, to start with. Certainly, for a family seeking holiness, praying together is a good start, particularly at meals. The other thing is to do charitable work together, not as an onerous burden but to show love to people, especially strangers. This promotes a proper sense of what love actually is, namely wishing for and working for the good of the other person. This is the good as seen from God's point of view.

(5) Culture

The question of culture has been part of pastoral work since the beginning of the Church. (See Saint Paul's address at the Areopagus. (Acts 17:16–34)) The problem for Clergy is that the study of culture got mixed up with political correctness somewhere along the way.[208] This has led, for example, as far as an African Bishop suggesting that African beer and corn bread be used for celebrating the Eucharist. The Bishop did not appreciate how history works. He was just imposing something and acting like a *deus ex machina*—a rationalistic approach more fitting to the Enlightenment than to Catholicism.

Pope Paul VI's Apostolic Exhortation *Evangelii nuntiandi* (December 8 1975) written after the Synod on Pastoral Challenges to the Family in the Context of Evangelization, is a good place to start. John Paul II also wrote about culture numerous times. Examples of his work can be found in *Evangelium vitae* (25 March 1995); *Solicitudo rei socialis* (30 December 1987); and about a dozen other texts.[209]

---

[208] Matteo Ricci's *The True Meaning of the Lord of Heaven* is a good example of properly thought out inculturation.

[209] Other texts are *Redemptoris missio*, *Laborem exercens*, the Jubilee messages, his speeches on his various journeys.

Both popes make the point that cultures inevitably include the products of concupiscence and sin. There are always some rich truths in cultures as well. It is up to the Clergy to make the appropriate moral judgments using the moral teaching of the Church. Cultural practices are not an automatic and fitting part of parish practices or the liturgy. Often, the appropriate Bishops' conference has already published on the different local cultural elements and their suitability.

For the work of the Bishop, Clergy and Laity, the constant issue when dealing with man-made cultures is that *Jesus Christ* is the truth of the world. *His* history of salvation is being extended into each culture by the Church. The moral teaching of the Church, because it is Jesus Christ's, is universally true for all mankind and is not relative to a culture. It is true because it is based on the data of revelation, the revelation of the Divine Word. (Cf. John Paul II, *Veritatis splendor*, 6 August 1993.)

The romantic view of cultures dominates today mainly because elites pander to particular cultural groups to get their votes, but elites usually don't know anything about any cultures (including their own) in any depth although they do know how to manipulate them. Theologically, the perfect human being is Jesus Christ. In fact, Vatican II taught that: "The truth is that *only* in the mystery of the incarnate Word does the mystery of man take on light." (GS 22) (Emphasis added.) Given the nature of the Incarnation, this is an unlimited statement. It cannot be limited by secular hypotheses about culture, history or political power.

Cultures always have some beautiful elements—unless one is considering the culture imposed by ISIS or by Nazism or progressivism—but, cultures are always far from complete in helping human beings to become more richly human. Cultures may in fact have values and practices that get in the way of a complete humanity. It takes continuous discernment by Clergy who have at least been trained in moral theology to identify them. Clergy cannot have a romantic view of cultures, or, as can happen, a hatred of their own culture. Both attitudes get in the way of what might be called inculturation. Once again, it must be said that Bishops' conferences have often studied certain cultural issues already and made formal statements about them. They should be consulted and taken seriously unless they too are merely following the talking-points of some political party.

(6) Teachable Moments

The sad thing is that priests usually do not use all the opportunities for teaching that get thrown in their paths. They do not always have to make them happen. Leaving a conversation just as conversation about the banal or reducing the giving of Holy Communion to the sick to a breathless rushed visit, does not manifest the meaning of Christ in that situation. This, of course, means that other people who are present there do not meet Christ to the degree that they could have if the situation had been handled better.

The longing for informality and casualness that permeates culture in the US is a real drag on pastoral work and on liturgy.

However, the greatest obstacle to doing pastoral work is our lack of awareness of our own prejudices and ignorance. Trust in the teaching of the Church! The Church knows more than we do. In two thousand years, she has encountered the same problems dozens of times and has worked out some kind of Christian response that is geared to respecting people, which is not the same as simply going along with whatever the people say at present. To do the latter is actually disrespectful of the people involved. They are entitled to hear the truth. That will promote their development as human beings.

Chapter Nine The Intellectual Life of the Priest

> Priests find mutual assistance in the development of their spiritual and intellectual life, that they may be able to cooperate more effectively in their ministry and be saved from the dangers of loneliness which may arise. Paul VI

(1) Introduction

The word "intellectual" in the title indicates an essential dimension of Catholicism and is not a reference to mere opinions that Catholics might hold. As was said earlier, human beings are created to function properly by using their intellect and their will. This is all part of the scheme of Creation. One cannot simply think as one likes because that leads to inauthentic human existence. Catholicism is here to lead people to authentic human existence. No form of Enlightenment thinking can achieve that.

The reason for this chapter is that, in the US, Clergy and Laity do not always think that Catholicism is so true that its teachings have to be applied in *every* situation. They are victims of the Enlightenment culture—which did not and does not believe that thinking involving faith is true—and they are victims of a certain amount of laziness too. The renewal of one's mind really is part of being a believer—Old Testament or New. The priest ought to be the one to help people do that. This is not a simple requirement. Instead, it reaches right into the heart of being a priest. It is only with the correct intellectual development and operation that a priest can avoid adding to the communion of evil and can advance the community of grace.

St. Paul explained much of the religious psychology behind the issue. For example, he explained: "Do not conform to the pattern of this world but be transformed by the renewing of your mind. Then you will be able to test and approve what God's will is—his good, pleasing and perfect will." (Romans 12:2) The word 'mind' in that sentence does not refer to some vague subjectivism or opinion, or some pious ideas. The Jews and Christians of the period knew that he was referring to the proper operation of the *intellect* of the individual. This is a problem for people who want to morph Catholicism into a touchy-feely religion with no intellectual content.

Some Clergy have never learned that being a faithful Catholic involves the perennial understanding of how human beings function. Human beings have two powers of the soul, the intellect and the will. One has to know (which involves faith) in order to make responsible choices (the will).[210] The most authentic operation of the human being involves thinking and acting in this way. It is authentic because it uses the powers of the soul properly. This is not a time-conditioned way of thinking that has

---

[210] Cf. John Paul II *Fides et ratio* and *Veritatis splendor.*

been superseded. It is the way authentic human beings function. This is verified from what we know from revelation. Thus, it is not one option among many valid ways of thinking.

Consequently, like it or not, a priest has to deliberately learn a lot about the *Catholic* worldview. This gives him a foundation for doing his pastoral work faithfully and completely, so that the faithful get what they are entitled to—properly thought out passing on of Catholic content—and the priest can attend to his own salvation in the process. The Catholic worldview does not pass on the prevailing agnostic secular worldview while adding a few Catholic bits and pieces to fool people that the information is Catholic. Examples would be—passing on agnostic psychology when Catholicism already contains a good and accurate psychology; passing on teachings from one's political party and so on. Catholicism involves the priest, body and soul, and that includes his mind and heart. The same must be said of the layperson. The priest works from God's revelation in the natural world and in history in order to minister in the name of Jesus Christ to people who will be learning to think properly at the same time.

It means that the priest simply cannot preach and face situations the way that pagans of his age and socioeconomic group would do. Inevitably, the situation of pagans does not contribute much accurate information to understanding most things no matter how well it is packaged. On the contrary, the priest is an agent of divine revelation in faith and morals. This way of conceiving the priesthood is essential for authentic priesthood. This would be one validly serving the Word. Then the priest will not fool himself that he knows more than revelation or fool the people that he is doing his job when in reality he is just a tool of the Enlightenment or a political party. This is the elephant in the room for US priests and priests in other countries, with either strongly leftist or rightist ideologies, as will be seen below.

The priest's worldview accumulates over the years, from his parents and family, his friends, his experiences, his seminary and so on. It includes insights from his prayer life, the Scriptures, Church life and documents. It also includes his learning about the world and society as Catholicism understands them, something that he will have to work at especially as new issues arise. Again, this is not an understanding among many possible understandings. It is one that fits reality. People are looking to the priest for the *Catholic* wisdom about the world and salvation history. They are not looking to him for chatter about baseball or a comedy routine. Laity work in the world and they know many things about it, but they do need some help understanding it in relation to God.

The pressure on Clergy and Laity to adopt secularist thinking is overwhelming. The media pour out this kind of thinking 24/7. So, the priest will need to work to present what he has learned and *is* learning from Scripture and Tradition in a coherent way that serves the ever developing or non-developing comprehension of his parishioners. They have been called by Baptism to live in this world, operating with a Catholic worldview and bringing this worldview to bear on each situation that they find—that is what Confirmation is about. After all, as the Second Vatican Council reminds us: "If [people] fail moreover to respond to that grace in thought, word and deed, not only shall they not be saved but they will be the more severely judged." (LG 14) The mention of 'thought' is important.

Laity need to know the revealed truth and the implications that follow from it. There is a further qualification: the Council again: "The Laity have the right, as do all Christians, to receive in abundance from their spiritual shepherds the spiritual goods of the Church, especially the assistance of the word of God and of the sacraments." (LG 37) The priest needs to be able to step up to inform them with the right tools to do the job. This is his duty. Also, the diocese or religious order has spent hundreds of thousands of dollars making sure that the priest has the right tools, at least in theory. This cost imposes a duty on the part of the Clergy to pass on the truth always and well.

Pastorally, with the priest's help or, in fact, quite often despite him—because some Clergy are so poorly informed or so politically biased—the people in the pews need to be developing their own participation in the Catholic worldview to better understand what their day-to-day experiences mean in ultimate terms. Accurate Catholicism is the best resource in the world for doing that, given that what the Church knows, is known from divine revelation and its implications! This revelation is from the God who made the universe so he is hardly uninformed about how it works and yet secularist thinking is convinced that he must be!

(2) Faith

The obligation to have a Catholic worldview should not be a surprise. However, it pushes against the common cultural idea of religion as merely a private thing to be held onto, or not, and the idea that religion is primarily about feelings (the Enlightenment again!).

What stands out against all of the efforts to diminish Catholicism, and what blunts them in some way, is first and foremost the fact of Catholicism's hold on divine revelation in faith. The US is not a Christian country (if it ever truly was!) so the primacy of divine revelation has to be asserted repeatedly. Starting with the revelation to Abraham and on into the New Testament writings, it is apparent that the act of faith, which is man's graced response to revelation, involves actual informational content.

This fact must be emphasized because after studying at the seminary, a priest may know that the faith can be expressed in a series of propositions or creeds. And yet, when he encounters people who have not had this training, the priest will find that some are working with Catholicism as a collection of feelings and experiences. As a priest he is going to have to try and elevate their faith to the point where it does have some doctrinal content—that it forms the very stuff of their minds!

There is nothing wrong with approaching Catholicism through feelings and experiences even though they may be incomplete at a particular point in time! Basically, the description of the Christian way of life for us is, in the words of Hans Urs von Balthasar, that "we can no more speak here of a religion of feeling than we can of a rationalistic religion."[211] Our effort must constantly be to get some grasp of the majesty, and the sheer fullness, of the human experience of God mediated by the Catholic Church. To make a small step forward—Hans Urs von Balthasar again—said that people must know that in the complete act of faith: "it is the whole man who has to respond to the whole form of revelation as it appears within the whole of the created world, and it is God who empowers him to give such a response."[212] This involves the graced human being, graced body and soul, that is in his body, his senses, his intellect and his will. In contrast, sin (the thinker's and other people's) clouds the intellect and the will. The quote from von Balthasar, once again, emphasizes the role of context in living properly.

The whole human being is involved in faithfully responding, with God's assistance, to the whole of God's revelation![213] A historical point: right up to the end of the Baroque period (1600-1750) thinkers understood things in terms of the whole man (woman) and they understood that this was the "'normal' experience of the Christian seriously seeking to live his faith."[214] Pick one of the early saints! This history is long and complex and not relevant here except to appreciate that for most of the intellectual history of the Church, this was the *normal* way that faith-experience was understood. Whether people were consistently good at it is another story.

---

[211] Hans Urs von Balthasar, *The Glory of the Lord I: Seeing the Form*, San Francisco: Ignatius Press, 1982, 298. (Abbreviation GL I)

[212] *GL I*, 297.

[213] Avery Dulles S.J.: "The Catholicity of the Christian faith means its fullness of truth and goodness and its dynamic capacity to perfect and divinize whatever is perfectible in human nature." "The Criteria of Catholic Theology", *Communio* (22), 1995, 304.

[214] *GL I*, 297.

After the Baroque, came the Enlightenment and the Romantic Period with their overemphasis on the role of feelings in religion.[215] (This was also the time of the rise of Jacobinism, more about that shortly.) So, the properly operating intellect had no place. A common assumption, from then on, was that the full meaning of whole areas of human life have their full meaning separate from God and his influence. This simply went unchallenged because 'we are in a new age when the Church has been superseded'.

(3) Politics

To start with: Catholicism says that Jesus Christ is the fullness of the meaning of the world because: "All things came to be through him, and without him nothing came to be." (John 1:3) This is a matter of faith. So, it is part of the Tradition that a priest cannot advocate for the political views of a party or some social justice group[216]—most of whom have very limited and often erroneous worldviews anyway. The unspoken part of this prohibition is that Clergy should not leave out certain Catholic teachings because their party does not agree with them!

Some worldviews mean well but that does not absolve them from their obligation to follow the truth. The intention is not the defining characteristic of the value of an action—as was pointed out in Chapter One. Furthermore, some party's views are agnostic and anti-human. Then too, hundreds of organizations can be found that already advocate any list of secular views, so the priest does not need to be the one to put them forward. Morally, he ought not to do it. Such actions deface the Church in its mission. When a Church official behaves in this way, it validly appears to others that he has found something better than Christ. He shows that, for him, Christ is *not* the fullness of the meaning of the world. Then, of course, there is the danger of, wittingly or unwittingly, making the Church a proxy for some secular organization.

Put another way: Catholicism's teaching does not need to be augmented by secular modes of thought. Someone does not need to add a secular anthropology, or a secular sociology, or a secular political theory etc. to 'improve' Catholicism in some way.[217] The Church is here for the salvation and welfare of humanity and the

---

[215] To see how far this can be taken, take a look at the work of the Protestant Friedrich Schleiermacher (1768-1834) who designed a whole religion based on the 'religious experience'.

[216] Cf. "Christ, to be sure, gave his Church no proper mission in the political, economic or social order. The purpose which he set before her is a religious one. But out of this religious mission itself come a function, a light and an energy which can serve to structure and consolidate the human community according to the divine law." (GS 42)

[217] Introducing secular thinking has measurable effects: "Secularization in Canada is set to shut One Third of the Churches," https://www.worldreligionnews.com/religion-

Church—as the presence of Christ on earth—knows more than enough to serve these goals and achieve them superbly by the grace of Christ. The Church has sometimes made horrible mistakes but that is due to the fact that sometimes even Church officials do not always know what Catholic teaching is in detail or how to apply it consistently. To quote a cliché: it is not that Catholicism has been tried and found wanting but rather that it is not often tried! Very often, Clergy and Laity take a shortcut in their thinking by drawing on cultural content—which is close at hand—like parroting what their political party says. They do this rather than doing the heavy lifting of finding out what the Church actually says and why and then making the effort to apply it accurately to the local situation.

Probably no seminary in the world offers a theologically grounded course in politics in its training program.[218] The oversight indicates that seminary organizers and the seminary programs themselves are often not clear how the intellectual content of Catholicism works. *Fides et ratio* showed them but how many people have read it? Bizarre as it may seem, modern seminaries are usually designed according to the Enlightenment concept of what an educational institution should be. That is, letting professors choose material according to their own lights. I met one seminary professor who was giving a history of the Church from the Marxist perspective! Or, they might organize their material the way that they want rather than synchronizing with other professors so that the same principle comes up across different courses at the same time. It is the institutional equivalent of merely dipping into the tradition of the Church with its diverse yet interrelated pools of truth. Letting professors present information in entirely their own way is drifting towards the Enlightenment notion of the independent *philosophe* who comes up with brilliant thoughts on the world on his own.

---

news/secularization-canada-set-shut-third-churches#.XJIpa4dem3U.twitter There is however a place for research in this scheme of things. For example, Benedict XVI said that "A notion of scholarly research that would consider itself neutral with regard to Scripture should not be encouraged." (VD 47) This applies to much more than the study of Scripture. Every reality needs to be studied with a hermeneutic of faith. So much so that when a kind of two-tier system develops where one study is agnostic and one is pious is a very poor academic study. Quoting Benedict again: "Unfortunately, a sterile separation sometimes creates a barrier between exegesis and theology, and this 'occurs even at the highest academic levels.'" (VD 35) Obviously he is talking about the study of Scripture, but the same principle applies to studies in anthropology, psychology etc.

[218] It is not even mentioned in the *Program for Priestly Formation*, fifth edition. It is worth noting, however, that some people would justify this gap by saying that Church and state are separate but see footnote 7.

Scripture, theology, biblical theology, Christology, anthropology, ecclesiology and the rest form an organic unity because there is only one Incarnate Word. Imagine, for example, a Christology course that only used academic analyses of the Scriptures and made no reference to the tradition of the Church to find out the interpretations of texts. Or imagine a course in ecclesiology that only used materials from secular cultural sociology without referring to the tradition of the Church. Courses like these actually exist. Unless the senior staff at the seminary are very good at theology and firm enough to ask the right questions of the faculty and to dig into the details of the syllabi, such courses will appear in seminaries.

A course in the theology of politics is doubly urgent today because, firstly, political thinking is the only lens that many people in the modern West have for viewing the world. Political thinking is also the laziest way to handle information. One just follows what the crowd, led by what their elite, thinks. And secondly, people who think politically do not have the philosophical and critical tools to deal with the world in terms of meanings and values that relate to the transcendent. They don't do the final step in knowing, namely, referring their concepts back to reality to see if they genuinely correspond to that reality.[219] This means that a conversion of mind must occur in the individual to show that the Catholic view has primacy simply because it is true. It fits reality. In the words of Paul again: "Do not conform yourselves to this age but be transformed by the renewal of your mind, that you may discern what is the will of God, what is good and pleasing and perfect." (Romans 12:2)

Historically, politicians have indeed made efforts to address many social problems, or they say they have, sometimes rightly, mostly wrongly, and sometimes terrifyingly badly or they have not even been aware of what the real problems are. Their actions are often wrong because their premises on what it means to be human, or in a relationship, or a community, or a country are usually weak and deficient. So, their actions have all kinds of unexpected side-effects. These efforts add to the communion of evil spoken of in Chapter One. This situation obliges the Church to repeatedly assert what faith and morals are and of necessity, it needs the freedom to do so.[220] Fundamentally, the situation of the Church is not a power issue but a truth issue. Catholic teaching is true. Cultural attempts at meaning are only valuable to humanity to the degree that they measure up to what Catholicism already knows, specifically in its field of faith and morals. For example, Catholicism is not going to try to explain Stonehenge. That is for archaeologists to do. But it is up to the Church

---

[219] See Thomas Aquinas, *Questiones disputatae de veritate,* https://dhspriory.org/thomas/QDdeVer10.htm#5

[220] Cf. *Fides et ratio.*

to explain what it means to be human, what community means, what genuine human society is, what religion is etc.

In the US, paying attention to politics is badly needed because political thinking already permeates seminaries, dioceses and religious congregations and because many Clergy and the diocesan administrations routinely flip between doctrinal thinking and political thinking when doing their work. Imagine if a medical doctor mixed what he learned at medical school with what he might learn from a witchdoctor! People function as if Catholic thinking and political thinking are interchangeable, which of course they are not. The one is based on truth, the other on what is politically correct, or in other words, what the mob's elite thinks at this moment.

Political thinking twists a person's thinking from a truth issue into a power issue and thus loses the truth. This is significant for the faithful because their salvation depends on knowing the truth. The underlying intent, whether consciously or not, from the Enlightenment on, has been to take down the Church and to diminish the presence of Catholic principles in society. On the contrary, the administration of any Catholic entity should actually believe that Catholic teaching is true—which it is—and then act as if it is true, all of the time, in every circumstance. Logically, political considerations should be subordinated to the truth issues. The Catholic worldview should be the first point of reference for making judgements about politics.

Lastly, a little mentioned aspect of the question on how truth is handled is that Catholic institutions in the US often also *export* the method of giving priority to handling truth politically. This means that they pass on some accurate propositions, but they include some propositions that reflect their political desires. So, in the middle of a talk on priesthood, the lecturer will throw in a statement such as "women should be priests." Personally, the lecturer thinks that all of his statements are of a piece. To him they all appear to fit together. They do not. The words of a lecturer should reflect the history of salvation. In other words, they are based on reality. The piece of watercooler logic is misleading to say the least. The authority of the history of salvation has been superseded in this instance.

Moreover, foreign students either come to the US to learn in universities, colleges and seminaries. They pick up this strange way of handling truth without even thinking about it. Or they study in schools overseas where they are taught by professors trained in this method in the US: 'If it is American it must be good.'

(4) The Church on Politics
The Second Vatican Council explained that "the norm of human activity is this: that in accord with the divine plan and will, it harmonizes with the genuine good of the human race, and that it allows men as individuals and as members of society to

pursue their total vocation and fulfil it." (GS 35) The divine will is to be given its proper place. It will become apparent that this norm is contradicted by those who are Gnostics—why this is so will become apparent shortly.

The Church *does* know what the genuine good of the human race is. That is part of its job. The words of the council should be the guiding principle for operating a parish, a diocese, or even for an institution's interaction with society.[221] From a Christian point of view, this ought to be the basic rule for conducting political parties or any other human activity, for that matter. In practice, it does not happen in this way because of hostility to the Church and the way the truth of the Church counteracts peoples' blind grasping for power.

Philosophically, the Modern period is marked by the detaching of the transcendent dimension of an action from its concrete temporal dimension. It is not necessary to go into the history here, except to say that before the Romanticism of the Enlightenment, the world was viewed entirely differently. The Church was viewed differently too. The earlier perspectives were not historical accidents but rather the result of people trying to apply the principles of Scripture and tradition in a precise way and not distorting their work by bending to current political correctness. The temporal actions of the individual and the Church were considered acts of the Church because they were done by or on behalf of the Body of Christ following the principles subsequently listed by Vatican II. There was no such thing as an action in society that was imagined to have nothing at all to do with the Church and its mission as it follows Christ in the world.[222] The Church was the only institution that had the tools to sketch out the transcendent dimensions of situations.

Yet the West did not appreciate this. For example, why did it recently fall to the Church to defend the proper use of reason, as happened in John Paul II's *Fides et ratio*? Was no one else going to do it? By peeling off the spiritual from the temporal, moderns lose the meaning and implications of their actions, particularly they miss all of the spiritual implications. So, they miss essential things like the proper perception of what it means to be human, or what is the proper conception of human society, etc? Hence, they misconstrue the meaning of their actions. Then they build on their misconceived actions and make the situation worse.

To point out one of dozens of possible examples: For safety reasons, it is now necessary to issue maps of the concentrations of hypodermic needles and concentrations of human faeces in the streets and parks of San Francisco so that

---

[221] One would think that this would be obvious but often Laity, Clergy and Chancery officials do not impart the full Catholic quality to their every action.

[222] Andrew Willard Jones, *Before Church and State: A Study of Social Order in the Sacramental Kingdom of St. Louis IX*, Steubenville: Emmaus Academic Press, 2017.

people can avoid them.[223] No one necessarily planned this outcome but the idea behind the problem was to give people every possible choice regardless of consequences. Officials do not consider what freedom really is for or how the larger society bears the consequences. (Context again!) There is a moral consideration here, namely that freedom is for beatitude and not for degradation, but if there is no referring to God's law when planning things then beatitude becomes whatever one wants. This is not mere piety but the defence of authentic human life and dignity. (San Francisco now has 9700 homeless people in the city. Los Angeles has 36 000 (2019))

In the language of the first chapter, a faithful Catholic—and everyone else—is duty bound to not add to the communion of evil. In fact, one must go further and advance the communion of grace and truth.

(5) Politics in the US

Frequently, politics appears as the real gospel in the US, at least in terms of the time that people spend on it. Too often every stitch of the meaning of a situation appears to depend on which crowd says what and not on the situation itself. The meaning of a situation seems not to depend on the *nature* of the situation, which is something that involves God and His revelation as hermeneutic reference points. Instead, the meaning of a situation rather depends on what certain people want it to mean at the time to gain political power.

Secondly, and frighteningly, the great coup achieved by the Left is the instilling of the now common notion that political thinking ought never be critiqued by Catholic moral principles allied with a false notion of the separation of Church and state. This idea is so ubiquitous that it is never even questioned. This leads to some strange anomalies such as, for example, the report that "Catholics continue to be the only major religious voting block that can shift from one election to the next," according to Mark Gray of the Center for Applied Research in the Apostolate (CARA) at Georgetown University.[224] Since the moral law does not change, how is this shift even possible?

Clergy everywhere should know about these problems precisely because the Church is often used as the stalking horse for bad politics. The reason politics is so important to a priest in the US, is that for the reasons just outlined, there is a massive *qualitative* difference between the two main groups of parties politically speaking.

223
https://www.americanthinker.com/blog/2018/02/interactive_map_of_needles_and_feces_in_san_francisco_has_great_user_interface.html
[224] Cited by *National Catholic Register*, November 10, 2016.

The two options (introduced in Footnote 11) for political action are love and power—modes that are contrary to each other. The first lines up with being in a world that has been redeemed or with being in a world that "has been made subject to futility." (Romans 8:20)

Generally, the basic objective realities for fully functioning human beings are rational moral thought, holding to the Natural Law, to the rule of law, to free trade and to principles of nationhood—all concrete aspects of the exercise of freedom, properly understood. This is part of the law of love. But in the US, in practice, one set of people does not base its thinking on these things, even if they use the words. The two main groups of people work from totally different *moral* foundations and many Clergy do not know enough moral theology to see this or the problems that it causes.[225] People who try to mix them are merely inconsistent but the ramifications are awful and ultimately they are responsible for their own errors in moral thought. Raising the issue just causes ridicule and flat-out denial which are the Left's responses to challenge and are no substitute for logical argument.

In the US, one kind of party follows the Natural Law with its ties to divine law and the rational obedience that follows from that. The *Catechism* explains that:

> The natural law is immutable and permanent throughout the variations of history; it subsists under the flux of ideas and customs and supports their progress. the rules that express it remain substantially valid. Even when it is rejected in its very principles, it cannot be destroyed or removed from the heart of man. It always rises again in the life of individuals and societies: 'Theft is surely punished by your law, O Lord, and by the law that is written in the human heart, the law that iniquity itself does not efface.'[226] (CCC 1954)

This kind of party follow the Natural Law and does it well or badly but that is another issue. They try to apply its principles in how they understand institutions, civil and private, as well as they can. They also propose laws and policies that embody the same principles. These are all based on the proper notion of love particularly as it pertains to individuals loving themselves, loving others and whole groups of people.

The other kind of party ignores the Natural Law. The objective reality is not their focus. They are concerned with power over others and that occupies their whole attention. As far as the intellectual questions are concerned, they operate with a form

---

[225] This is a concern because Catholicism is about the moral life. Priests are supposed to pass on the doctrine of the moral life. If they do not know enough moral theology, then why are they functioning as priests?

[226] St. Augustine, *Confessions.* 2, 4, 9

of Gnosticism. As far as the questions of interpersonal relations and social transactions are concerned, their strategies are those of the Jacobins.

Starting with Gnostic thinking itself: Gnosticism is:

The doctrine of salvation by knowledge. This definition, based on the etymology of the word (*gnosis* "knowledge," *gnostikos*, "good at knowing"), is correct as far as it goes, but it gives only one, though perhaps the predominant, characteristic of Gnostic systems of thought.

Whereas Judaism and Christianity, and almost all pagan systems, hold that the soul attains its proper end by obedience of mind and will to the Supreme Power, i.e. by faith and works. It is markedly peculiar to Gnosticism that it places the salvation of the soul merely in the possession of a quasi-intuitive knowledge.[227]

At the outset, it should be said that Gnosticism was identified as a heresy by Catholicism early on for serious intellectual and moral reasons like forgetting that "it is I who bring both death and life." (Deuteronomy 32:39) It should be emphasized that thinking in the Gnostic way does not involve faith and reason in the proper way, so it is not really thinking in the full human sense. It is important to highlight the lack of faith in those who think in the Gnostic fashion. Furthermore, even in the short description above, it is clear that Gnostics imagine that they have some kind of superior knowledge and so do not learn from the deity. The leftist elite literally has become his own deity.

In the political groups that think in the Gnostic way, their elite have the above-mentioned quasi-intuitive knowledge of how society should be governed. It goes without saying that any governing that gets done will be done by the elite. Crudely put, the elite 'just know'. They know everything, including what is moral.

They *know* without even doing the heavy lifting of finding the substantiating data. In fact, for them what is 'right' often ignores the data. That is data from a theological perspective which is the only one that offers the complete view of the meaning of something and even includes references to statistical data. So, in the example of the needles and faeces (above), the complete data would include some projections of moral requirements as well as future problems and possible solutions. Of course, there is also the consideration of whether letting people have ready access to drugs without some efforts at retraining them is in the best interests of everyone. The same with the faeces. What are the duties of a city towards the homeless so that they live and behave like human beings? What space ought the city dedicate to the homeless?

---

[227] J. Arendzen, "Gnosticism," *Catholic Encyclopedia*, 2009.

What toilet facilities ought the city to provide and where? Most of all: from what understanding of freedom should the city operate?

Furthermore, the corollary of the elite knowing is that it is understood by all that those who are not part of the elite *do not know*. They abdicate their responsibility to know—not a properly human way to act—and then do the strangest thing. Each individual hands over his consciousness and his conscience, to the elite. It seems as if they are just begging for some authority to submit to. This absolves them from having to do the heavy lifting of thinking for themselves using faith and reason and then taking responsibility for their decisions. The elite thinks for them. It gives them the content of their minds, makes their decisions for them and they follow along in lockstep. As a result, there are millions of nominal Catholics who will automatically vote for people who pour tens of millions of dollars into abortion mills and who do many other deadly things. They will vote for people whose policies actually generate death, joblessness, poverty, violence and so on. Here is the core of the problem— does one fill one's mind with God and his law or with the ideology of the Left?

Since before the French Revolution, the Left has been both Gnostic and Jacobin.[228] Jacobinism depends on the emotions. According to Simon Schama, the Jacobins were noted for their militant egalitarianism, for teaching a public macro-morality.[229] Thanks to Schama, we know that: They violently attack any opposition. They oppose established authorities. They use a rhetoric of conspiracy and the denunciation of traitors. They are anti-capitalist and anti-modernist with many tests for political purity. One more difference between the Left and Catholicism is that Catholicism maintains a micro-morality: "We transform the world by focusing on our own personal morality and transformation."[230] The morality is sought out by each individual, often from the Church and it is applied to his/her life. Again, this formulation of things is not merely one option among many acceptable options. The Catholic micro-morality of individual freedom and responsibility is the only option for a human being to function in a properly human way, and one that truly develops each single individual.

---

[228] Jacobinism is so named after the college in Paris where the political group with these practices met in pre-revolutionary France—Couvent des Jacobins de la Rue Saint Jacques.
[229] Attorney-General William Barr delivered remarks to the Law School and the de Nicola Center for Ethics and Culture at the University of Notre Dame, South Bend, IN, Friday, October 11, 2019. By macro-morality, he means a perspective where people's "morality is not gauged by their private conduct, but rather on their commitment to political causes and collective action to address social problems." This is diametrically opposed to Catholic morality. One would think that Catholics would know this!
[230] Ibidem.

137

For the Left: imagining that they have superior knowledge (Gnosticism) means that they have utter contempt for their opponents. Hence, the Jacobin modes of speaking, the lying, the hyperbole, the threats and the insults, demonstrate that power will be grabbed by the party at *any* price, with any loss of human dignity, without *any* compromise. The party will also hold onto power at any price. The lying, the threats etc. all appeal to the lower instincts, not something to be encouraged and aided by Clergy or Laity. The problem for the Church when Clergy involve themselves with the Left—and by my guess, in the US over 50% do—is that Clergy are involving themselves with terrible acts (killing babies, using people's sufferings to game the system, using government institutions to terrorize people etc.) that their party involves itself in. They associate themselves, by a civil act, with the people who commit these terrible acts or at least those who finance them and promote them. There is no subsequent civil act to take back part of what they have publicly announced that they support.

The party often acts in the name of good intentions, but as was explained earlier the words that they use do not mean what the general context implies. The good intentions are only the window dressing to conceal the grab for power. In addition, good intentions do not completely define a moral act (Chapter One). For Catholics there is such a thing as being an accessory to other people's actions!

The lying, name-calling, hyperbole and all of the other misuses of communication are all signs of the extraordinary Jacobin disrespect and sheer disdain for the people being addressed. People are entitled to be addressed with the truth and only with the truth. They are also entitled to be addressed in a positive way. The principle to be used is that the teaching of the Church applies to everyone because it is universal truth for all of humanity. That the teaching is portrayed as being only for certain people is another artefact of the Enlightenment. It is anti-human in a number of ways.

Spreading partial truths set off the disruption of the human communion. William May indicates just how deep the problem gets: "the sins of individuals when accepted and endorsed by others, soon become the practices of a society, becoming embedded in its culture, mediating to us false understandings of ourselves and of what we are to do, inviting us, sometimes with pressure, to do what is wicked."[231] Catholics cannot associate themselves with this process. See too, the concept of social sin. (Chapter One.)

---

[231] William May, *An Introduction to Moral Theology*, Huntington IN: Our Sunday Visitor Publishing, 1994, 187.

A last point: it is rarely mentioned that the Left abuses symbols too. To quote a friend: "they will use any symbol for any purpose as long as they increase their power." Generally, this is part of the Left's strategy of deception, with power being the goal. It includes an eclecticism in the taking up of symbols—"I shall invoke this symbol at this time, if I increase my power as a result." The leftists wearing Kinte cloth to show support for a certain group of people was just one example. The cloth actually is the badge of a Ghanaian tribe, the Asante, who were the major slave trading tribe in Ghana. Misusing the symbol shows the true agenda of the wearer.

Another classic illustration was Hillary Clinton's use of a "reset" button as a prop in a meeting with the Russian Foreign Minister. "On 6 March 2009 in Geneva, U.S. Secretary of State Hillary Clinton presented Russian Foreign Minister Sergey Lavrov with a red button with the English word "reset" and the Roman alphabet transliteration of the Russian Cyrillic alphabet word перегрузка ("peregruzka"). It was intended that this would be the Russian word for "reset" but actually was the word for "overload" (The correct translation would be перезагрузка ["perezagruzka"].)[232] The research had not been done properly so the gesture of the reset button actually said something completely different. The Left's poor grasp of reality comes out here. There is a whole established phenomenon called the Russian language and it has rules. The disdain of the Left when using symbols means that they are reduced to being props for whatever is going on in the mind of the elite at the moment. For them, the external reality of the Russian language, in this case, did not deserve the proper level of research even though the meeting between the two officials would be reported around the world.

There are millions of other cases of misappropriation too. A rainbow flag being used to adorn a church sanctuary. Ecclesiastical vestments being loaned to be used in a fashion show. The pulpit being used for advocating contrary doctrines and so on. What each of these things actually means is apparently irrelevant. They are just a stage prop for the particular member of the elite who is seeking attention at this time. Just as with words and technical terms, the elite uses anything that once had meaning as a screen on which to project their own imagined superior insight.

A closing example would be the Bastille on the eve of the French Revolution. It was evoked as the great symbol of aristocratic oppression. When it was broken into with great fanfare, only seven prisoners were found in the prison and only three of them were, by any stretch, political prisoners. Yet, the Bastille was demolished, and the stones were sold. It is the classic symbol that is not really a symbol despite all of the hype. Make enough noise and anything can represent anything. This is simply

---

[232] Wikipedia.

emotional manipulation and has nothing to do with honest communication which is what Catholics are all about.

(6) The individual Catholic

The individual Catholic has an amazing task in life—"The grace of Christ is operative in every person who, following a correct conscience, seeks and loves the true and the good and avoids evil." (CCC 1716) Notice that the individual is to use all of his powers and use them correctly to live a full life. In other words: Catholic Clergy and Laity are called to something called the integrity of operation. The person both knows the divine law and makes sure that his every word and action complies with it. This is the absolute opposite of Gnosticism! Also, Catholics cannot be Jacobins because they treasure and promote the dignity and freedom of each individual to grow towards beatitude rather than promoting the advancement of their party at any cost. In this way, they are recognizing each individual as a person. Each person is unrepeatable and unique so that they cannot be treated as mere individual units.

On its face, when Catholics do these actions, they cut across the role of the Church as the institution that supports the development of institutions according to the proper understanding of being human, being community, being a society, and being a country.

However, on the contrary, the Left does not just repurpose institutions for their own advancement but as Schama noted, the rhetoric and activities of the Jacobins meant that when they came to power, they have so damaged the human fabric of society that they literally "make their [own] subsequent governance impossible."[233] As one example, in the modern period, the guru of the Left, Saul Alinsky, proposed that the strategies of the Jacobins be used again. So, in modern leftist rhetoric for example, it is routine for the Left to accuse any other party of doing what the Left is doing itself. This reversal of the relation between language and situation makes the formulation of a law—if it is to be acted upon—almost impossible. Legal terms can mean anything at any time, making the whim of the judge the arbiter of a situation when a conflict is brought to court.[234] Journalists can no longer report because that is no longer their function. They are there to advance the party and their 'reporting' becomes passing on calumnies and detraction.

---

[233] Simon Schama, *Citizens - A Chronicle of the French Revolution*, New York: Thrift Books, 1989, 527-532.

[234] For example, the question of a judge's advancement might be tied to how they decide cases. Cf. Raymond J de Souza, "Cardinal Pell's Acquittal Contains Message for Retired Professionals: Get to Work!" *National Catholic Register*, April 14, 2020.

For the Catholic who is trying to function in the world, for example, ought one watch a TV channel that works in the Jacobin way? This means that one is supporting the process of calumny and detraction. And, adding to the communion of evil in the process. There is no way that a Catholic can associate themselves with this kind of behaviour otherwise they are being polluted in the process.

Allied to this point is the fact that, to the best of my knowledge, the Left has never originated a new worthy state institution. Even the notorious leftist state security organizations all existed before the leftists came to power. They may have improved them i.e. made them more terrifying, but the initial idea had already been planted by the previous regime.

Adding a nuance to the preceding point: the Jacobins need pre-existing institutions from which they can feed. They need law courts that their members can use from which to legislate. Even though the court is not the place to do this. They need churches from which to propagate a new form of Jacobin religion. They need media through which to agitate and terrorize the population and so on.

One of the better tools in the Left's toolbox to convince everyone that every issue in society is merely political—no higher order ontological thinking is required. For them, the philosophy of Gnosticism is quite satisfactory for dealing with the situation in hand. In contrast, the Church has been the advocate of the higher order thinking of faith and reason because that is what human beings are designed for, in order to function best. Some Church hierarchy and Laity often passively go along with political thinking even though, for more than two thousand years, there has been a solid reason why metaphysics has been part of Church reasoning. It is required to explain the Church's anthropology, sociology and moral theology. It can do this accurately because it transcends politics and political considerations.

In addition, the Left's elite has produced ideologies like the 'New Soviet Man' in Leninism, the myth of the Aryan in National Socialism, the myth of the State in Maoism, and the myth of the Progressive Man in leftist thinking in the US. These are just a few of the more egregious examples of twisted anthropology from the last century. It would be difficult to total the number of people killed by blindly imposing these various ideas on society, but it runs into the hundreds of millions.[235] This catastrophe appears to be insignificant to the Left. It is mere collateral damage or as Stalin once said: "It is a mere statistic." (Compare these distortions of the

---

[235] Freedom of access to abortion is a purely ideological position because anti-human policies are not acceptable under Natural Law. Since Roe v Wade (1973) there have been 61 million abortions in the US.

understanding of human nature with the basic principles of human nature laid out in Vatican II's *Gaudium et Spes*.)

These ideologies have operated at horrific cost to those subject to them and the rest of humanity pays the price too. The ideologies distort history so badly that the rest of the people in the world have to subsidize the decades-long recovery of whole countries. Or other people have to go to war to pick up the pieces when the leftist ideologies fail. The carnage justifiably horrifies those who follow Natural Law such as many Catholics, for example.

Karl Marx exemplified Gnosticism very well because he simply *knew* the solutions to the social problems of his time. However, the deficiencies in his knowledge about the social and anthropological factors involved were appalling. Consequently, hundreds of millions of people around the world have died as a result of versions of his thought being imposed. The casualties and the wave of degradation of human beings generally show the horror of enforcing a form of thinking without knowing anything about the real nature of human beings, human community, human spiritual life and the common good. In other words, without knowing the Natural Law. The Church knows these concepts better than anyone else because of its openness to revelation, but that does not mean that specific Clergy and Laity know them and apply them regularly and consistently.

Adolf Hitler too, simply *knew* what had to be done in depressed post-First World War Germany. His politics gave rise to the Nazi State and the death camps so that Jews could be obliterated, and Jewish property could be taken from the Jews and redistributed to 'ethnic' Germans.[236] This does not even begin to include the 'removal' of the rest of the 'undesirables'. Similarly today, the Left in the US advocates the myths of its elite: socialism,[237] redistribution, progressivism, the superiority of the good of the state over the good of the individual, no free enterprise, equal suffering instead of equal opportunity, contraception, abortion, promiscuous life etc. all in the name of an agnostic version of freedom.

Any study of history makes it apparent that the policies of the Left always involve terrible human costs. It is apparently taken for granted that for every policy there is an acceptable level of suffering and death. Just to take one example: regarding abortion, the 60,000 abortions of black babies in New York City in 2016 alone and

---

[236] Peter Fritsche, *Life and Death in the Third Reich*, Boston: Belknap Harvard University Press, 2008.

[237] Hadley Arkes, "The Church and Socialism: The Fallacy that will not go away," *The Catholic Thing*, September 10, 2019, at https://www.thecatholicthing.org/2019/09/10/the-church-and-socialism-the-fallacy-that-will-not-go-away/

every year are not even part of the social conversation.[238] In reality, the costs to the rest of humanity are stupendous—never mind to the babies themselves! The loss to society of thousands of babies per day with all of their spiritual and physical potential is incalculable. The accompanying moral degradation of society from promoting this carnage beggars the imagination (see again the 'communion of sin' in Chapter One.) There is also a terrible additional suffering and psychological damage to the mothers and to families. Even the abortionists themselves are dehumanized. But the Left believes that the costs are acceptable because their elite gets power and wealth as a result and the masses have their 'freedom'. Also, the mass of the Left has their sought-after authority figures, to whom they can submit. However, it turns out to be freedom to live with the horrors they have committed and to blithely diminish the moral standing of the rest of humanity too as a result. In the process, the Left gains positions of influence in society, the media and the Church.

The Left is anti-human in another way too. They diminish the value of humans by opposing each individual's true freedom, true worship, true life, true identity and much more. These concepts can only be properly understood by reference to Divine Revelation and not by what the leftist elite *says* is freedom, worship, etc., at the moment. In other words, the Left ignores the criteria of human authenticity. Its operatives and their supporters lose sight of the principle that Vatican II explained as follows:

> It grows increasingly true that the obligations of justice and love are fulfilled only if each person, contributing to the common good, according to his own abilities and the needs of others, also promotes and assists the public and private institutions dedicated to bettering the conditions of human life. Yet there are those who, while possessing grand and rather noble sentiments, nevertheless in reality live always as if they cared nothing for the needs of society. (GS 30)

Of course, the council used these words in the full sense of their context and history in *Catholic* social terms. It would take a book to fully describe the rich fabric of human authenticity, but the council at least touched on the main points. These are ignored by the Left themselves in the way that they act. At the same time, in their style and tactics, they deprive their opponents of their own rights to act in an authentic fashion in society as well.

The Jacobin tactic in society includes suppression of opposition voices: from simply eliminating topics from conversation at the table, to censorship and active harassment, the Left has no equal. Historically, one can show that the modern Left in the US, has its roots in the thinking of Benito Mussolini, with all that fascism did and

---

[238] https://lozierinstitute.org/abortion-reporting-new-york-city-2016/

143

does to control the message.[239] Two modern day examples in the US will suffice: (i) the following and harassment of Fox reporter James Rosen and his family by the National Security Agency (reported 20 June 2013); (ii) the government's spying on the Senate Intelligence Committee (reported 31 July 2014). More examples are to be found in the many topics that are *not* covered by the majority of the media.

Leftist thinking is so markedly unreal—in the sense being used in the Tradition—because it has no regard for history as the term is normally understood. It does not take cognizance of previous history even though the past serves us and at the same time makes demands on us. As the *Catechism* explains: "a society endures through time: it gathers up the past and prepares for the future. By means of society, each man is established as an 'heir' and receives certain 'talents' that enrich his identity and whose fruits he must develop." (CCC 1880) The *Catechism* continues: "Each community is defined by its purpose and consequently obeys specific rules; but 'the human person . . . is and ought to be the principle, the subject and the end of all social institutions.' (GS 25)" (CCC 1881) The statement about the human person is something that has several thousand years of tradition behind it. It is the key to all of the objections about the Left all throughout its history. Catholic anthropology includes the principles of the morality of association. On the one hand, these are contradicted by Gnosticism and on the other, they are contradicted by the political strategy of Jacobinism.

Moreover, the category of history is an essential component of rational thought. For the Left, only the present matters because that is where gaining power takes place and so the elite do not need any memory of the past. The party itself has no past. The egregious things it has done in this country and others have no call on party members now.[240] For example, at present, the Left is insisting that statues of leftist Southern civil war heroes must be taken down. In fact, the Left started the Civil War and lost it and tried to reverse the result. The statues are of old party members! For the party, this is not incongruous because there is only the present.[241] However, one history professor did raise the question of statues as *reverencing* military leaders which deserves serious

---

[239] Jonah Goldberg, *Liberal Fascism – The Secret History of the American Left from Mussolini to the Politics of Meaning*, New York: Doubleday, 2017.

[240] The Left has given the US: the Civil War; the attempted reversal of the outcome of the Civil War, the killing of thousands of freed slaves, the imposition of segregation (Cf. Ron Chernow, *Grant*, New York: Penguin Press, 2017.) and the re-imposition of segregation (Woodrow Wilson). It has also given the KKK, Jim Crow laws and so on. All things that can be verified by a little reading.

[241] Hillary Clinton's senior thesis at Wellesley College was entitled "There is only the Fight: An Analysis of the Alinsky Model." https://en.wikipedia.org/wiki/Hillary_Rodham_senior_thesis There is only the present!

consideration.[242] But human beings are historical in their very being (historicity). So historical facts are part of any thought process, because it is part of the context of their humanity. It is inescapably part of thinking about what human beings ought to do and what they should repent of having done.

The way that human beings are created means that the meaning of history will eventually come out in society. The cracks show up very soon but at what cost? Interestingly, the black historian Colson Whitehead thinks that "those who enable historical amnesia are accessories to crimes against humanity"[243] Can Catholics go along with avoiding the lessons of history? The simple answer is no because Catholicism truly affirms authentic humanity and history is part of the required anthropology.

Furthermore, in the Catholic sphere, if history is ignored then the concept of Church 'tradition' has no meaning either and this is serious for Catholics and for human beings generally because Scripture and tradition are God's revelation. (*Dei verbum*, Vatican II) Given that the Church is tasked with safeguarding revelation in its entirety in order to serve humanity, having Catholics who reject history undercuts all aspects of the work of the Church.

The Deposit of Faith disappears too. Not recognizing the historicity of individuals, the Church and society means that for the Left, words in the teaching of the Church only mean what the present elite wants them to mean at this present moment. If I am a leftist, I can say the opposite thing tomorrow and not feel any shame at all. I will also not be challenged on that even though I have diminished the authenticity of myself and of everyone in the situation that I was speaking about. One cannot ignore the serious historical problem that developed after the Second Vatican Council and that is where a portion of the community teaches what opposes the Deposit of Faith.[244] This is a complex piece of history in itself but just pointing to it indicates the major theological difficulty for authentic Catholicism that is involved.

For Catholicism, there is a memory, within the tradition, that has immense potential for helping people find the accurate meaning of things. Everything starts with the fact that the Tradition of the Church is unique because "both of them [Scripture and Tradition], flowing from the same divine wellspring, in a certain way merge into a unity and tend toward the same end."(DV 9)[245] That is to say that Church Tradition is

---

[242] Fox 5, DC, 2020/06/05
[243] In the words of his reviewer Frank Rich. *New York Times Book Review*, July 21, 2019.
[244] Cf. George Weigel, "Joseph Ratzinger, Theological Reformer," Denver Catholic, Archdiocese of Denver, at https://denvercatholic.org/joseph-ratzinger-theological-reformer/
[245] This is tough enough to impart in orthodox Catholic institutions who do work with the Natural Law.

itself *part of Divine revelation* and it is fundamentally interlinked with the divine revelation in Scripture and not apart from it. Subverting the historicity of tradition in any way interferes with peoples' complete reception of revelation and imposes a purely man-made interpretation on something that actually interprets itself because only God can explain God. (God is present precisely to do this interpretation.) Implicit in this process is the very real probability of misinterpreting Scripture.

Hermeneutically, words such as 'marriage,' 'family,' 'justice', etc. all get to the core of what it means to be human *if* they are considered in the light of Scripture and Tradition. Revelation has shown what the words truly mean in the history of salvation. However, these terms get morphed into completely different concepts by the Left. Tomorrow, these terms will mean something else again if it suits the advancement of the party.

In general, the Left's thinking is thinking separated from its true context. Put differently, the Left does not feel bound by the whole context of a situation. So, one can, in their view, claim the mantle of social-justice-advocate and ignore the serious moral problem of voting for candidates who support abortion. Part of the context for making a judgement about the morality of such a vote would have to include the number of deaths by abortion as well as the disproportionate number of black babies killed by abortions. Catholics are required to trudge through the list of criteria for a moral act because they are required to act morally. No one is exempt ever.

When the Left uses words, they do not use them with an intellectual context, or they do not have more of a context than the elite want to allow at the time. For them, words are merely sounds used to catch someone's attention. Their words are noises that come out of their mouths and have no more purpose than to manipulate people by catching their imagination. For example, the normal hearer thinks that the word 'justice' from a leftist means 'justice as it is understood in Western tradition'. But that is not the case. The hearer is led along by this illusion but not in the direction of discussing actual justice. In fact, there is a manipulation of the audience going on behind the words. The deception lies in having the hearer thinking that the Left is speaking about one thing when in fact they are talking about something else—basically let us handle justice and we will get it right.

For the Left, terms of art, in the fields of law, government, trade or finance etc. do not derive their meaning from their historical context—a set of concepts that are bonded with the history of the institutions using the terms. Yet, this is precisely the process required by Natural Law thinking for communication between moral beings for moral purposes.

On the other hand, those outside of the Left, instead of blindly following the party elite, they defer to the reality of the Natural Law. Consequently, they reflect on the role and function of a particular institution and its history. They defer to those with expertise in the institution's use of the terms and who can referee the usage of terms so that they are used with some consistency and accuracy. They then have some guarantee that they are involved in truly human communication, one that elevates the speaker by allowing him/her to speak the truth. Truthful communication also elevates the hearer who is being treated in a manner corresponding to his/her dignity and who is being presented with the truth. This is authentic human communication. Thus, calumny (making false claims to damage someone's reputation) and detraction (disparaging someone purely to belittle them) are not the currency of communication and yet they seem to have become commonplace in the media and around the table.

Catholics are obligated by the nature of human dignity itself to only communicate the truth. Hence, Catholics need to know that calumny and detraction are still sins. Calumny is a serious sin because one makes *false* statements in order to damage someone's reputation. The sin of detraction involves making *true* statements in the wrong forum about someone in order to damage their reputation. Politics cannot be an arena in which the moral law is suspended. The Left, however, does just that. Catholics cannot morally 'slip the leash' for a while. They are bound by the moral law, for their own good. Their purpose on this earth is to become saints. Tossing that goal aside even for a moment shows how poorly they understand their position and how precarious it is.

Going back to the meanings of words: In Natural Law terms, 'government', to take one example, means the elected institution that leads a country for the common good of its citizens, the protection of the good of the country and its sovereignty. Then, as the *Catholic Encyclopedia* explains: "The power of the State is limited by the end for which it was instituted, and it has no authority to violate the natural rights of its subjects."[246] For the Left, 'government' is an institution that is the platform for the elite to develop their own power and wealth. Overall, the 'great' figures of the Left have authority and so the Left's team wins. The context, in other words the rest of the people in the country and in countries overseas, is irrelevant.

Regarding institutions: It is self-evident for anyone who studies history, that leftists subvert institutions from the inside. This means that they do not use institutions for the purposes for which they were intended. They use the institutions to propagate their policies which is not the same thing as serving the common good. For example, some US administrations appointed alleged Communist sympathizers and

---

[246] W. Kent, "Divine Justice", *Catholic Encyclopedia*.

Communists to the administration.[247] This was despite the fact that Communism has a history that is long and uniformly bad and historically it has been the opponent of the wellbeing of this country even to the extent of opposing the US in dozens of proxy wars with appalling consequences. The amounts of blood and treasure consumed in opposing Communism should have given a clue to how subversive these appointments were, but the Left does not recognize history even that of their own country. The appointments appear so incongruous *because* they contradict of the anti-Communist context of any administration of the US.

Another example: law courts can become weapons for the party to exercise its agenda rather than as places where the law is applied without fear or favor. Also, lawsuits can become weapons to bankrupt opponents or even incarcerate them.

Catholicism, on the other hand, has a great concern that institutions only be set up to enlarge the common good. This is yet another problem with Catholics advocating and supporting leftist policies. Regarding Catholicism itself, it develops the Church to serve God and humanity, and never as a tool for power or to propagate untruth.

The need for personal integrity is more in the spotlight now that there are fewer common standards of behaviour in society anymore. It is central to Catholicism that people grow to a greater integrity due to grace. In addition, the Church used to be able to rely on what was called 'common decency'. When this was the case it would not have been possible, for example, for a paediatrician to say: "in this particular example if a mother is in labor, I can tell you exactly what would happen, the infant would be delivered. The infant would be kept comfortable. The infant would be resuscitated if that's what the mother and the family desired, and then a discussion would ensue between the physicians and the mother." (Governor Ralph Northam, Fox News, January 30, 2019) The previously accepted standard of care of newborns—keep them alive at any cost because they are so precious and unique—apparently no longer exists. Now that common decency is no longer common, every single moral requirement is going to have to be identified and taught repeatedly and inculcated back into the culture. People who seek integrity will learn each of these moral standards and implement them. Clergy especially!

It is also rarely mentioned that, at least nationally, the Left overwhelmingly dominates the popular media. About 90% of major media personnel are leftists. Many media personnel are former party officials or employees. Their information handling is often done in the style of the Left and for the goals of the Left. The problem is that Clergy frequently do not know where to go to get accurate information. If they are

---

[247] Cf. Karen McQuillan, "Barack Obama populated the US Government with Communists," *The American Thinker*, https://www.lifesitenews.com/opinion/barack-obama-populated-the-us-government-with-communists

leftists, they only want to hear what comes from the mothership. Some Clergy associate themselves with the media propagating these ways of thinking by listening to them and then passing on what they hear. They then proceed to do their ministry on a false foundation with a false understanding of revelation and the world.

(7) The Other Choice

The other possible choice of political parties involves choosing one that follows the Natural Law grounded as it is in Divine Revelation. By the nature of the case, such a party knows its own history and the history of the nation it is serving. Members of such groups try to follow divine law. (They have made terrible mistakes and still do, but they at least have some very high and objective standards to measure their mistakes against and on occasion they do.) One must also acknowledge that not all members of the other possible political choice are consistent because their thinking is sometimes just as muddy and not always properly human either. They sometimes pick up bits and pieces of policies from the Left for a whole host of reasons that cannot be examined here. These obvious flaws, however, do not nullify the real possibilities and higher moral achievements of choices founded on the Natural Law.

Such groups of people promote the development and fulfilment of *individual* human beings and ideally never do things at the expense of another human being. (The problem with identity politics?) Every individual is precious as an individual and not as a member of a class. Natural law offers the principles to be used as the foundation of institutions and for authentic communication to serve each individual with the fullness respect.

From the Natural Law perspective, each institution serves the general good by serving some area of the human project. Thus, they work to achieve the good of all. Even the IRS is meant to do that! Such institutions have internal checks and balances so that they are not used for purposes beyond their original brief. Over and above that, society herself is supposed to have checks and balances applying to every kind of institution so that they do not usually get perverted or pervert society.

Tragically, the fundamental leftist myth—that is bought unquestioningly by so many—is that the teaching of the Left is not to be measured against Catholic teaching and critiqued using Catholic moral principles. Somehow, for the Left, political thinking is morally untouchable. They see it as a privileged area beyond the moral considerations that would expose the flaws in Gnosticism and Jacobinism very easily. The Church has an anthropology, a psychology, a sociology of community and institutions. These sketch out the main principles drawing on Divine Revelation. Nevertheless, Bishops and religious superiors often just go along with the myth even though the Second Vatican Council had a substantial teaching on the proper role and, more importantly, on the limits of the political dimension of life.

Another myth is that the Left cares more for the poor. Historically, this can be shown to be false. The party that fought to protect slavery, produced the KKK etc. gave the lie to this early on. Today nothing has changed—consider the violence, poverty, lack of jobs and problems with jobs in leftist controlled cities. Consider the piles of needles in the parks and human faeces in the streets of San Francisco and other leftist controlled cities! Consider the thousands of homeless in such cities. Consider the thousands of abortions, particularly of black babies in leftist controlled cities.

So, for Catholics, when acting politically, it comes down to either following leftist ideology or the Natural Law. There is no other alternative. One either follows subjective criteria (following someone who 'knows') or one follows objective criteria (Natural Law). Anecdotally, a slight majority of Clergy would seem to be of the Left. Evidently for them, Catholic teaching is not true or at least not true enough to be followed completely. Their following of an incomplete form of Catholicism indicates that they do not believe that it leads to the highest common good for all humanity—something that is apparent from the understanding of Jesus Christ found in tradition and Scripture. One should ask, why are they still functioning as Clergy?

Regarding the meaning of leftist language: It is essential to look at the *behavior* (an objective phenomenon) of the Left because they use religious terms like they use other terms and that is as manipulative tools and not as labels for parts of reality. For example, most 'Catholic' leftists are convinced that they are devout Catholics. This is false. Their confusion is based on the illusion that words can mean anything they want them to mean at any time.[248] "I am devout if I think I am." In such a person's mind there is no objective standard against which they can be judged. What gets lost is the objective meaning of words.

Most words precede us. They come to us complete with a meaningful context and we do not get to define them at all. To work with this verbal structure requires real humility. The illusion that the meanings of words can be changed at whim guts the concrete every-day presence of Catholicism itself and turns religious discussion into a power-game. This game seriously interferes with the real work of dioceses and religious congregations. In fact, it simply nullifies it because most leftist concepts are the opposite of Catholic concepts. In which case, 'Catholic' activities are being done to advance the party.

Just a reminder: the two options of following the Natural Law or seeking out power do not simply reduce to the Republican and Democrat parties in the US. The reason is that *everyone* is bound by the lack of conversion indicated by the 20-

---

[248] Or it could be due to bad catechesis which is an ever-present danger, and which illustrates how crucial the presence of a good priest is.

minute law. Most faithful are not that converted. People are usually going after some aspect of power in society and more rarely after the implementation of the Natural law-based activity in society. People are amazingly inconsistent. Another reason for priests to be consistent.

Now, the problem with having so many Catholics operating at least occasionally in terms of an ideology is that this phenomenon conceals the unity of the Church. In turn this conceals the unity of the God who made the Church. In fact, the leftists have found their own god, one that lies in the subjectivism of the elite that they follow. This is not a rhetorical statement. Conceptual unity is fundamental to the Catholic presence. According to Paul: "I urge you, brothers and sisters, in the name of our Lord Jesus Christ, that all of you agree in what you say, and that there be no divisions among you, but that you be united in the same mind and in the same purpose." (I Corinthians 1:10) The unity of the Church depends on the unity of minds in the Church community. Ultimately, the mind of the Church lies with the Holy Spirit, but people cannot see the Holy Spirit. They can, however, see Catholics at work and at play. That is where the unity of the Church is evident.

This unity is only brought about by participating in the One Truth. The Church bears no similarity at all to the unity of a country that contains conflicting currents of thought which might be imagined as a political template for the Church, and a faulty one at that. The Catholic unity of mind is a unity that completely involves all of the faithful body and soul unified by the Spirit of God. The involvement and the unity indicate the presence of the moral unity in the teaching of the Church. It is necessary so "that the cross of Christ might not be emptied of its meaning." (I Corinthians 1:17)

The key point is that undermining the moral unity of the Church undermines its public presence as a community unified in Christ. For example, contraception damages that unity right down to undermining the authentic unity of a married couple who practice it. For example, contraceptive activity by the faithful has implications. It means that

> the innate language that expresses the total reciprocal self-giving of husband and wife is overlaid, through contraception, by an objectively contradictory language, namely, that of not giving oneself totally to the other." (CCC 2370)

The couple is just applying the contradictory language of leftist thinking to what is a sacramental union.

Analyzing the *Catechism*'s statement: Firstly, because of this divisive choice, one has the tragic public contradiction of the human authenticity brought by Christ. Then further, the teaching that sees serious flaws in contraceptive behaviour is undermined by individuals living as if contraception is not even a moral problem. The integrity of humanity itself is diminished each time that contraception is used. It is the communion of sin once again.

Secondly, approaching contraception as a merely political issue suggests that authentic 'giving oneself totally' is not the key to husband-wife relations. Apparently then, for them Christ is not the source of the truth of human morality or of the grace to practice it. Contracepting couples are nominally part of the faith-community by Baptism and yet do not value what Christ means for them and for the world. Contraception is not solely a private, personal activity as was clear from John Paul II's teaching on the communion of sin.

This counter-witness, or perhaps even more strongly, this public revolt against God's order, is the reason that this chapter has to appear in a book on priesthood. The real issue is always to be faithful to the Natural Law and to use that to make judgements on political matters.

(8) The Theology of the Intellectual Life

Priests participate in the continuing and restoring expression of the Divine Word into the world through the Church to the degree that they want to—even though they are ordained to do this completely. The Divine Word is universally true as part of its nature as the Divine Word. It is not true conditionally or only for a certain group or only for a certain time. This is basic to the nature of the presence of the Word himself. So, to quote Benedict XVI:

> If all things 'hold together' in the one who is 'before all things' (cf. Col 1:17), then those who build their lives on his word build in a truly sound and lasting way. The word of God makes us change our concept of realism: [Now] the realist is the one who recognizes in the word of God as the foundation of all things. (VD 10)

Hence the problem for the leftist 'Catholic'. The Word is the truth of the world and that is why believing in Jesus Christ is not a side-issue to the central goal of grabbing power and steering the Church in the direction of being a tool of socialism. (See Hadley Arkes, "The Church and Socialism: The Fallacy that will not go away.")[249] The truth manifested in the Word and his Body the Church is the complete opposite of the concepts put forward in socialist ideology. In the latter, where the state knows all and the elite imagine themselves to be the heart of the state, the elite are the sources of meaning for everything in society. They have become Christ!

---

[249] Hadley Arkes, "The Church and Socialism: The Fallacy that will not go away," *The Catholic Thing*, September 10, 2019, at https://www.thecatholicthing.org/2019/09/10/the-church-and-socialism-the-fallacy-that-will-not-go-away/

Historically, the two closest recent parallels to this process are the Positive Christianity developed by the Nazis in the thirties and the efforts in modern China to make Catholicism operate according to the principles of Communism. Closer to home is the effort to make the Church adopt the ideology of socialism—under the rubric of progressivism. Underneath all of the word games, this is the problem at its root. It is the denial of the full stature of the Word. Apparently, the Divine Word needs the help of today's socialism. In contrast, the truth of the Word is all encompassing, manifesting itself in all the fields of human endeavour, again and again.[250] But, for the leftist, the party has more authority and more knowledge than Christ.

The origins of the thinking of the Left can perhaps be traced back to people as far back as Jan Hus, Wycliffe, through Martin Luther into the Enlightenment, all of these figures were anti-ecclesial and anti-traditional in the Catholic sense. There were always other elements to their ideology as well. All sought to create ecclesial communities that were structurally and conceptually contrary to the Church. It was said earlier that, underneath the word games, the Left is all about dismantling institutions and it is doing that to the Church. So, the Left in the Church is not merely a slightly different way of thinking, it is a way of emptying every principle and every concept in Catholicism.

A suitable symbol of the Left might be the disaster at Chernobyl in Ukraine (1986), for example. The two reactors were built ignoring the commonly known principles of nuclear reactors—because the Left knows better—one of the reactors had a melt-down and polluted most of Europe. The clean-up is still going on (2020). Many countries, all non-socialist, have had to contribute to the 100-year project of containment and clean-up. The lying to the millions of people, locally and internationally, that accompanied the unfolding of the events, is very much in line with the standard operating procedure of the Left. The deaths and suffering of so many people have not yet been fully responded to.

Furthermore, Catholicism is a way of life, not merely a religion, despite all the Enlightenment's efforts to paint it in that light and to paint it into a corner as a result. As a way of life, Catholicism institutes a positive, constructive and life-giving civilization, a civilization that is focused on the common good and can bring people to the fullness of worship and the consequent fullness of life. Yes, it has often failed to maintain its authenticity, and the perpetrators must bear that guilt forever. The failures are due to human weakness, laziness and immorality but that does not

---

[250] See John Paul II's *Fides et Ratio*!

153

change the possibilities of the doctrine and the grace, it just shows that the human mediators of the doctrine are fallible as are the mediators of socialism.

Here are a few suggestions on how to develop one's intellectual (and spiritual) life in terms of participation in the work of the Word of God.

(9) The Divine Office

Speaking of the Divine Office, Paul VI said: "The hymn of praise that is sung through all the ages in the heavenly places and was brought by the High Priest, Christ Jesus, into this land of exile has been continued by the Church." (Constitution of Promulgation, Revision of the Divine Office)[251] This continuation takes place in part (the other part is the offering of the official sacrifice of the Church) through the daily recitation of the Divine Office, the official prayer of the Church. The priest prays the Breviary because it is essential to his participation in the communion of prayer of the Church and it is essential to who he is personally and vocationally. It is required by Canon Law for the same reasons.

These two 'areas' of the priest's life—prayer and sacrifice—gradually converge into a constant transaction with the Spirit, if the priest is diligent. Primarily, the priest is an official of the Church making the official prayer to the Father, through the Son in the Spirit. This service participates in the ongoing worship of God by the whole Church, on earth and in Heaven. Then too, it sanctifies the priest's day reminding him constantly what he is about and who with. By praying the Breviary, he enters more and more deeply into the unfolding of the Kingdom of God in the world through the Church and in his own spirit.

In itself, praying the Breviary consists of reciting extracts from the Scriptures and extracts from the Tradition of the Church. By doing this, the priest is immersed, daily, in the two interrelated streams of Divine Revelation.[252] This activity serves to bring the priest into contact with what is most real and least subjective in his situation as a participant in Christ's presence in the world.

This is one way that the Scriptures come to be part of the history and life-experience of the priest himself. The more mindfully he reads them—and literally, *prays* them—the more they become part of the intellectual and spiritual furniture of his mind. It is very difficult to explain this experience to people who are not on the way to living in the expanded spiritual world of the praying person. The Breviary does not necessarily provide new *data* that can be gotten elsewhere. Imagining the experience that way would be to throw a shadow on the rich changes that take place in one's mind, once one is exposed to the Divine Word present in the words on

---

[251] November 1, 1970.

[252] See *Dei verbum*.

the page. To make a crude illustration: one hears about pornography 'rewiring' people's minds. We can say that encountering Sacred Scripture and the sacred tradition will 'rewire' our minds too, to bring it far more in line with its true nature by the Spirit. As the Synod on the Word of God reminded us: "The word of God is at the basis of all authentic Christian spirituality." (VD 86)[253]

An underappreciated aspect of the scriptural experience is that it gives one exposure to reality, technically, the exposure to being, both the divine Being and the human being in all of the multiplicity of human relationships. It is the experience of reality in constant interchange with God. Since God not only created us, He also persistently redeems and sanctifies us.[254] The exposure to real being in all of its depth, in every historical event (historical books) and in every verse of the Wisdom literature, shows us authentic human existence. And the books on the law show us the divine law, the ordering of human being. These are all things that are applicable to leading the Church, in the celebrations of the sacraments, in homilies and in simple day-to-day conversation.

Both revering Scripture and reading it lead priests to realize that "while in the Church we greatly venerate the sacred Scriptures, the Christian faith is not a 'religion of the book': Christianity is the 'religion of the word of God', not of 'a written and mute word, but of the incarnate and living Word'." (VD 7)[255] The living Word spoke throughout the Old Testament and the New Testament. This is important because "being Christian is not the result of an ethical choice or a lofty idea, but the encounter with an event, a person, [Jesus Christ] which gives life a new horizon and a definitive direction."[256]

The other part of revelation occurs daily in the Tradition of the Church. One way that priests experience the Tradition is through the Office of Readings. And they do it in a prayerful milieu. The pressure from an Enlightenment culture to avoid the tradition of the Church can be overwhelming but, in fact, historically, the Enlightenment's teaching about the Church is inaccurate.[257] (Take a look at the

---

[253] See Colossians 1:9-11

[254] This is the non-Pelagian view of the world! Pelagius thought that people can get along without grace which has been demonstrated to be untrue. Pelagian thinking lies behind many of the casual attitudes to the Breviary.

[255] Benedict XVI is quoting Saint Bernard of Clairvaux, *Homilia super missus est*, IV, 11: PL 183, 86B.

[256] Benedict XVI, Encyclical Letter *Deus Caritas Est* (25 December 2005), 1: AAS 98 (2006), 217-218.

[257] One characteristic of the Enlightenment is their lack of knowledge of the history that preceded them much like the Left today. They did not appreciate the standard of development of the world before the *philosophes* came on the scene and they had a very

statements about the Church in the famed *Encyclopedie!*[258]) So, the priest, even before his ordination, has to resist the sheer lunacy of avoiding the Tradition of the Church in the hope of serving his people better. (Martin Luther rejected most tradition in favor of making his own ecclesial community according to his own lights.) To do so cuts one off from the torrent of grace and truth to be found there.

For some reason, some students find that their seminary training is oppressive, and they fear that it will not be relevant to the real world. Nevertheless, well planned or poorly planned, intellectual training at the very least shows something of what the Church teaches and what the Church has taught. The Breviary offers samples of texts from the Fathers right up to the Second Vatican Council. The council itself said: "the Church, in her teaching, life and worship, perpetuates and hands on to all generations all that she herself is, all that she believes." (DV 8) Clearly what is handed on (tradition from *tradere*-to hand over (Lat.)) obviously is more than texts, but some of the traditional texts appear in the Office of Readings. These texts are texts that the priest reads while immersed in his pastoral work right now. He does his pastoral work, celebrating liturgy, visiting the sick, preaching retreats, helping out at the local soup kitchen, with the words of Augustine and Basil and some unnamed homilists buzzing around in his head.

However, praying the Breviary, is not a purely instructional experience where the priest learns from some writer how to do a particular aspect of his pastoral work. First and foremost, he is exercising the receptivity of faith. Praying the Breviary models how Christians enter communion with God. It is a kind of immersion in living salvation history, a phenomenon far beyond our comprehension, while joining the Church community at her prayer.

## (10)	The Catholic World

In the US, cultural pressure often makes Catholicism into a purely private interior interest. This thinking is a present-day artefact of the Enlightenment and it biases most US culture and education. The priest, as a representative of what really superlative culture can be, has to have at least a general knowledge of the vast contribution of Catholicism to human culture, something that continues to this day. The prevailing public image of Catholicism is that it is mostly irrelevant—and more recently, vice-ridden. There is a strong Pelagian component to this kind of thinking resting on the assumption that considerations of grace (and therefore by implication,

---

selective take on the classical world. This is the way that the Left's thinking can be forgetful. The events of the classical world have no claim on them. Rather the classical elements are used as ornaments for their own thinking.

[258] Denis Diderot, *Encyclopédie*, or its original title, *Dictionnaire raisonné des sciences, des arts et des métiers*. 1751-1772.

sin) has no place and in fact contributes nothing to the modern state of affairs. (How Enlightened can you get?)

On the other hand, it is impossible to overstate the contribution of Church members—or families, or institutions like dioceses, religious orders, hospitals, orphanages, universities, art workshops and all the rest—have made to the world for over two millennia. The individual priest will not get a grasp of the wonders of the Church's past unless he seeks it out himself. So, it is vital for the functioning priest to have some kind of overall conception of what has happened in the extraordinary life of the Church. This requires some serious reading, and some serious listening to music, speeches, plays and poetry. Some serious attention ought to be paid to works of art and buildings as well. Just as important, a priest needs a deep appreciation of the Church's uncountable works of charity and let us not forget all of her contributions to international law, finance, architecture, and the rest. Science, psychology and research in so many fields owe much to their being started and developed by Catholics. Of course, the towering contribution of the Church is the many sacrifices of the Mass offered through the centuries and the thousands and thousands of men and women who followed the will of God completely and became saints.

Now a priest cannot be an expert in all of this, but he has to have at the very least a collection of anecdotes that he can dust off at the appropriate moment. It really helps Catholics to hear what other Catholics have done. People will stand in awe of the manifold works of the Holy Spirit in our history when they discover where the great holiness, much of art and science come from. This is also where the stories of the saints come in but, as important as they are, they are not the whole story. The rest of the Catholic story lies in the stories of 'ordinary' Catholics who frequently were not saints but who have made contributions in different fields, nonetheless. The essential thing is to get past the stage of being embarrassed by Catholicism. That is a mindset fresh from the intellectual pressures of the Enlightenment.

The Enlightenment hoped to supplant Catholicism and it still tries quite successfully today. To get a grip on what this means, one can, for example, read one of the histories of the French Revolution such as *Citizen* by Simon Schama. Watch for the images of Catholicism, the suffering of Catholics and the Left's constant recourse to using Catholic symbols and images to present their own secular narcissism and solipsism—like their secular 'liturgies', for example, or when they used cathedrals for their own purposes.

The priest being, in some sense, a Catholic intellectual helps other believers join in the transformation of the mind about the meaning of the world and humanity, a change that is brought about by Christ. Then there is the sheer magnificence of

Catholicism and its superb understanding of the nature and purpose of the world. The core issue is obviously believing in Jesus Christ, but of course, this is done in the context of the all-pervading divine Trinity and his Church. Conceptually, there is no purely secular history, but everything is a history of God, his salvation and his providence. Within that history the Church has done wonders. Yes, there have been fools and there have been sinners but why dwell on that? That derogatory attitude in itself is a relic of the Enlightenment and is not the whole story. Fools and sinners appear in every walk of life and in every ecclesial community. And yet Catholicism is about the *whole* story of God's salvation as its name suggests!

There are certain concepts that the priest simply has to know. Hopefully these will have been covered in the priest's seminary training, but some seminarians are full to the brim with longing to get out of the seminary and be made Bishops. They are sometimes too full to allow much of the wisdom of the Church to enter in. So, once the priest is in a parish and he knows that he is not going to be made a Bishop tomorrow, then he can settle down to fully serving his people by telling them of the glories of Catholicism.

This short chapter is not the place to give a full description of the conceptual side of Catholicism. There are thousands of textbooks that do just that. However, this chapter can point to the kind of resources that a priest should lay hold of to function better as a pastor.

One final point: speaking about the intellectual life of the priest is really saying that the priest has a mind. The anti-intellectualism that runs through some groups of priests plays into the anti-intellectual notions of religion that come from the ongoing Enlightenment tradition. This has its parallels in the anti-intellectual currents in law, politics and economics, etc. that are encouraged by the Left. Moreover, there are increasing attempts to diminish the role of expertise and hard-earned competence in most walks of life. In a sense, one must talk about the priest being a professional, in the sense of his obligation to know a lot about Catholicism and to be reading each day on the topic.

Having a brain, being created with an intellect and a will, is one of the major ways that priests are in the image of God and means that they ought to use their brains in the way that God intended. Uninformed priests will become more and more irrelevant except for weddings and funerals. Informed priests, on the other hand, are the resource that informed Catholics will turn to all through life. Now to resources . . . .

(11)   The Scriptures
The priest needs to be a man of the Scriptures. Much, much better than TV, the Scriptures are the root of the many liturgies of the Word that the priest will be celebrating. Even the simple act of checking the footnotes in the New American

Bible[259] for the various readings will, over time, give the priest a store of the basics of the theology of the Scriptures. Some Scripture courses at seminaries are courses in how to read the Scriptures agnostically (as if they had been written in a university!) but this is not what the priest was ordained to pass on to his parishioners. The Scriptures are the inspired Word of God and should be treated as such. The Scriptures are the Church's book and they are best read in the tradition of the Church—which most often means reading them in liturgies. (Cf. VD 52)

The Synod on the Word of God, with its teaching summarized by Benedict XVI is one of the giant collections of the Church's understanding of how to handle the Scriptures, the best since Vatican II's *Dei Verbum*. Benedict's document is called *Verbum domini*. It is well worth the effort to appreciate the massive significance of the Holy Scriptures.

Between what he learns in his prayer with the Breviary, the proper treatments of the Scriptures and his own personal prayer, the priest can start to enter the scriptural world with its constant reference of being to God. This is the prelude to making *this* world a scriptural world, one that operates with constant reference to God.

Another good resource is a computer—not for the usual reasons of filling time or watching porn, but to gain quick access to the documents of the Church—one part of the Tradition—on the Vatican website. One should, at least, know the basic teaching of Vatican II, and of the last few popes, as well. Then of course, on the same site, there is the Code of Canon Law.

(12)   Internet Sites that are useful:
The *Catholic Encyclopedia* (newadvent.org). This is the 1918 version of the *Encyclopedia*, but it still has many good articles. By good is meant that they use a consistent epistemology not jumping from solipsism to Marxism to Humeanism on a whim. Acting on a deep interest in Catholicism literally means that one develops a routine of looking things up. If I am going to celebrate a baptism, let me read about Baptism before I do anything else. Then, once I know what I am participating in, I can look at the rite itself as well as the readings.

Some other useful sites are . . .

The National Catholic Register at ncr.com—very good site full of Catholic news. Good columns

Catholic World Report at catholicworldreport.com—more news. Good columns.

The Catholic Thing – thecatholicthing.org Good daily columns

---

[259] The standard text used in the liturgies of the Sacraments.

Catholic News Service – catholicnews.com

Catholic News Agency – catholicnewsagency.com

(13) Pro-Life

Candidates for priesthood rarely grasp the full implications of the pro-life stance of the Catholic Church all at once. It is not simply a policy decision. We serve a God who is the God of life. (Matthew 22:32-34) Our existence itself is a wonder of God's Providence. Consequently, the prolife stance of the Catholic Church is not a mere policy but is in fact a theological aspect of the nature of the Church herself. The fact that God became incarnate as a human being means that human life is extraordinarily precious. As a result, Clergy constantly have to learn more about the theology of human life. There are websites such as the Priests for Life (priestsforlife.org), the Sisters of Life (sistersoflife.org), Human Life International (hli.org) and many others that are very useful, in two senses, to inform us and to show us other people working on putting forward the Catholic meaning of life in the world today.

Allied with the pro-life stance of the Catholic priest, there is a whole worldview that constantly has to be put forward and argued against, and that is the worldview where contraception and abortion are no longer seen as sinful and are judged merely in terms of convenience. The Church teaches the intellectual and moral problems with analysing life merely in terms of convenience. The whole world would change dramatically if the pro-life ethic was consistently promoted and followed by the Church. For example, if the Church consistently taught about the horrors of abortion *and* offered support and even adoption to every mother who wanted to kill her child, these actions alone would change the world on their own.

Don't forget lifesitenews.com. Always up to date.

(14) Catholic Current Affairs

One needs to develop a Catholic general knowledge. This is where aggregation sites like New Advent (newadvent.org) are so useful. One gets basic info about teachings coming out of the Vatican and the US Bishops Conference as well as some good articles on current Catholic issues. There are also some articles offering Catholic commentary on social issues. There are a number of other sites that do the same thing. The point is that the Church is not just an institution among institutions. Reducing the Church to that alone would be to impose an Enlightenment view of society on the Church. However, the Body of Christ spans everything in terms of helping people find the true meaning of everything. No other institution can make such a claim and then back it up with such a long history of doing just that.

Another news site can be found on the Vatican website at https://www.vaticannews.va/en.html. This gives a listing of current news at the Vatican.

One competent vaticanista is Sandro Magister who writes for the Italian *L'Espresso Republica*. One example of his writing can be found at http://magister.blogautore.espresso.repubblica.it/2020/02/12/francis%E2%80%99s-silence-ratzingers-tears-and-that-never-published-statement-of-his/ His column site is called *Septimo Cielo* – Seventh Heaven. It has translation function.

The Vatican site itself can be found at http://w2.vatican.va/content/vatican/en.html. There, one can find everything from the important texts to the activities of the current Pope. Within the listings of the Pope's activities one can find all the speeches that he makes. These are particularly useful when the Pope is visiting a location or an institution that you want to mention. For example, when Benedict XVI spoke to the German Federal Parliament and brought out something of the theology of law at http://w2.vatican.va/content/benedict-xvi/en/travels/2011/outside/documents/germania.html.

Lastly, the news and activities of the US Bishop's Conference are also very helpful. These can be found at http://www.usccb.org/. The site also has the daily readings, the texts of the books of the Bible, and descriptions of the way that the many departments of the Conference function.

(15)   Observers of Catholicism

A feature of the modern digital era is the sheer number of commentators on Catholicism from all parts of the political spectrum who are ready to comment on anything and everything. Some are very well informed (eg. Sandro Magister). Others not so much. Some have a long history in the business and others very short. The point is that some people bring a great deal of specialized knowledge to the task and others are shooting from the lip. So sometimes there is something useful to be gained but some work is needed to separate the wheat from the chaff.

It is up to you which commentators you choose to follow on a regular basis. I would recommend thecatholicthing.org for some great commentary every day.

The research process may seem tedious, but it is part of the fascination of Catholicism that some very intelligent people reflect on the activities of Catholics. One takes insight from wherever it comes. Also, Catholicism is authentic enough to stand all the criticism.

Chapter Ten The Spirituality of the Priest

> There is an essential aspect of the priest that does not change: the priest of tomorrow,
> no less than the priest of today, must resemble Christ. John Paul II

(1) Introduction

According to John Paul II, "the priest, who welcomes the call to ministry, is in a position to make this a loving choice, as a result of which the Church and souls become his first interest, and with this concrete spirituality he becomes capable of loving the universal Church and that part of it entrusted to him with the deep love of a husband for his wife."[260] The pope has captured the shift in focus that happens through grace and love so that the individual priest moves from self-love to love of others—the "Church and souls" that John Paul II refers to.

The focus on love means that the explanation of priestly spirituality lies in examining the ancient concept of priesthood as *amoris officium*—the office of love.

(2) Amoris officium

Saint Augustine used the term *amoris officium* in his *Tractates on the Gospel of John*, where he commented on John 21:12-19. The Gospel text is:

> Jesus said to them, "Come, have breakfast." And none of the disciples dared to ask him, "Who are you?" because they realized it was the Lord. Jesus came over and took the bread and gave it to them, and in like manner the fish. This was now the third time Jesus was revealed to his disciples after being raised from the dead.

When they had finished breakfast, Jesus said to Simon Peter,

> Simon, son of John, do you love me more than these?" He said to him, "Yes, Lord, you know that I love you." He said to him, "Feed my lambs." He then said to him a second time, "Simon, son of John, do you love me?" He said to him, "Yes, Lord, you know that I love you." He said to him, "Tend my sheep." He said to him the third time, "Simon, son of John, do you love me?" Peter was distressed that he had said to him a third time, "Do you love me?" and he said to him, "Lord, you know everything; you know that I love you." [Jesus] said to him, "Feed my sheep. Amen, amen, I say to you, when you were younger, you used to dress yourself and go where you wanted; but when you grow old, you will stretch out your hands, and someone else will dress you and lead you where you do not want to go." He said this signifying by what

---

[260] To priests taking part in an assembly organized by the Italian episcopal conference (Nov. 4,1980): *Insegnamenti* III/2 (1980), 1055.

kind of death he would glorify God. And when he had said this, he said to him, "Follow me."

This is an account of one of the resurrection appearances of Jesus and the heart of the encounter is the testing of Peter, 'Do you love me?' followed by the instruction to Peter – 'feed my sheep'. The key term here is 'love'. Everything turns on Jesus' question to Peter: 'Do you love me?' By this act, the future minister of Christ is committed to Jesus Christ out of the deepest love and consequently to Christ's 'sheep' as well, whom he loves.

However, this ministry can be abused too. Saint Augustine commented: "Let [the priestly office] be the office of love to feed the Lord's flock, as if it was the signal of fear to deny the Shepherd. Those who have this purpose in feeding the flock of Christ, that they may have them as their own, and not as Christ's, are convicted of loving themselves, and not Christ, from the desire either of boasting, or wielding power, or acquiring gain, and not from the love of obeying, serving, and pleasing God."[261] At the end of his sentence, Augustine pointed to three positive actions on the part of the priest that make good the three denials of Peter. The actions, of obeying, serving and pleasing God, are the threefold repetition of Jesus' charge to "feed my sheep." It is these actions taken together that comprise the *amoris officium* of the priest.

(3) The Unity of Life and Work

The treatment of the *amoris officium* of the priest (above) presents the authentic priest as a continuing and *coherent* spiritual-physical phenomenon *in the world*. The need for coherence in the priestly life has been highlighted by the recent negative events when some Bishops and priests failed to integrate their lives and responsibilities with the spiritual power and tasks that Christ has given them.

One may describe the coherence as a unity of the priest's spiritual life and the priest's work. This insight was put forward by Vatican II, for example. In *Presbyterorum ordinis*: "by adopting the role of the good shepherd they will find in the practice of pastoral charity itself the bond of priestly perfection which draws their life and activity to unity and coordination." (PO 14) These words appear in an article on the difficulties of the priest's life today (the 1960's) where the answer to the difficulties of life, for the priest, is not simply to do work, have a pious devotion and have leisure time, but rather to go right to the core of his priesthood where work and devotion overlap. It lies in "joining himself with Christ to acknowledge the will of the Father."

---

[261] Saint Augustine, Tractate 123 (John 21:12-19), *Tractates on the Gospel of John*, Nicene and Post-Nicene Fathers, First Series, Vol. 7. Edited by Philip Schaff. (Buffalo, NY: Christian Literature Publishing Co., 1888.)

This is *the* trademark of the life of Jesus. Only thus is the priest joined to the Good Shepherd whose food was to do the will of the Father. (John 4:34) The Catholic priesthood is living the will of the Father continuously and correspondingly being fed by that.

Practically, one saw it in the life of John Paul II himself, who as Bishop of Krakow, used to ask his staff, which doctrine would help them to deal with a particular problem? He ran his office this way. This is how true Church doctrine is. It is not a simple commodity whose distribution creates a job for priests. Church doctrine crystalizes the mind of Christ and it was up to Wojtyla and his staff to apply it in their circumstances so as to do even mundane things in obedience to God's will—'may your will be done on earth.'

The Program for Priestly Formation in the US sheds further light on this unity: "Priestly life lived in configuration to Jesus Christ, Head and Shepherd, must necessarily manifest and give witness to the radicalism of the Gospel." (PPF 26) Thinking about the unity of life and work leads precisely to the radicalism of the Gospel. The Gospel—which is about following the will of the Father—is so radically transformative of human life that there is no substitute for it in all of created reality. The priest will find it transforms his life from being a bundle of unsatisfied needs that are dealt with piecemeal, into being a coherent act of loving understanding—the definition of the very inner life of God! To the priest, the Gospel is so radical that the priest makes his choices drawing from the light of the Gospel.

(4) Radically Configured to Christ

Historically, the Christ was expected to come and fulfill the Jewish roles of Priest, Prophet and King. (The roles are also known as Offices.) Another way to express this is to say that Christ lived the *form* of life of the ultimate priest, prophet and king. In the history of philosophy, "form" is a special word indicating the proportion between the parts of something—in this case the life of Christ—the integrity of his form, and the radiance of meaning that comes out of the form of that something.[262] The priest has to work and pray to be using the fact that he has been trans-*form*-ed into Christ's form of life. He is not being transformed into a gentleman or a bourgeois bachelor.

Rather than being a mere occasional occupation, priesthood takes over a man's life. Chapter Four spoke of the disciple's life being appropriated by Christ. So, the priest is not like a modern bachelor who on occasion has the job of fulfilling the functions of a Catholic priest. The fashionable and comfortable life of the well-off priest makes a joke of the claims about being the presence of Christ who deliberately lived a lower-class life. The middle-class priest shows that the

---

[262] Cf. Hans Urs von Balthasar, *The Glory of the Lord – A Theological Aesthetics IV: The Realm of Metaphysics in Antiquity*, San Francisco: Ignatius Press, 1989.

priesthood might merely be a job to pay for his other interests. Instead, theologically the priest is a walking sacrament, the Christ walking in the neighborhood.

Turning to the Offices of Christ himself: Jesus is the Priest. (cf. Hebrews 4:14) Christ's priestly existence has the constant form of sacrifice, of returning all to the Father, of following the will of the Father, without ceasing. Among other things, this sacrificial form of life can be seen in the availability of Christ. One incident is illustrative: Jesus' encounter with the woman with the hemorrhage. (Matthew 9:20-22, Mark 5:25-34, Luke 8:43-48.) Jesus was on the way to the house of Jairus, because of his sick daughter, and a woman in the crowd touched his garment hoping to be healed from her illness. Jesus was intending one thing and yet out of the sheer goodness of his presence, this woman was healed. Ultimately, the sacrificial life of Jesus leads to his sacrificial dying on the Cross. He gave his life with all that that entails, and salvation pours forth on the earth. Generally, "Jesus' words and actions during his hidden life and public ministry were already salvific, for they anticipated the power of his Paschal mystery." (CCC 1115) Today's priest has the power to do the same thing.

The form of Jesus' sacrifice on the Cross looks horrible but in fact it radiates redemption and sanctification. Every Eucharist from then on simply draws on the sacrifice of the Cross. So, from then on: "The holy Eucharist completes Christian initiation. Those who have been raised to the dignity of the royal priesthood by Baptism and configured more deeply to Christ by Confirmation participate with the whole community in the Lord's own sacrifice by means of the Eucharist." (CCC 1322)

For the priest, most centrally, his sacrificial priesthood involves the offering of the Eucharist. In addition, it involves hours of prayer, endless visits to the sick, comforting the dying, preparing people for marriage and so on but salvation is also being wrought in history by these emotional and sometimes painful moments. These moments contribute something to the priest's fulfilling his own life of sacrifice as well. They also make him grow up into a mature adult who can be with people in their suffering.

Jesus' life has the prophetic form as well. Everything he does teaches the will of God. Holy priests do the same thing. Everything that Jesus does proclaims the will of God and his love. Jesus also knows the scriptures and the tradition that, each in their own way, express the revelation of the Divine Word through the power of the Spirit. The holy priest passes on their content too. So, for example, the priest does not even try to follow the same life as a bachelor, by dating, following the bar scene, spending money on anything that he pleases, trying to garner as much leisure time as possible. Rather his life fills with prophetic actions.

Is the enormity of the life-change, from life before the seminary to life after the seminary, made clear to potential seminarians? On the positive side, the prophetic priest prays as much as he can, does charitable work, his language is not the vulgar language of the movies. His conversations are not about the vulgar subjects: "No foul language should come out of your mouths, but only such as is good for needed edification, that it may impart grace to those who hear." (Ephesians 4:29) So, the priest is a public visible example of a counter-cultural life. He serves the Spirit of God and not the spirit of this world. (cf. I Corinthians 2:12)

More positively still, the priest speaks prophetically which is not like being 'prophetic' in the post-modern sense of speaking warm fuzzy words. Instead, he simply speaks the Good News of the Gospel. The post-modern sense of prophecy involves speaking about current fads, such as, for example, climate change, a phenomenon that has actually been with us for millions of years. The priest's prophetic words do not aid groups trying to get power over people and resources.

Thirdly, the life of Jesus is kingly. It is a new kind of kingship, especially given Pilate's public announcement of his kingship in a proclamation at the top of the cross. He was "the one who has been born king of the Jews." (Matthew 2:2) Further, he has come to bring the whole world under the sovereignty of God after its rebellion. Yet, he is a different kind of king: "If I, therefore, the master and teacher, have washed your feet, you ought to wash one another's feet." (John 13:14) The aristocratic priest has no place here.

Yet there are still the aristocratic parishes where a certain kind of aristocratic priest is placed to 'best serve' the lay aristocrats. It would take a book to cover the history of compliance between the priest and the wealthy Laity. It seems to be a question of servicing those who are sources of diocesan funding. Not that the wealthy are not parishioners too but preaching to them involves leading them to be better Christians just as it does for the poor. This ministry is not a chance for the priest to join the life of the wealthy.

Jesus' kingship means that he also speaks with authority. Comprehending the life of the priest under the kingship of Christ involves knowing some history: an expectation of status and wealth got attached to being a Clergyman even though the one that they ostensibly serve, 'had no place to lay his head.'

The expectation of wealth and power has never really gone away for some diocesan and religious Clergy as they seek out the bourgeois life. The other dimension of the historical problem was that the Clergy were state officials and consequently they got tied into the state in various ways. This continued, for example, in the Napoleonic organization of the Clergy through the Department of Cult in France (19th cent.), and under the Nazis (20th cent.) with their 'positive Christianity'. It still is evident in countries where many of the Clergy are tools and advocates of the ruling juntas and in the modern West where so many Clergy are advocates and tools of a political party. (See Chapter Nine)

More personally, the priest is kingly in organizing his own life so that his energies are directed into positive things—as Augustine once put it, one's body is under the command of one's soul and one's soul serves the will of God. Interiorly, even the fantasy life of the priest comes under the Lord's kingship. Furthermore, the priest is obviously responsible for his parish and for the Church at large. His spirituality must have space and time for this responsibility—to do it as well as possible, and then to reflect theologically on what he has said and done. The goal of all of his work is that people become holy, God is worshipped, and the poor are cared for.

(5) Reflection

The priest has to be a reflective person, asking himself daily: what did I do? How did I do it? How can God increasingly express his love through me?

A lot of the priest's spirituality has to do with love. But few have absorbed a real theology of love. Thomas Aquinas wrote about the virtue of love: "According to the Philosopher (Ethic. viii, 2,3) not every love has the character of friendship, but that love which is together with benevolence, when, to wit, we love someone so as to wish good to him. If, however, we do not wish good to what we love, but wish its good for ourselves, (thus we are said to love wine, or a horse, or the like), it is love not of friendship, but of a kind of concupiscence. For it would be absurd to speak of having friendship for wine or for a horse." (ST II II q. 23 a.1) Love is wishing for and working for the good of others. Most emphatically this is the person's good as God understands it.

It takes real maturity to give all of one's attention to other people and not feel that this is a loss or that one is being deprived in some way. Ultimately attending to others is to experience the glory of Christianity. Selflessness is in the end a spiritual issue.

(6) Eucharistic Spirituality

One important feature of a priestly spirituality is the Eucharist. Vatican II spoke of the liturgy as "the primary and indispensable source from which the faithful are to derive the true Christian spirit; and therefore, pastors of souls must zealously strive to achieve it, by means of the necessary instruction, in all their pastoral work." (SC 14) Hence, the spirituality of the priest, at some point, has to translate into his finding the 'true Christian spirit' himself and helping the faithful to also find 'the true Christian spirit'.

The priest's personal spirituality of the Eucharist is absolutely essential for finding this spirit. John Paul II explained: "The Eucharist is both a mystery of faith and a 'mystery of light'."[263] In the very next sentence, the Pope explained what he meant. The priest "in some way relives the experience of the two disciples on the road to Emmaus: "their eyes were opened, and they recognized him" (Luke 24:31)." (EDE 6) They had this experience 'at the breaking of the bread.'

The underlying dimensions of the mysterious Emmaus experience point to some worthy ideas for priestly spirituality. Thanks to John Paul II: The first idea is the way that the Eucharist builds the Church: "Just as the Church 'makes the Eucharist' so 'the Eucharist builds up' the Church; and this truth is closely bound up with the mystery of Holy Thursday." (DC 4) The gospel accounts indicate two dimensions of the Holy Thursday events: the consecration of the bread and the wine, and the washing of the feet. Meditation on these two things just keeps on opening up avenues for prayer and reflection.

Secondly, given this book's interest in the intellectual side of the priesthood, it is significant that John Paul II refers to the "faith and that disposition of mind," that everyone contributes to the eucharistic celebration to be drawn into the union caused by Christ's sacrifice. (DC 4) The Spirit draws the faithful into the Eucharist but precisely as persons using the powers of their souls – intellect and will—as fully as they can and relying on the elevation brought by grace.

In his *Dominicae cenae*, John Paul II pointed to the following features of the Eucharist:

(1) Firstly, the celebration of the Eucharist is "a holy and sacred action. Holy and sacred, because in it are the continual presence and action of Christ." (DC 6) The priest is not adding anything or improving the Eucharist in some way. The priest is totally immersed in something that God is doing: "'the Holy One' of God, 'anointed with the Holy Spirit,' 'consecrated by the Father' who lays down his life of his own accord and takes it up again, and the High Priest of the New Covenant. For it is he who, represented by the celebrant, makes his entrance into the sanctuary and proclaims his Gospel. It is he who is 'the offerer and the offered, the consecrator and the consecrated.'" (DC 8)

The American desperation to constantly remodel things, imposed onto us by commercial interests or our own egos, coaches people into a view of what is

---

[263] John Paul II, Apostolic Letter *Rosarium Virginis Mariae* (16 October 2002), 21: AAS 95 (2003), 19.

important: new-is-important. In fact, on the contrary, in God's work, the Eucharist, the faithful and the world are being renewed and not vice-versa.

(2) Then, "the priest celebrant who, by confecting the holy Sacrifice and acting 'in persona Christi,' is sacramentally (and ineffably) brought into that most profound sacredness, and made part of it, spiritually linking with it in turn all those participating in the eucharistic assembly." (DC 8) (The concepts of '*in persona Christi*' and '*in persona Christi caput*' were extensively treated in Chapter Four.)

The reference to the Emmaus experience above points to the personal and interpersonal dimensions of the spirituality that are involved. Luke described the experience more fully, "their eyes were opened, and they recognized him, and he disappeared from their sight. They asked each other, 'Were not our hearts burning within us while he talked with us on the road and opened the Scriptures to us?'" (Luke 24:30) Consequently, the eucharistic encounter itself involves participation in both the word (Jesus explained the Scriptures) and the sacrifice (the Eucharist as an event added to the Tradition). In the midst of these events, the faithful people will recognize Christ himself.

(3) John Paul II's third point was that the Eucharist is a true sacrifice. Here John Paul II means 'sacrifice' in the sense of 'the handing over to the sacred'. (What does the priest himself understand by the 'sacred'? Is the sacred a part of his spirituality?) The celebration of the Eucharist is the moment when the priest is "authentic" and performs "a true sacrificial act that brings creation back to God." (DC 9) Consequently, actions like the offertory procession, and the idea that the gifts to be offered represent the gifts that each person brings to the assembly, are significant moments of meaning leading up to the meaning of the offering of the sacrifice. Here the pope refers to the words from the Eucharistic Prayer III as a summary of what he is saying: "Look with favor on your Church's offering and see the Victim whose death has reconciled us to yourself. Grant that we, who are nourished by his body and blood, may be filled with his Holy Spirit, and become one body, one spirit in Christ. May he make us an everlasting gift to you." Does the priest, at the Offertory, specifically and consciously emphasize these aspects that will subsequently be mentioned in the Eucharistic Prayer?

The representation of Jesus' sacrifice through the offering of the bread and wine means that: "For the bread and wine presented at the altar and accompanied by the devotion and the spiritual sacrifices of the participants are finally consecrated, so as to become truly, really and substantially Christ's own body that is given up and his blood that is shed." (DC 9) That someone would make such a sacrifice, and that it is God himself who does it, is a substantial concept that opens up many further avenues for meditation. Lastly, von Balthasar makes a further point about the Eucharist: "In this surrender of himself the Son is the substantiated love of God given to the world, a love which in this handing over of self becomes 'glorified' and 'gives thanks' (is eucharist): the Father to the Son, and in visible and audible form (John 17) , the Son to the Father."[264] Here von Balthasar is pointing out the Trinitarian dimensions of the sacrifice. In other words, the celebration of the Eucharist exposes us to the eternal inner life of the Divine Trinity—this is the most fundamental concept in a priestly spirituality.

This thought concludes our brief reflection on priestly spirituality. *In toto*, priestly spirituality is trinitarian, priestly and communitarian.

---

[264] *GL I*, 571.

Chapter Eleven The Priest and St. John Vianney

(1) Introduction

Saint John Vianney (1786 -1859) was named the Patron Saint of Pastors by Pope Pius X in 1929. (One good biography of St. John Vianney is Alfred Monin's *Life of Saint John Vianney: Cure D'Ars*, London: Burns and Oates, 1907.)

On June 19th, 2009, Pope Benedict XVI initiated the Year for Priests. This was on the 150th anniversary of the birthday of Saint John Vianney. In his letter to mark the occasion, Pope Benedict XVI quoted a phrase from saint John Vianney himself: "The priesthood is the love of the heart of Jesus."[265] Here lies the very core of the spirituality of Saint John Vianney and of every priest. Pope Benedict expanded further on this theme:

> In his time, the Curé of Ars was able to transform the hearts and the lives of so many people because he enabled them to experience the Lord's merciful love. Our own time urgently needs a similar proclamation and witness to the truth of Love: *Deus caritas est* (1 Jn: 4:8). Thanks to the word and the sacraments of Jesus, John Mary Vianney built up his flock, although he often trembled from a conviction of his personal inadequacy, and desired more than once to withdraw from the responsibilities of the parish ministry out of a sense of his unworthiness.

Here is the fundamental aspect of the life of the priest—that the priest is the presence of Christ for people, often the only one that they will personally encounter. This meeting does not come without a cost. In Benedict's words again: "a priest cannot devote himself to their salvation if he refuses to share personally in the 'precious cost' of redemption." This is part of the sacrificial Christological posture that to be embraced by the priest and it means taking on the full cost of being a priest as well.

In the 1960's, one occasionally heard the phrase from Clergy, "I don't do windows." Yet the Patron of Pastors accepted that his life has to conform to the life of Jesus Christ in terms of being personally costly. This was very evident in his practice of spending hundreds of hours in the confessional, and of giving the penitent a small penance and then doing the rest of the penance himself. John XXIII went further in his encyclical on the priesthood: "Not even [the priest's] thoughts, his will, his feelings belong to him, for they are rather those of Jesus Christ who is his life." (*Sacerdotii Nostri Primordii*) The taking over of the priest's life is total!

Moreover, as one learns about John Vianney's life, one learns about the priesthood. Also, keeping the Christology of the priesthood front and center keeps one's image

---

[265] l'Abbé Bernard Nodet, *Le curé d'Ars. Sa pensée - Son cœur*, éd. Xavier Mappus, Foi Vivante, 1966, 98.

of the priesthood from being a mere secular occupation that one can lay aside from time to time.

(2) Some of John Vianney's History

His parents were Jean Marie Matthieu Vianney and his wife Marie Beluse. They were astonishingly pious people, in terms of their prayer and Marie offered her son to God and the Blessed Virgin even before his birth.[266] He later said of himself that he had a deep devotion to Mary "even before I knew her."

A striking feature of his early life was his parent's hospitality to the homeless and the poor. They would feed them and put a roof over their heads for the night. John Vianney would help settle the visitors into the barn. He especially liked to help homeless children. He also taught them their prayers.

The French Revolution took place in 1789 and the years after. When Napoleon brought some order out of the chaos, Catholicism became a tool of the central government as it happens so often in Enlightenment governments For John and his family to even go to Mass was a very risky affair. They went in secret, always on the second floor of an out-of-the-way building like a farmhouse so as not to be too visible. At that time, Clergy who refused to work for the French State risked their lives to bring people the sacraments.

In 1809, while he was considering his vocation, he was conscripted by the state to serve in the army. He ran away up into the mountains. Vianney stayed in a village up there and worked for his keep until the Emperor Napoleon gave a general amnesty to runaway soldiers. The second time that John was conscripted, his brother stepped up and took his place in the army.

Vianney studied under the Curé (parish priest) of his home parish in the town of Écully. After two years, he was sent to a seminary, le Petite Séminaire of Verrières for his philosophy studies. He had to adjust a great deal due to his previous lack of studies and lack of culture generally, but he soon impressed his fellow seminarians by his constant faith. At the seminary, he demonstrated a remarkable spirit of humility and distrust in his own abilities. Then he was sent to the seminary in Lyons. According to Abbé Monin, "the inferiority of [his academic] attainments has been much exaggerated."[267] Even though he had to answer questions in French because of his appalling Latin, his answers on theology and morality were always judged to be very good.

---

[266] All quotations here are from Alfred Monnin's *Life of Saint John-Baptist Vianney: Curé of Ars*, London: Burns and Oates, 1907.
[267] Monin, 36.

John Vianney was ordained on August 9, 1815. He was 29. After his ordination, John was assigned as Parochial Vicar to the parish at Ecully. The Pastor there was Abbé M.Balley, a saintly man who prayed with his vicar each day and set the example of a good pastor. Vianney quickly learned to spend much time in the confessional, so much so that he barely had time for his daily Mass. He only ate one spartan meal a day. Interestingly, according to M. Monnin, John Vianney "did not have two weights or two measures; he made the perfection which he preached to others the inflexible rule of his own actions."[268] He gave his salary to the poor and wore an old cassock. He was a prime example of the man of integrity mentioned earlier. Notably, although the Clergy in his district were the usual mixed bag, John Vianney did not pick up their bad habits.

After Abbé Balley's death, Vianney was appointed as the Curé of Ars, a tiny village in the Dombes region of France. The Vicar-General of the diocese said to him: "Go, my friend, there is but little of the love of God in that parish; you will enkindle it."[269] *Amoris officium* again!

(3) The Parish

Summarizing Vianney's approach to the parish, M. Monin says: "They felt that he loved them, not only as a whole in a general way but with the discriminating and individual love of the Sacred Heart himself."[270] He spoke to everyone and knew enough about the people's lives to converse with them until he could introduce religious aspects into the conversation.

The renewal of the parish started off when he instituted perpetual adoration of the Blessed Sacrament. He encouraged more participation in the sacraments especially as regards receiving Holy Communion more frequently. He also added the celebration of evening prayer in the parish church each night. In other words, the parish became "a Christian oasis."[271] Remember that he was working in France in the agnostic and anti-clerical world that had been left by Napoleon. As another of his changes, he refurbished the run-down parish church.

In 1825, Vianney opened a home that he called La Providence—Divine Providence. It was to house destitute girls and orphans. These were the people who were most at risk in the terrible poverty in the countryside of that time. The home depended on donations from the faithful and a couple of Vianney's miracles (yes really!) in the home did not hurt either. He also opened up a free school for little girls in the parish. The girls learned to read, write, sew and knit. He himself taught them

---

[268] Monin, 45.
[269] Monin, 41.
[270] Monin, 45.
[271] Monin, 52.

catechism each day. The classes also began to fill with the pilgrims who had started to come to the village in the hopes of seeing the holy pastor himself.

Vianney developed a number of penitential practices for himself, from limiting his food to sleeping on boards. Fasting played a big part in his life too. He was constantly aware of his lack of suitability to be a priest.

Monin has a great deal to say about Vianney's various encounters with the Devil. We will not spend time on them.

All through his time in the parish, life was not a bed of roses. Many people caused him a great deal of suffering. There were people who felt that their previous experience of getting spiritual direction from Vianney was being taken away by the fame of the little Curé. Gossip about the number of female penitents who went to confession also roiled the parish. Many problems were caused by the Curé's efforts to get his people to find other ways of spending their time besides drinking and dancing.

Then the pastors in the neighboring parishes were jealous and they refused to give absolution to anyone who went to Vianney for confession. His consolation to himself was that he was not fooling everyone. He imagined that least some people, his detractors, saw through him and saw him as he really was. He even signed a petition that was being circulated complaining about him.

Not only did he suffer from the visits of the Devil, and from the locals but also in his relation with God himself. Vianney had a terrible feeling of being lost by God.

During a period of thirty years, crowds of people—tens of thousands—went to the town of Ars on pilgrimage, to see the holy pastor, to participate in his Mass, go to confession, and to hear him teach.

Personally, he suffered greatly from the sin that he saw all around him: "My God, how long shall I live among sinners?"[272] Nevertheless in 1835, he was personally dispensed from the annual diocesan retreat precisely because the Bishop realized that there was the greater need of him in Ars itself. He could not escape the classic situation of experiencing the conflict of being the wheat among the tares.

Someone describing his preaching, said that: "His language was easy and abundant. His subject was the end of man which is happiness in God. Sin sets us afar off from God; repentance brings us back to him."[273] Vianney lived a life of constant toil except for his six hours of sleep. He spent most of his day in the confessional and the

---

[272] Monin, 149.
[273] Monin. 169.

miracle was that he could keep doing this year in and year out for thirty years, winter and summer.

In 1843, he started to get sick and was given an assistant even though seeing another priest at the altar gave him "heartache."[274] His sickness got more serious and he was anointed. At this time, he suffered greatly from attacks by demons. He needed to take a break from the parish, but the parish could not bear to see him go.

In addition, Vianney was one of the first people to develop a devotion to the apparitions of Mary at La Salette. These were the apparitions of Mary that occurred at La Salette in France, in 1846.

During the forty years of his ministry, John Vianney also started religious communities for educating girls and boys. He started a Congregation of Missionary Priests as well in the diocese. Their work was to preach parish missions. Before he died, Vianney went to the trouble of making sure that the congregation was financially sound.

The house that Vianney lived in was very simple and almost bare. There was a bed in his room and not much else. The other rooms were empty except for a large wardrobe in one of them full of very expensive vestments – a gift from a local count. Hundreds of books were found in the house after his death. So, the later stories about his ignorance were overdone.

Visitors to Ars, and there were tens of thousands of them, always came away with a sense of great reverence.

In 1843, Vianney became seriously ill. After a great deal of prayer and rest, he had a miraculous recovery. The people carried him to the chapel so that he could give thanks. For a while, he had to be helped to the chapel just after midnight for his daily Mass because he could not go the whole night without nourishment. This was the time in the history of the Church when the fast ran from the evening meal to the time of next morning's Mass. When he received the last rites, he answered a question about the truths of his faith: "I have never doubted them."

This time was also marked by the first of his three times of great spiritual conflict when he wished to leave the parish and go into a monastery. He always came back to the realization finally that his vocation was to work in the parish of Ars until he died.

A second time he tried to leave it was because he wanted to retire into solitude. Again, rumours spread quickly around the parish and the people spent their time between blocking his movement from the parish and praying for him. When he finally agreed to stay, he was visited with extraordinary graces. Vianney was also

---

[274] Monin, 177.

becoming more and more knowledgeable about the way that Satan used apparent inspirations from Providence as ways to manipulate him to leave.

The extraordinary priestly spirituality of John Vianney requires far more space than can be dedicated to it here. Personally, people spoke of his compassion and his efforts to communicate. Interestingly, Monnin refers to his 'visibility' whether he was feeling sick or well, tired or full of energy: "He had the same heart on earth as he has in heaven."[275] His religion was a religion of love, not the modern confusion of love and tolerance or self-indulgence but of genuine love in the sense that Christ taught. He went into a state of ecstasy when the Blessed Sacrament was exposed. Most importantly, he worked for the salvation of souls, morning, noon and night. The wave of confessions and conversions that flowed around him cannot begin to be described.

John Vianney passed away in 1859.

---

[275] Monnin, 234.

Chapter Twelve Priesthood in a time of Scandal

(1) Introduction

The child-abuse and same-sex scandals of the early 2000's and of 2018 in the Church are a poignant reminder that the Church has always been a Church for sinners. Not that she encourages sin or turns a blind eye to it despite recent events! These sorry times that have left so many victims are part of a much larger phenomenon in the US. US culture itself includes a degree of child abuse—a fact that is rarely acknowledged. Furthermore, there is nothing intrinsic to Catholicism that causes these outrages. Roughly 90% of child abuse in the culture takes place in families. It also takes place in every religion, every school district, every sport etc. This is in no way to excuse the horrors that have occurred. It certainly does not excuse the utter hypocrisy of some of the Catholic Clergy when they do the abuse or cover it up.

A scandal involves a pervasive wave of revulsion and anger at some real or imagined phenomenon. It involves a complex cloud of reactions. Bishops, priests and their people all get caught up in the cloud of anger and protest that justifiably gets added on to the weight of their already busy lives. Out of a sense of justice, it certainly has to be dealt with both legally and pastorally. Whether it is acknowledged or not, the events even tear into the daily lives of those who are not directly involved and more importantly into their world of beliefs and ideas. The scandal bites even more deeply when it occurs within the Catholic Church that has a serious love for humanity and its advancement and that claims a moral authority in the world.

When considering what the Church does, the vital point to keep in mind is that the Church is holy because of Jesus Christ, whose body it is. Jesus Christ is a gift from God to the Church. So, the holiness of the Church does not depend on the holiness of its members. The Church is holy because Jesus Christ is holy! He is present in the Church, so the Church is holy. Whatever the officials do in the Church, there will always be good and bad officials. Whatever lay people do in the Church there will always be good and bad laypeople. The individual priest often has almost nothing that he can do personally about what other priests, Bishops or laypeople do. Earlier, Fr. Longenecker referred to the status of Catholic priests as one of "indentured servitude."[276] He was not entirely kidding. This almost complete helplessness is part of the servitude of a priest. As far as causing officials to be replaced, even officials who engage in reprehensible behavior, the average priest can mostly only pray and endure and be with his people. Sometimes a judicious letter might help! So, that is not a good place to start discussing the scandals even when considering one who is

---

[276] https://dwightlongenecker.com/why-was-the-mccarrick-abuse-hushed-up/

innocently tangled in an apparently scandal-ridden Church. The best starting point is a theological one, one that deals with the nature of hypocrisy itself.

(2) Hypocrisy

Recently, scandal has become the norm in some dioceses and scandal does seem to be everywhere at least in the public perception.[277] The pandemic has got everyone's attention for obvious reasons, but the investigations will continue for a while in some states. People might forget that they will find the same rate (or higher) of incidence of these appalling acts if they look at some school districts, other churches and in some families. Putting that aside because it does not help an individual priest trying to live and work as a pastor, there is a theological dimension to the scandals.

The word "hypocrite" occurs frequently in the mouth of Jesus, in the gospels. This even means something for us today because Jesus represents true religion. True religion involves the true relationship of an individual to God and neighbor. One feature of true religion is that its participants act in accordance with what they say they believe. For example, Jesus said: "Woe to you, teachers of the law and Pharisees, you hypocrites! You clean the outside of the cup and dish, but inside they are full of greed and self-indulgence." (Matthew 23:25) They 'clean the outside of the cup' meaning that they observed the tiny details of Judaism but in fact they are 'full of greed and self-indulgence' because they use their positions to gain more possessions and power.

The mention of 'self-indulgence' is key because as Aquinas tells us, most of the sins that people commit are due to self-indulgence. For our purposes, the mention of hypocrisy is essential from an ontological point of view because being intellectually consistent is the only way that human beings can show their integrity and live

---

[277] The mention of the 'public perception' is essential because a catastrophic response to the abuse cases can miss the very real point that the Church for the most part is functioning normally as much as it can in a pandemic. I am not referring here to the leadership or management side of things but to the everyday life of the faithful in tens of thousands of parishes. People are receiving the sacraments. They are being prepared for Marriage. The sick are being visited and so on. People are still loving their neighbour or not. Yes, for the abused and their families the abuse may well be catastrophic in many ways, and often is, but for the vast majority of Catholics, living the life of a faithful Catholic is unchanged. Also, the individual Catholic's duties and responsibilities have not changed at all even if his/her priest or Bishop has failed miserably. And most priests and Bishops have not. The separation has to be made between reading the Church and the individual's part in it politically or theologically. If the Church is merely a political party, then anything anyone does that is questionable has consequences for a person's support of the party. But if the Church is theological—and it is— then Christ is present and a person's service is a participation in Christ's service and his mission, even when it is mediated by fallible human beings, and it has not changed at all.

authentic lives. Hypocrisy is a serious public fraud especially when one claims to be a follower of Christ—in other words, where someone is saying that they believe in a way of life where consistency between belief and practice is a distinguishing characteristic.

One account of how central truth is to the whole project of being an authentic human, can be found in the *Catechism* where it says that:

> Man tends by nature toward the truth. He is obliged to honor and bear witness to it: 'It is in accordance with their dignity that all men, because they are persons . . . are both impelled by their nature and bound by a moral obligation to seek the truth, especially religious truth. They are also bound to adhere to the truth once they come to know it and direct their whole lives in accordance with the demands of truth.' (CCC 2467)[278]

What is notable here is the importance of the truth to someone for their development as a human being. It is relevant in both their private and public roles and so it is fundamental to the intellectual life of the Catholic. The truth is vital for someone coming to fuller humanity. Once individuals know the truth, they order their lives accordingly, because humans seek the truth by their very nature.[279] Truth leads to their salvation. So, whether it is cardinals, bishops, priests or deacons, the members of the hierarchy not only have an obligation to organize their lives according to the truth, they have taken on the responsibility of being examples of true living for everyone else. However, this is not politically correct of course because some imagine that each person has their own truth. But revelation says that the truth of Jesus Christ is for everyone. So, both Clergy and Laity have to learn the truth that they will go on to teach and express in everything that they do: "Put on the Lord Jesus Christ and make no provision for the desires of the flesh." (Romans 13:14) Furthermore, the hierarchy are called to live and teach the *whole* truth all the time. The Laity have the same obligation.

These obligations, for which the hierarchy are paid and cared for, mean that they are impelled not only for spiritual reasons to teach the truth and to live it, but also for justice sake! Any hypocrisy on their part is a crime on many levels. For example, the money that they get comes from the collections in parishes and from donors. The money is only given to support them in doing authentic ministry and to live authentic lives.

Mostly, the money is given for the poor. The question should be asked why was the four billion dollars that was spent on the penalties for the abuses and the cover-ups even available? (Obviously some of that sum came from insurance policies.) Why

---

[278] The *Catechism* is citing Vatican II's *Dignitatis Humanae* 2.
[279] John Paul II, *Fides et ratio*, 4.

was the money not spent on the poor? Why were the hierarchy sitting on it? It was not given for that purpose.

Now, every culture contains a certain level of hypocrisy. The hypocrisy in US culture is probably due to the Enlightenment separation of the concept of humanity from truth just as much as it is due to sin.[280] Pastorally, one comes across hypocrisy particularly among those who have mastered the surface features of being righteous. That behaviour takes one back to the time of Jesus: where for example, Jesus explained that, 'Isaiah was right when he prophesied about you hypocrites; as it is written: 'These people honor me with their lips, but their hearts are far from me." (Mark 7:6) The point is that the lips and the heart are meant to be in concert—the basic principle of authentic Christian life.

Hypocrisy was the most frequently condemned sin in the mouth of Jesus because it absolutely contradicts what he came to do. Hypocrisy denies the very meaning of Christianity itself. Christianity involves God revealing his interior life namely revealing the eternal processions of the Divine Word and the Divine Spirit. The presence of Christianity depends on each 'faithful' individual participating in the presence of Jesus Christ, who is who he says he is. Theologically, people are created through the Word and so human existence is 'worded' meaning, among other things, that the very words that people utter should be expressions of the Word that created us.

Nevertheless, it must be said again that the Church is indefectibly holy because of the presence of Christ. The holiness of the Church does not depend on us.

(3) Response to a Scandal

When scandal happens in the Church, a number of things take place at the same time: there are victims to be cared for, there is a real sense of shock among orthodox members of the Clergy; there is a feeling of grave concern for one's parishioners and for the Church herself; there may or may not be leadership from the ordinaries—this will vary from diocese to diocese or religious order to religious order; and there is a revulsion at the hypocrisy manifested by those members of the New People of God who are publicly tasked with living morally and spreading the truth by doing so.

When a scandal happens, the fully functioning priest immediately takes certain concrete steps: the first is to report if he knows something about a scandal as long as he did not hear about it in confession. Reporting to ordinaries is probably accompanied by reporting to secular authorities too depending on which country is involved. The priest very definitely continues to pray the Office of the Church.

---

[280] The essential ontological link between humanity and truth was mentioned above.

Getting distracted from the routine of priestly life, something that is a precious safeguard of that life, has its own negative effects. Setting these things aside adds to the communion of evil described in Chapter One. It is vital to remember this because morale among the Clergy will plummet when a scandal takes hold.

The second step is to participate regularly in the sacraments particularly those of the Eucharist and of Healing. Of course, these activities are already part of the priest's duty to his people and are a boundless spiritual service to laypeople, but they also serve the priest himself as well. Liturgy has a way of showing the priest who he is again and again. Of course, the Eucharist does this *par excellence*.

Thirdly, even before a scandal, it is worth a lot to the priest himself to find a group of priests who regularly get together to pray and discuss. Frequently, they will be the only social group with whom he can discuss things in depth. Normally Clergy conversation is mind-numbingly shallow! This group will be the only one that has a chance of understanding his experience. In the group, he can perform the same service for others. The group can also be a place where he can discuss almost everything and know that it will not be spoken of outside the group. For a while at least, during the scandal, there may be no other more formal structure to rely on. (The internal forum with one's spiritual director still remains!) Sometimes Bishops and ordinaries are developed enough to organize larger gatherings for prayer, discussion and support, sometimes not.

(4) Staying Well-Informed

The priest is obliged by the very nature of a scandal to work hard at being well-informed about what is going on. It is profoundly true that the truth counts—truth about Jesus Christ, truth about the Church and its teaching, truth about the scandal. As was said above, human beings are intimately involved in the truth, by their nature. Then, according to the instruction from the Congregation for the Doctrine of the Faith, *Donum veritatis*: "The truth which sets us free is a gift of Jesus Christ (cf. John 8:32). Man's nature calls him to seek the truth while ignorance keeps him in a condition of servitude." (DV 1) There is real servitude in not knowing what is going on. The priest's parishioners will not trust him either unless he demonstrates that he is well-informed. He will often be the closest voice of reason!

The backstop for all questions about theology should be the *Catechism*, the 1983 *Code of Canon Law*, and the Rites. They cover most of the issues unless people are trying to manufacture theology or construct Church practice politically. By 'politically', I mean someone formulating 'doctrine' or introducing idiosyncratic behaviors in liturgies according to what political pressure groups want. Authentic doctrine and authentic practice do not get formed in this way. Hence the need to have a comprehensive grasp of the fact that the priest is the nexus of many areas of truth. The priest will also have to think through how to answer some of the possible questions that he will get.

Back to the point about trying to form doctrine politically: this activity comes up against a reality that cannot be denied, namely the Judeo-Christian history—although the Nazis and modern-day leftists try to deny it, often using force. The history of the Church has taught that, as Vatican II explained: "The Church and the political community in their own fields are autonomous and independent from each other." (GS 76) They are two substantially different realities, so making secular social policies appear to have the force of doctrines means confusing two completely different kinds of things. This point is not generally understood but it is a fact and has to be taken into account.[281] This issue was treated in more detail in Chapter Nine.

For the priest, being informed does not mean participating in gossip. The sins of others can lead Clergy into sin. By their nature scandals give rise to calumny and detraction. These are still sins, and serious ones at that! So, being informed means being capable of explaining things that can be explained, in the right forum obviously, and leaving aside those things that cannot be explained in a particular forum because they are not appropriate. Wallowing in the details is definitely not good for people generally.

(5) Responding to the Anger

Scandals cause a lot of anger and that anger will be around for a long time. The priest himself is going to be angry at the betrayal of the Church, his parishioners and himself.

Some Clergy will face some very awkward questions, sometimes from very angry people. Always there is a point in the discussion when one realizes that comfort is what is really being sought. Yet aside from empathy there is really only comfort in prayer and penitence. These are the ecclesial responses to the anger. How many parishes do pray regularly *for* the Church aside from the obvious moments in the Eucharist? Naturally, if he hears about incidents of abuse, the priest should file a complaint with the police and the diocese. The priest should also check if he has further legal obligations under state law and diocesan law. One cannot be passive— one should ask and ask regularly to see whether there have been any updates in the law. This is all just part of being well-informed.

Then there are many people who are going to be blazingly angry and yet will not ask questions. In fact, some might even leave the Church out of anger, as a way of punishing the Church. If they mention it to me, I always say that they should get the

---

[281] The problem arises when the policy is formulated, and it leaves out part of the context of the issue.

abuse figures for the church that they will be joining. As a response, if there is the possibility of having gatherings, or if one can ask people to come and chat individually, that might help parishioners a little. It will help people if they know that their shepherd is equally shocked and at the same time very much interested and available. Prayer and scripture reading should be a part of any outreach. Sometimes the prayer or the reading will reach people far more deeply than any ordinary words. The Parable of the Wheat and the Tares might be very useful (Matthew 13:36-43) but it is not an excuse for the sorry abuse situation.

For the individual priest, making personal contact and being available is crucial to sustain and perhaps it might even regenerate the personal links with parishioners and between parishioners that should be part of any community but those that are most especially part of a community in Christ. Sadly, it may take a scandal to show people what real Christian community looks like once again. (See chapter on the priest and the Laity.)

One impossibly difficult thing for priests to handle is the sometimes-obscene details about the kinds of abuse activities whether they are Clergy or not. We have a duty to children to allow them to be innocent as long as possible. Childish innocence is a precious commodity, but a priest cannot restore informational innocence once it has been lost—no one can. TV and the Internet have already made that impossible. Personally, I think that the priest should at least not spread the details even in discussion with other Clergy. Indulging in prurience is wrong. Also, I think that parents particularly have some deep-rooted instinct to protect the innocence of their kids. This may be the root of some of their anger. Anger at betrayal is also certainly another big part of it.

Finally, one of the great shocks for Clergy today is that life as one had known it in the past is not going to continue. The old idea of the ladder of promotion, from minor parish to major parish, and perhaps even to Bishop in a minor diocese and then to a major diocese has effectively been dealt a death blow, fortunately! The Clergy whose mindset is still founded on this model are going to have a struggle trying to function in this new suspicious world. They are going to have to deal with constant suspicion even though everyone knows that most abuse, numerically speaking, occurs in families. The suspicion is going to make some priests and Bishops gun-shy. They will avoid doing some of the things that they ought to do as pastors.

(6) The Pandemic

At the time of writing the pandemic was a new phenomenon and unprecedented as well. Clergy have been discovering what they can get up to when they are disconnected from the normal parish routine. The most basic thing to keep in mind is keeping to the routine for prayer and the breviary. Staying healthy is crucial too.

Being informed about the social aspects of a pandemic is a big part of the priest's service to his people and to the Church.

Chapter Thirteen The Priest and the Program of Priestly Formation

> Priests are called to a specific vocation to holiness in virtue of their new consecration in the sacrament of Holy Orders, a consecration that configures them to Christ the Head and Shepherd. John Paul II

Some of the theology of the priesthood that appears in the Program of Priestly Formation is well worth studying. The abbreviation PPF will be used here. In the US, the Fifth Edition of the PPF was issued in 2006, approved by the full US Conference of Catholic Bishops and by Rome. This document also applies to all religious seminaries in the US, even though the religious are still entitled to their own spiritual formation programs and to preserve their rights and privileges.

The new priest will likely bear the imprint of the edition of the PPF that was current during his formation. Of course, this depends on just how good the programs at his seminary were and how diligent he was in absorbing them.

The Program for Priestly Formation (5ᵗʰ edition) was laid out based on the Post-Synodal Apostolic Exhortation, issued by John Paul II, called *I Will Give You Shepherds: On the Formation of Priests in the Circumstances of the Present Day*. This came out in 1992 and is known by its Latin words: *Pastores dabo vobis*. The Exhortation was specifically addressed to the question of priestly formation and is the presentation of the deliberations of the Synod on Priestly Formation. The Preface of the PPF also notes two other papal documents, by John Paul II, that were used, *Novo millennio ineunte* (At the Close of the Great Jubilee of the Year 2000, 2001) and *Ecclesia in America* (The Church in America, 1999). Now, briefly following the subdivisions in the PPF . . .

The Preface
The Preface of the PPF describes the history of the treatment of priestly formation starting with the Vatican II documents.

(1) Introduction
The introduction to the PPF starts from the most historically and theologically accurate starting point for understanding the Church community. It says that the formation community is "a continuation in the Church of the apostolic community gathered about Jesus, listening to his word, proceeding towards the Easter experience, awaiting the gift of the Spirit for the mission." (PDV 60) This focus elevates the discussion of formation to its proper level.

The essential term for beginning the study of formation is *context. Pastores dabo vobis* explains: "God always calls his priests from specific human and ecclesial contexts, which inevitably influence them; and to these same contexts the priest is sent for the service of Christ's Gospel." (PPF 5) This is not mere contextualism but in fact a recognition of how the real presents itself. The human community in all of its complexity is the real acting 'space' of the seminarian and later of the priest. In the specifically ecclesial context, there are two dominant factors, the current of renewal initiated by Vatican II and a strong missionary thrust that was also taught by Vatican II, even though it was opposed by parts of the Left after the council.

The PPF points out that the US context both shows people's thirst for spirituality as well as the strong secular character of the culture. There is also a weakness of ethical standards and a large unchurched population in the US. Trends of globalization and emphasis on diversity are strikingly present. One might even say that diversity has become one of the macro-ethics of the new Left. Then, lastly, candidates for the priesthood themselves are culturally diverse and struggling with secular culture.

(2) The Nature and Mission of the Ministerial Priesthood.

In the seminary, all formation is to be based on "the truths of the faith." (PPF 13) The primary truth is that priesthood is grounded in specific Trinitarian foundations. According to John Paul II: "the nature and mission of the ministerial priesthood cannot be defined except through this multiple and rich interconnection of relationships which arise from the Blessed Trinity and are prolonged in the communion of the Church, as a sign and instrument of Christ, of communion with God and of the unity of all humanity." (PDV 12) Thus the Trinity is the foundation of formation as well as of the spirituality of the priest.

Further, the mission of the priest, in Christological terms is that: "Priests are called to prolong the presence of Christ, the One High Priest, embodying his way of life and making him visible in the midst of the flock entrusted to their care." (PDV 15) The priest participates in the continuing missions of the Divine Son and the Divine Spirit in the world through the Church.

Then, the Church includes "the priesthood, [that] along with the word of God and the sacramental signs which it serves, belongs to the constitutive elements of the Church." (PDV 16) By its foundation, the Church is apostolic (one of the signs of the true Church) and "through the priesthood of the Bishop, the priesthood of the second order is incorporated in the apostolic structure of the Church." (PPF 17)

Priesthood in Presbyteral Communion
The actions of priesthood only occur within a communion that is united to Christ sacramentally through the hierarchical communion with his Bishop. (PPF 18) And

so, "the ordained ministry has a radical 'communitarian form' and can only be carried out as a 'collective work'" (PDV 17 in PPF 18) Hence the need for bonds of spiritual fraternity and cooperation between the Clergy. In a frantically individualistic culture, the PPF has its work cut out. Seeing the intense training that is needed to get soldiers to coordinate and sports teams to cooperate, something similar would be needed for those who would be Clergy.

Priesthood: Diocesan and Religious
The two kinds of priests have so much in common that they follow the same program of formation in the US.

(3) The Life of Priests

The word "life" in the title of this section is important. It refers to the totality of the priest's existence and its being centered on Christ— "the one thing necessary." (PPF 20) The PPF then specifies that: "priests are called to a specific vocation to holiness in virtue of their new consecration in the sacrament of Holy Orders, a consecration that configures them to Christ the Head and Shepherd (PDV 20)." (PPF 20) The document is aiming at training priests to have a totally integrated life where "the specific arena in which their spiritual life unfolds is their exercise of ministry." (PPF 23)

The PPF emphasizes that the ministry is "*amoris officium*," using St. Augustine's phrase. It is a work of love. Then the PPF devotes the whole of article 26 to describing a dozen ways in which the priest is conformed to Christ. Articles 27 - 29, treat the fact that religious who are Clergy draw on their religious charism to give shape to their exercise of their priesthood. They reiterate that the two types of Clergy do need to have the same human, intellectual, spiritual and pastoral formation as per the PPF. These areas of human being cover the four areas of the priest's life that were mentioned earlier.

(4) Priestly Vocations in the Church's Pastoral Work and the Admission of Candidates

Various Responsibilities in the Church for Vocations
Everyone in the Church has some kind of responsibility for promoting priestly vocations: the Church, the Bishop, the family, the presbyterate, the vocation director, the seminary and seminarians themselves. Everyone in the Church participates through prayer and by active collaboration in the work of encouraging vocations at every possible opportunity.

The Discernment of Vocations
The Church community plays an essential part in the discerning of vocations in individuals. Judging whether one has a priestly vocation is not a purely private

discovery. John Paul II described the problem in discernment when people act "as if God's call reached the individual by a direct route, without in any way passing through the community" (PDV 37) In addition, the various members of the community have a positive contribution to make to the carrying out of the initial process of discernment that results in the candidate entering the admissions process for the seminary.

The Admissions Process

Admission of candidates to the seminary is judged on the basis of the individual having "a right intention, . . . a sufficiently broad knowledge of the doctrine of the faith, some introduction to the methods of prayer, and behavior in conformity with Christian tradition. They should also have attitudes proper to their regions, through which they can express their effort to find God and the faith" (PDV 62) At least at the early stages, the formation staff follow the principle of gradualism where the candidate has to be judged to be advancing in development in the different areas of human existence at the very least. In each case, the PPF describes the required thresholds of development in each of the developmental parts of life, namely, in the "human, spiritual, intellectual, and pastoral" areas. (PPF 37)

The PPF recognizes that there had been a recent increase in the diversity of the students when the document was written, having "not only differing personal gifts and levels of maturity but also significant cultural differences" as well. (PPF 38) Interestingly, regarding the present concern about the scandals, the majority of the various forms of abuse chronologically seem to have been committed before the PPF's were introduced. There has been a steep decline in the number of cases in the last twenty years despite all of the hype to the contrary.

The PPF also sets a very stringent standard for finally accepting a candidate: "Bishops, religious superiors, and rectors must have moral certitude about the psychological and physical health of those they admit to the seminary." (PPF 39) This was said in the face of the institutions of formation being staffed with personnel from all kinds of formation backgrounds. It would be worthwhile asking the question: How much retooling and changing of personnel was done as a result of the issuing of this version of the PPF? Another valid question would be: do seminary personnel understand the theology of the issues regarding homosexual Clergy? Lastly, without being facetious, do the seminary personnel understand the intellectual requirements of the Catholic priesthood?

In conclusion, the PPF also noted that the data gathering about a candidate to make an evaluation could also be useful for the student's own personal efforts to work on his development, both spiritually and psychologically.

There is an emphasis on the seminarian's understanding of his own sexuality in the PPF, because of the vast amount of research in the subject. So then, the PPF could lead the student to understand that "sexuality affects all aspects of the human person in the unity of his body and soul. It especially concerns affectivity, the capacity to love and to procreate, and in a more general way the attitude for forming bonds of communion with others." (CCC 2332) This concept of the overall influence of sexuality militates against current efforts to minimize the Church's concern for sexuality and the related gender issues. The secular efforts treat sexuality as a side-issue and they suggest that it doesn't require much consideration in a student's formation. This issue will return again because the Church is constantly having to lay out the Judeo-Christian understanding of sexuality and the absoluteness of this understanding! The history of salvation is understood in gendered terms.

(5) Norms for the Admission of Candidates

Central to the admission process are the seminary's efforts to develop evidence that: "the applicants give witness to their conviction that God has brought them to the seminary to discern whether or not they are really called to the priesthood, and they should commit themselves wholeheartedly to carrying out that discernment." (PPF 45) Having these norms for the discernment process makes for a more well-grounded decision. It is simply more realistic and appropriate to the situation.

In addition to their other criteria, the PPF noted that: "Applicants from diverse ethnic and cultural backgrounds should be given every encouragement." (PPF 49) It should be noted too that formation staff themselves also range widely in quality. They come from many programs of varying quality themselves—another important point. Moreover, the formation program is expected to carry out the additional tasks engendered by candidates who don't fall within the traditional parameters of the seminary population— "Seminaries are responsible to ensure the possession of adequate resources to serve the formative needs of such applicants." (PPF 49) It is not clear how practical this is because getting staff to cover all the different eventualities will not be easy. These provisions are a nod to the increased cultural sensitivities of the times. Nevertheless, the PPF loses sight of the basic uniformity of the values of Catholic civilization and the fact that Catholicism can motivate and help most kinds of people to develop the faith in almost any circumstances gets lost.

The PPF details what the program expected in terms of psychological, developmental, and linguistic standards to be satisfied in the approval process. The writers are particularly clear that: "Any evidence of criminal sexual activity with a minor or an inclination toward such activity disqualifies the applicant from admission." (PPF 55) The candidate's debts must be considered too.

Administratively, several kinds of documents are required from the candidate—baptism certificate; confirmation certificate (PPF 63)—and the fulfillment of canonical requirements as well. (PPF 64) Even a physical examination is required. Wisely too, they include a caution about the frequent immaturity in the faith of recent converts.

(6) The Formation of Candidates for Priesthood.

In this section, the PPF starts where it should with the theological foundation of formation: "Formation is first and foremost cooperation with the grace of God." (PPF 68) Secondly, the program notes that formation is fundamentally ecclesial and yet usually not at all in the sense that the student imagines because he probably has not done much ecclesiology. Again, *Pastores dabo vobis* appears as the gold standard for the criteria in the areas of "human, spiritual, intellectual, and pastoral formation." (PDF 70) The writers of the PPF emphasize that there are very specific requirements for the priesthood in each of the above areas, over and above the requirements for other baptized people.

Going back to the ecclesial nature of formation: from the perspective of the Church, the candidate is expected to be "not just a well-rounded person, a prayerful person, or an experienced pastoral practitioner but rather one who understands his spiritual development within the context of his call to service in the Church, his human development within the greater context of his call to advance the mission of the Church, his intellectual development as the appropriation of the Church's teaching and tradition, and his pastoral formation as participation in the active ministry of the Church." (PPF 71) It is the ecclesiastical context—there is the word again—that describes and enables the different developmental areas to be integrated by the candidate.

It is great that this requirement is in place. However, newly ordained candidates are joining a population of priests that often was not formed in this way. The sheer complexity of the mix of active priests itself generates many of the difficulties that are now surfacing in the recent history of the Church. The fear of consistency, that remains from the sixties, has had all kinds of effects. I think that it is tied to the fear of insisting on and enforcing uniform theological standards. Otherwise, the Bishop or the religious superior will not be popular and not get the cooperation of his Clergy.

The quote from PPF 71 (above) highlights how the different areas of growth are integrated. Then, PPF 73 simply repeats the interrelationships on which this integrity rests by saying: "Clearly human formation is the foundation for the other three pillars. Spiritual formation informs the other three. Intellectual formation appropriates and understands the other three. Pastoral formation [goes on to] express the other three pillars in practice."

Now, considering the dimension of human formation in more detail . . .

I.   Human Formation

Theologically, to start with, the center of all human formation is Jesus Christ himself, who, "in his fully developed humanity, he was truly free and with complete freedom gave himself totally for the salvation of the world." (PDV 5) This is a scriptural insight because Jesus Christ "comes from the human community and is at its service, [and] imitating Jesus Christ 'who in every respect has been tempted as we are, yet [is] without sin'" is the route to authentic formation. (Hebrews 4:15)

As a kind of background, PPF 76 offers a compendium of the basic human traits that a good priest definitely needs. Much time is also to be spent on the "education for chastity, a virtue incumbent on all Christians and in a unique way embraced in celibacy, ought to present it as a 'virtue that develops a person's authentic maturity and makes him or her capable of respecting and fostering the 'nuptial meaning' of the body'. (PDV 44)"

The program is aware that a great problem for Clergy is loneliness. Yet, loneliness itself, seen in the right light, can become "holy solitude." (PPF 79) The other side of loneliness is to produce communities of Clergy that minimize the experience of long periods of loneliness. In a culture grounded in individualism, this is as much of a duty as developing a spirituality of loneliness. Particularly, there is an epidemic of loneliness in the US itself.[282] This is another way that the Church can serve the US population, namely to demonstrate how to deal with loneliness.

The PPF also offers elements of a pedagogy in human formation, so, for example: "In general, human formation happens in a three-fold process of self-knowledge, self-acceptance, and self-gift—and all of this in faith." (PPF 80) One might ask how a seminary sees that it is actually pedagogical throughout the day, requiring critical awareness on the part of staff and seminarians. The question is answered in PPF 80. The document then lists all of the various kinds of personnel and the interrelationships that are established in the seminary community.

The above three requirements (PPF 80) can be fulfilled when each person is consciously doing what they were hired to do and working on their own growth at the same time. For example, this process then can counter the "Uncle Ted"

---

[282] University College of San Diego, "*High prevalence and adverse health effects of loneliness in community-dwelling adults across the lifespan: role of wisdom as a protective factor.*" https://www.eurekalert.org/pub_releases/2018-12/uoc--sls121218.php

phenomenon for seminarians.[283] Seminarians will not be fooled so easily when someone takes an inordinate interest in them nor will they be cowed when tat person has authority.

PPF 80 targets the formators themselves: "These formation advisors/mentors and directors should be priests. They observe seminarians and assist them to grow humanly by offering them feedback about their general demeanor, their relational capacities and styles, their maturity, their capacity to assume the role of a public person and leader in a community, and their appropriation of the human virtues that make them 'men of communion.'" (PPF 80) This is also where the specific question about stopping homosexual sub-groups forming in the seminary should arise. As more investigations into seminaries publish their results, the details of this phenomenon and many others will surface.

A related question is the one of appointing homosexuals as formators. As the result of superiors and ordinaries trying to be openminded, sometimes whole tiers of formators in the seminary structure can be homosexuals. The issue of how much one adheres to the Natural Law will be part of the discussion. One ought to follow it completely. The alternative way of thinking is to turn to an ideology instead and that is where the difficulties arise. The ordinaries are not themselves acting in ways that are consistent with the Natural Law even though that is part of their job. Being 'even handed' in an ideological way—putting the ideology above the teaching of the Church—is all that is needed to sometimes create problems later for the Laity and Clergy in the diocese or the religious province. Being 'even handed' assumes that the two options of sexual orientation are simply equivalent, and scientifically and theologically they are not.

Norms for Human formation

Aim of the Human formation Program
The aim of the program can be summed up in the words: "This program must have a clear focus on the ordained priesthood as a vocation that brings the candidates to full human and spiritual potential through love of God and service of others." (PPF 84) The seminarians' human and spiritual realization of themselves through the priesthood is a crucial insight to hang on to. The culture pushes so many other very short-sighted 'fulfillments' and yet here the seminary offers the real fulfillment for a few specified men.

---

[283] 'Uncle Ted,' refers to Bishop and later Cardinal McCarrick and his currying favour with seminarians.

The Goals of Human Formation

The concept of the real fulfillment of a seminarian leads to the fact that: "Candidates should give evidence of having interiorized their seminary formation." (PPF 84) Then follows a highly detailed description of the results of a human formation.

The Candidate for Human Formation

Preparation for Celibacy

Article PPF 90 explains that "sexuality finds its authentic meaning in relation to mature love." This is love as the Church understands it, as Christ understands it: "No one has greater love than this, to lay down one's life for one's friends." (John 15:13) They might have added the distinction of including love of Christ, platonic love of women and fraternal love of men. The PPF identifies many skills and practices to bring these about. Most importantly, and here the political approach to sexuality must be replaced by the clear commitment to the fact that "a candidate must be prepared to accept wholeheartedly the Church's teaching on sexuality in its entirety, be determined to master all sexual temptations, be prepared to meet the challenge of living chastely in all friendships, and, finally, be resolved to fashion his sexual desires and passions in such a way that he is able to live a healthy, celibate lifestyle that expresses self-gift in faithful and life-giving love." (PPF 94) In the past, some Bishops, Clergy and seminarians have treated some of the Church's teachings as optional. How to call everyone to live by the standard of the Church's teaching is not yet clear because it would involve the responsible people using their authority when the need arises. It may involve seminarians having to learn what the responsibility of a church official is.

Preparation for a Simplicity of Life

The first article in this section is worth quoting in its entirety: "Human formation should cultivate a spirit of generosity, encouraging the seminarian to become a man for others and to curb expectations of entitlement. Manifestations of undue materialism and consumerism in the seminarian's behavior should be confronted and corrected." (PPF 97) The article should be applied to Bishops and cardinals first to present some kind of public example and thus some kind of credibility. These expectations are really Christian, but their Christian basis should be argued for in some detail rather than assuming that everybody gets it. Article 98 then does a good job explaining about the counter-cultural nature of these expectations. It is rarely understood or admitted that Catholicism is a new culture (civilization) because it is based on love and not on concupiscence or power. Since religious Clergy must also follow the PPF, these articles need to be taken seriously in religious institutions too. The thing is that religious vows fit in very well with the notions of selfless love.

Preparation for Obedience

One of the highpoints in a well-developed notion of human well-being and integrity is the capacity for obedience. PPF 100 says: "The exercise of authority and the response of obedience are works of grace, goodwill, and human effort that play a part in the life of every priest." That is obedience on the part of the priest/seminarian. Then the article concludes with the objective theological principle for obedience on which everything rests namely to "manifest in heart and mind, the adherence to the Word of God and the Magisterium." Authority and obedience as patterns of behavior have been denigrated by the culture and it is very difficult to reinstate the correct revealed foundations of these two modes of action.

There is also the problem that formation staff sometimes want to be friends with the seminarians. Only a mature formation staff who can differentiate between their personal and professional roles and articulate them when necessary. This is a tough one to achieve. The maturity of the formation staff will decide on the success or failure of the seminary.

Yet even with formation staff, they are only as good as the point at which they can identify when they stopped growing and stopped learning. It takes maturity to do that. If they are honest, few people have really gotten to grips with profoundly understanding the Church, for example, or their place in it. When do they go to the effort of adding to their knowledge? But more disturbing is that they sometimes do not understand the foundations of the principles of the theology of the Church in revelation.

Then, further, concerning the seminarians and their functioning in an obedient way: "Seminaries should expect of seminarians a spirit of joyful trust, open dialogue, and generous cooperation with those in authority." (PPF 101) This is very optimistic. Seminarians know exactly who can wipe out their imagined vocations and how easily they can do it! Also, the foundations of the acts of trust, dialogue and cooperation are going to have to be completely rebuilt after recent events. Maturity in candidates should be the watchword.

Resources for Human Formation

Faculty and staff have to establish the basic principles of human formation for the seminary as well as set the example. The investigations into a couple of seminaries (eg. Buffalo, Boston) may shake up how the precious resource of healthy well-developed staff is used. One sign of proper human development is a spirit of genuine collegiality in the seminary: "The entire seminary staff, composed of priests, religious, and Laity, constitutes another significant group, who can model collegiality for the seminarians. Ways to foster the unity of this larger circle should also be developed." (PPF 104) The degree of collegiality is a sure indicator of the maturity of the formation staff. Another thing that overlaps with the practice of collegiality is the understanding of the Church as collegial—one of the features of *communio*. Notably, Laity themselves can have the same voids in their understanding of the Church that Clergy do. As with some other Catholic institutions in the US, sometimes not too much care is spent maintaining the integrity of the day-to-day passing on of the Catholic intellectual life. It is as if there is an unspoken belief that Catholicism is not terribly consistent. Not surprising in a Protestant and majority leftist country!

II. Spiritual Formation

This section in the Program for Priestly formation bases itself on John Paul II's statement that: "For every priest his spiritual formation is the core which unifies and gives life to his being a priest and his acting as a priest." (PDV 45) In other words, the priest's spiritual formation is the light that illuminates every thought and deed of the priest. In themselves, every aspect of the priestly spirituality involves being "configured" to Christ. This means that "their spirituality draws them into the priestly, self-sacrificial path of Jesus." (PPF 109) In this way, Christ does not remain a mere historical figure but rather he is the first-born of a whole new way of being in which priests participate by ordination. He is profoundly present in the life of the priest.

Article PPF 110 then goes on to list all the different elements of a priestly spirituality. In general, the particular interest of the document is in forming life-long habits in spirituality in the candidate. Community life too gets a specific mention: "The seminarian is able to enter into significant, even deep, relationships with other persons and with God. He is to be a 'man of communion'." (PPF 112) Communion is a theological term that was recovered in theological thinking before the last council. The term had been used long before as pointing to a group that is borne by the Holy Spirit and that communicates gifts of grace and truth among themselves. The hyper-individualism in the US means that this is a difficult area of growth to lay hold of. However, it does provide a far more profound and accurate virion of the Church than a purely juridical idea of Church.

The intellectual side of spirituality (PPF 113) is emphasized in the program as well, especially in terms of the gathering of information on the lives of the saints and the people of God. One cannot overestimate the impact on one's life of knowing the life of a saint in detail. The intellectual dimension of the faith needs to be emphasized because the intellectual integrity of the faith is often queried in the US culture and the western world in general. Also, the fact is that about half of the members of the culture do not routinely chase after intellectual integrity. Instead, they are committed to Gnosticism (detailed in the chapter on intellectual life) with all of its terrible problems.

Prayer

The PPF's discussion of prayer starts by referring to regular participation in the celebration of the Eucharist and in the morning and evening praying of the Breviary. PPF 118 details the need to observe the *norms* for the liturgy: "Priest faculty should be particularly observant of the liturgical rubrics and avoid the insertion of any personal liturgical adaptations, unless they are authorized by the liturgical books." Again, the program is emphasizing the collegiality and communion of members of the Church. Respecting the common rules is a mundane but obvious way to maintain communion. One does not approach the liturgy as a private actor, so careful instruction is required in how to celebrate the liturgy. Regarding the Breviary, the seminarians should gradually include all of the hours of the Divine Office so that they will have been doing this routine of prayer for at least a year before their deaconate ordination. The praying of the Breviary also draws the seminarian into the corporate nature of the Church as offering one worship in the one Christ to the Father.

The document picks up many of the traditional tools of spirituality, namely the liturgy of Penance, spiritual conferences, and instruction in "meditation, contemplation, *lectio divina*, and daily examen must be provided." (PPF 123) Consequently, there is no way that the priesthood can be perceived as a mere occupation.

Spiritual Direction

The practice of spiritual direction is taken very seriously by the PPF, with the directors needing careful identification and then being suitably trained and approved. Directors ought to have the complete confidence of the seminarians who "should confide their personal history, personal relationships, prayer experiences, the cultivation of virtues, their temptations, and other significant topics to their spiritual director." (PPF 124) The work of the directors forms the so-called 'internal forum' that gives the seminarian a trustworthy spiritual space within which to reflect and encounter Christ properly.

III Intellectual Formation

There is a theological foundation from John Paul II to this aspect of seminary life as well. In his *Pastores dabo vobis*, John Paul II says: "For the salvation of their brothers and sisters, [priests] should seek an ever-deeper knowledge of the divine mysteries." (PDV 51) There is a substantial meaning to the word 'knowledge' here. It shows the profound connection between one's spirituality and one's intellectual life. The PDF quotes St. Anselm's adage *credo ut intellegam* to illustrate the requirement of a spirituality in order to have a valid intellectual life. John Paul II's *Fides et ratio* explains this saying in much more detail! In fact in the same encyclical, he included a section on the other side of this saying and that is *intellego ut credam*—'I know therefore I believe'. It is the contention of this book that this is the area where many problems in the US Church can be found.

Hence, in the document's very neat summary, the goal of the intellectual formation in the seminary is to produce priests "who are widely knowledgeable about the human condition, deeply engaged in a process of understanding divine revelation, and adequately skilled in communicating his knowledge to as many people as possible." (PPF 138) There are skills involved here but there is also a most fundamental reality and that is the priest's union with Almighty God. Americans are great at passing on skills, a very useful competence to have, but someone who is absorbed with God will know and communicate even better still.

Importantly, this kind of formation is "ecclesial" in the sense that it, first of all, follows magisterial teaching. (PPF 138) Secondly, the ecclesial nature of the intellectual life means that it involves all the different aspects of Church life, the Scriptures, the tradition, the prayer, the sacraments and the community life.

The Context of Intellectual Formation

Summing up, the PPF considers the difficulties of teaching the students with widely differing abilities ranging from those who have specialized knowledge to those whose familiarity is only at the level of a poor catechetical knowledge. (PPF 140) In a sense, an institution cannot do all things, even with the best will in the world. This provision of the Program requires a substantial dedication on the part of some staff members who are involved with a particular student and the same kind of dedication from the student himself.

Stages in Preparation for Theology

According to the PPF, the pedagogical stages of theological studies take place successively in the "high school seminary, college seminary, cultural preparation programs, and pre-theology." (PPF 141) This may no longer be the case according to present day statistics. Nevertheless, the PPF has something to say about this somewhat dated picture of intellectual growth.

High School Seminary

To start with: "In the high school seminary, students acquire the basic skills and knowledge that enable them to pursue higher education. Catechesis should occupy a central position in the program of a high school seminary. This should include a solid foundation in spirituality and Catholic moral values." (PPF 142) Given the rapid secularization of society, this may actually have to be the practice of Catholic education in general. The Program is giving the complete scope of any child's education in the face of the raging secularism of the age.

College Seminary

The college seminary is distinguished by its double aspect: training in the liberal arts and training in philosophy. (PPF 147 – 151) Again, this could apply to all Catholic colleges, seminaries or not.

Philosophy receives a special mention in the Program. It is essential in this time of careless, sloppy thinking. Quoting from *Fides et ratio*: it is essential to note "the intimate bond which ties theological work to the philosophical search for truth." (FR 63) Then the PPF articles 155 -156 lay out the details of the subjects to be studied.

Importantly, "philosophical instruction must be grounded in the perennially valid philosophical heritage and also take into account philosophical investigation over the course of time." (CIC 251) This perennial philosophy is a line of thought that has been current for millennia. In fact, up until the Enlightenment it was widespread and considered authoritative. Recently, the Church has been trying to reinstate it, at least since the time of Leo XIII, and a number of Catholic universities are making efforts in that direction. There is an integrity to this way of thinking that is organically related to the nature of the human being, something that is lost when one learns Marxism, socialism and so on instead.

The program's list of studies repeatedly asks that the students learn to see the context of the materials that they are studying. The importance of context was emphasized previously, and it re-appears here. The PPF makes a good point because students are often not able to establish the context of their concepts for themselves. They have to deal with the agendas of their professors who may not have grasped the context of their thinking either. A second kind of contextual issue is that "from the beginning, students should learn to relate theology to the larger mission of the Church in the public sphere." (PPF 159) This is simply applying the general concept to the specific situation of theological study.

Cultural Preparation Programs
On a related point, PPF 160 notes that seminary programs should help candidates to learn about US culture. Considering that many US students do not know the history or many aspects of the culture of this country, this is a vital point. Again, the PPF is addressing the matter of context. Of course, history is not the only aspect of culture. The various 'philosophies' and ideologies that drive so much of US culture ought to be known as well. Then there has to be something about the legal system as well as something on the entertainment industry, the system of commerce and so on. I would add here that the student ought to have a really good grasp of Catholic culture too. The great figures like Dorothy Day, Flannery O'Connor and Walker Percy, some of the great music and plays like the Dialogues of the Carmelites and so on are crucial to lift the student out of the secular morass that the culture obliges them to wade through day after day.

Pre-Theology

The Program is very systematically laid out and far too detailed to go into here. The articles PPF 161 and 162 detail the required content of the pre-theology courses. These courses are for those who "lack the philosophical and theological background and other areas necessary to pursue graduate-level theology." (PPF 161) Evaluating what the incoming candidates have already done has to go beyond looking at the course names on the student's academic record. The names may mean everything or nothing at all. It cannot be assumed that the students have studied something appropriate even when the title looks alright. As with so many of the other proposals in the PPF, the list of required courses should be limited by the practical considerations of time.

(7) Graduate Theology

This is where the formation system for priests recognizes that the faith has real content. So, the PPF says: "Theology in seminary intellectual formation is truly to *be fides quaerens intellectum*, faith seeking understanding. This direction is not the same as the approach of religious studies or the history of religions." (PPF 163) This is a particularly valuable point because the latter two disciplines are secular efforts to examine religion. They miss the true nature of Christianity because it is so much more than a religion. They also treat all religions as identical phenomena which they are not. The secular academy's trying to find a neutral observation point from which to study Catholicism simply does not reveal much about Catholicism. The study of Catholicism involves faith which specifically means not being neutral. (The notion of a neutral observer's point is false anyway!) Further, because graduate theology involves the growing faith of the seminarian, the study needs to be integrated with the liturgy.

It is in the study of theology that a lot more course ought to be synchronized to stay true to the integrated nature of truth itself. Modern courses in seminaries sometimes tend to be along the lines of what the professor wants to do today as if no other education is going on in the seminary building today. This is motivated by the Enlightenment concept of the professor as the virtuoso thinker and the seminarians are sitting at his feet gathering the pearls. In fact, the Church is the thinker and the professor is simply trying to adequately share what the Church thinks to the best of his or her humble ability. The concept of the 'mind of the Church' is not a mere pious holdover from former times. It is a properly valid theological concept that ought to be guiding the design of the syllabus.

The content of seminary studies is ultimately pastoral and so the material must be taught in such a way that it can be presented in preaching. And it goes without saying—but it does nevertheless have to be mandated given the present state of tertiary education in the US—that the content ought to be congruent with the teaching of the Magisterium.

Integration of Intellectual Formation with the other pillars

The four pillars of the seminary formation program are the human, the intellectual, the spiritual, and pastoral. (PPF 164) These are closely interrelated because of the nature of a human's authentic participation in truth and because one is dealing with a single human being at a time. The human being develops as he takes in information. The resulting intellectual development helps and is helped by his spiritual development. The student's intellectual and spiritual formation help the individual develop to the point where he can do pastoral work adequately.

Norms for Intellectual Formation

The PPF gives a detailed account of the expected structuring of the academic programs of High School Seminaries, College Seminaries, Pre-Theology Programs, and Theologates. Material far too detailed to be examined here.

IV PASTORAL FORMATION

This is the fourth pillar of formation. To start with, "all four pillars of formation are interwoven and go forward concurrently. Still, in a certain sense, pastoral formation is the culmination of the entire formation process." (PPF 236) The priest is being trained to *function* as a priest, not merely to be one. Functioning means that "in virtue of the grace of Holy Orders, a priest is able to stand and act in the community in the name and person of Jesus Christ, Head and Shepherd of the Church." (PPF 237) Jesus Christ is the one who sets the example and who acts through the disponible priest.

The PPF gives an exhaustive list of the different dimensions of pastoral work: the proclamation of the word; the sacramental dimension; the missionary dimension; the community dimension; skills needed for public ministry; a personal synthesis for practical use; an initiation into various practical, pastoral experiences, especially in parishes; cultural sensitivity; religious pluralism; formation for a particular presbyterate and a local Church; the poor; leadership training; cultivation of personal qualities. The complexity of the pastoral scene and the amazing range of training that has to made available can be overwhelming. One caution is that the possibility of getting incorrect information on cultures is high due to the political correctness that has crept into discussions of culture and society.

The key to pastoral training, according to the PPF, is "supervision." (PPF 240) The supervisors require "an almost instinctive way of thinking theologically in pastoral situations, and a habit of prayer that permeates the ministry." (PPF 240) Of course, this means that they have to have substantial training in theology and practical pastoral work.

Norms for Pastoral Formation

The document gives a correspondingly detailed set of norms. One key concept is that "however the pastoral formation program is organized, it must pay attention to the seminarians' need to root a life of service in personal prayer." (PPF 253) Prayer once again comes to the fore as the central existential feature of the priesthood.

V. COMMUNITY

As a starting point, the PPF restates the opening proposition of the PPF, namely, the community "is 'a continuation in the Church of the apostolic community gathered about Jesus' in which men called to share in a unique way in the priesthood of Christ relive today the formation offered to the Twelve by the Lord." (PDV 60, 61) Originally, this quote was applied to the formation community. Now it is being applied to the Church community and its relation to the world community.

This citation is followed by a view of community, not from the historical-theological perspective, but from the theological one: "The seminary's life in community mirrors ecclesial communion, which itself is rooted in the Blessed Trinity." (PPF 259) It is this perspective that gives some idea of the true scope of community. It mirrors the Divine Trinity and helps people to learn to participate in the life of the Trinity. It is in this authentic life that the development in the four pillars of formation takes place. (PPF 260) This community helps the seminarian to develop the capacity to live the public religious life of the Church. (PPF 261) In a parallel fashion, the seminary community helps the seminarian live the personal and interior spiritual life of a follower of Jesus Christ.

The Norms for Community

The PPF finds itself in a dilemma here. It asks for a handbook for the community life of the seminary. Yet, at the same time: the document recognizes that "the rule of life addresses the essentials of community living while avoiding excessive detail that would stifle individual initiative or talent." (PPF 266) However, knowing the essentials is crucial for developing the ecclesial experience. The norms need to be ecclesial so as not to settle for what the socialists imagine are 'community norms' in some secular sense.

The list of norms includes the traditional elements of seminary community life: the Eucharist; the rector's conferences; daily routine; 'house rules and values'; etc.

Significantly, PPF 269 emphasizes that: "Matters pertaining to celibate and chaste living must be included in the seminary rule of life. This rule must also foster simplicity of life, encouraging fasting, almsgiving, and the asceticism demanded by a Christian life and the priestly state." Considering the theological interrelationships of all of these values, they will have to be more than explained. This is where getting to know the seminarians is crucial because only then, can one learn what charitable works they do; how they spend their money; what kinds of entertainments they participate in; and where they go with their friends, if they have free time. It is interesting that this article gives a list of the values advocated for religious life as well. I say 'advocated' because religious are often no better at achieving these values than are diocesan Clergy.

The above article's concluding words are: "The rule of life must encourage appropriate respect for those in authority, and [encourage] a mature sense of obedience." This is clear from the theology of priesthood itself due to the participation in the priesthood of the Bishop. However, there is also an essential obligation on the part of the Bishop to have "helpers" (LG 20) and "assistants" (LG 21), but also that he view them "as sons and friends." (LG 28) Nothing in the PPF refers to this dimension of the relationship between Bishops and priests.

The second half of the Program for Priestly Formation offers a substantial amount of material on the administration of the formation process. That will not be presented here.

Chapter Fourteen Who You will meet

As for the proud minister, he is to be ranked with the devil. Christ's gift is not thereby profaned: what flows through him keeps its purity, and what passes through him remains dear and reaches the fertile earth. Augustine of Hippo

(1) Introduction

Catholic priests are a quirky group to say the least, much like any random group of laypeople. However, in a mysterious way, all are part of the hierarchical community of saints and sinners who make up the physical and spiritual Church. Their peculiarities serve another purpose too and that is providing occasions of grace because Christians are nevertheless to always "love your enemies, and pray for those who persecute you, that you may be children of your heavenly Father, for he makes his sun rise on the bad and the good, and causes rain to fall on the just and the unjust." (Matthew 5:44, 45) This set of principles ground a mindset that expresses the concrete way that Christ is made present upon the earth by our full participation, by intellect and will.

In the case of the priest, the power of the presence of Christ takes poor concupiscent human material and transforms him to mediate grace and truth. But this is not demonic possession. It is not the mindless taking over of the person but an elevation and enhancement of the individual man by the grace of the sacraments for the Church. By baptism, God's grace means that, "as man in his intellective powers participates in the Divine knowledge through the virtue of faith, and in his power of will participates in the Divine love through the virtue of charity, so also in the nature of the soul does he participate in the Divine Nature, after the manner of a likeness, through a certain regeneration or re-creation." (ST II-I q.110 a.4) Nevertheless, there is another factor. In the words of Aquinas, once again: "the common and habitual course of justification is that God moves the soul interiorly and that man is converted to God, first by an imperfect conversion, that it may afterwards become perfect." (ST II-I q.113 a.10) So there is the potential for raising the degree of the priest's conversion. Charitably let us say that the newly ordained priest enters a priestly population made up of men who are at very different degrees of personal conversion.

Priests are guaranteed the sacramental grace for many aspects of their ministry, but their personal development and capacities for ministry continue to depend on their cooperation with grace. Hence there are priests who switch their Christianity on and off. There are priests who are Christian 24/7. And there are those in between. In addition, the presbyterate is a divided community where more than half are leftist and about 10% are homosexual. (Purely anecdotal figures!) Then, Clergy come from many different formation programs all with differing results. Furthermore, they have varying ages and psychologies.[284] Looking at things in more theological detail . . .

(2) The Saints

For the new priest joining the diocese or religious community, the first group to identify is those who are on the road to sainthood. These men pray a lot. They are orthodox men who love the Church and who do their ministry whenever it is needed. They contribute much to the community of the Clergy and the Laity, and they are as positive as they can be about their Bishop and superiors. The qualification is in there because Bishops and superiors get it wrong on occasion. Having the 'saints' around makes one's own priesthood seem much more possible, at the very least in terms of not being simply overwhelming. More positively, they make the true priesthood very evident by the radiant holiness of their ministry and because they pray for the Clergy and the Church at large. These are not the men who will cause a new priest any problems except that by being consistently Catholic, they are very humbling people to be around.

The group that will cause much heartache is, first and foremost. . .

(3) The Hypocrites

In the first century, there were three groups of people in the society around Jesus: there were those who believed in the future salvation of Israel, those who were not interested in the future of Israel, and then there were those religious authorities whom Jesus called hypocrites. (eg. Matthew 23:13) Apparently, those groups who are not interested in God's role in the world will always be around, but the real problem for a priest will always be the hypocrites.

It is stunning to meet priests whose words and actions show that they do not believe parts of Catholic teaching. Publicly, they often are not particularly vocal about it, but it is apparent when they discuss theology and when they preach and particularly in what they leave out of their preaching, teaching and initiatives. It probably comes up in the confessional too if one could eavesdrop. These are the hypocrites. One might include the abusers in this group as well.

---

[284] Note: It must be said, sad to say, that the conversations of Clergy are sometimes pretty dull. It's football, the weather and not much else. What this anecdotal insight means is that the custodians of the greatest truth in the world often choose not to discuss it. However, rather than treating theology as a commodity to be handed out at liturgies or on retreats, an alternative might be realizing that the truth is the Word, *present and active*, and so worth chewing over and discussing and reflecting on. This process helps men to interiorize the faith and furthers their conversion.

Their rejection of doctrine is not initially due to malice. Sometimes it has to do with them feeling superior to the Church, something that comes naturally for those on the left. Or when they were trained, they had teachers who knew more than the Church. It is hard to convince people just how insidious the leftist insurgency is in the Church. It is the Enlightenment all over again, only it is not *light* that is being shared.

From the sixties on, for historical reasons, some Bishops and religious superiors settled into the secular mindset. It seems to have been a reaction to some earlier periods of stringency about doctrine. Bishops and religious superiors wanted to be popular and some still do. There are, of course, Bishops who are simply ill-informed. Who keeps them orthodox?

They know on some level that it is wrong to have political views that do not gibe with the Church's moral teaching. They also know on some level that it is wrong to think that the Church is mainly about money[285] and institution-building more than about the truth.[286] In these instances Catholic teaching comes second. So one can, on the one hand, appear to promote genuine humanity but, on the other hand, they regularly vote for abortion; get involved in identity politics rather than the politics of the individual; they subscribe to the socialist myths about society; they confuse these myths with Christianity; they ignore history especially the history of their own political party; they ignore tradition; they condone the morality of the promiscuous Left and they hate certain groups of people. This appalling situation exists regardless of what they say because "truth" or any other words they use do not have quite the same meaning for them as it would for orthodox Clergy.

By avoiding what is known from revelation, including the reality of the Natural Law and by ignoring the history and purpose of social institutions, the leftist Clergy create a kind of cult. In fact, the study of religions does identify a phenomenon called syncretism—the mixing of two religions together. However, syncretism comes up against the problem that unadorned Catholicism is actually true because it is based on revelation, and it is true in an integrated way because the truths are logically related to each other. This means that Catholicism, by its nature, is not just one option in a range of 'reasonable' but imagined alternatives. Hypocritical Clergy are only committed to one of these imagined alternatives. Furthermore, it should be noted that doctrinally no priest or Bishop can 're-do' Catholic teaching to fit the latest social thinking for a number of reasons that have to do with the nature of God's revelation in history and the purely subservient role of the Clergy.

---

[285] The pandemic is going to force a lot of reflection on financial priorities.
[286] See Philip Lawler, *The Faithful departed—The Collapse of Boston's Catholic Culture*, New York: Encounter Books, 2010.

The temptation to 'redo' things in a solipsistic culture like the US comes as no surprise. However, finding this thinking in someone who has spent years learning Catholicism in a seminary is embarrassing but it does indicate the quality of some seminary training and the quality of some seminary management.

When approached, religious superiors and Bishops say that they could not possibly even suggest that their men vote differently, for example. This has been allowed to go on for so long that such thinking has become the norm and is part of everyday life. But perhaps ordinaries could start by explaining the problem. Many men do have enough good will to at least pay attention.

The leftist inclination of some Clergy and Bishops has two further features: first it suppresses the very fact of the truth of Catholicism itself. Historically, the Left is notorious for suppressing contrary views. This is not trivial because the Enlightenment has been saying that Catholicism is not true for three hundred years and it is still saying it. The long sad history of orthodox Clergy not getting certain posts and of orthodox faculty not getting jobs and promotions in Catholic institutions is easily uncovered. The other feature is a process that occurs in all leftist political operations throughout history, namely the dismantling of Catholicism. Leftists insert inconsistent propositions in streams of otherwise orthodox theology. What is happening is that the leftists re-purpose Catholic institutions to gain more power for their 'side'.

For them, institutions have no intrinsic function based on their founding principles to serve the common good. Yet, ideally, all institutions come out of the Natural Law concepts of what it means to be human, the value of the individual and the meaning of community and the common good. The Left, on the other hand, re-tailors institutions to increase their power. Institutions simply become tools of the ruling elite.

Now the hypocrisy: scripturally the problem with hypocrites was that the morality of their lives contradicted the values of the religion that they led, taught and represented to the world and whose economic system paid them. Alongside the authentic presence of the Jewish religion, at least parts of the Jewish establishment contradicted that teaching and nullified the public witness to authentic Jewish religion. There is no way to understate the damage that this 'parallel' institution did to the concrete presence of Judaism in the world, over the centuries. Don't forget that Judaism was already supposed to be a lesson for the nations. (eg. Psalm 9:11) The presence of the hypocritical counter-religion must have been very apparent to outside observers in those days. Nevertheless, the goal of seeing the true religion in the People of God and give glory to God did not go away. Christ himself came to preach to the nations.

With the coming of the New Testament, Jesus Christ is the true religion, the true obedience of man to God that happens right in the union of the two natures in the one being of Christ. The rest of us participate in that submission to God through the grace of Christ. The hypocrisy of nominal Catholics today involves presenting a fake version of Christianity out of ignorance, laziness or malice. What is worse is that some men are using the offices of the Church to put forward this fake form of Christianity under the guise of true Christianity while using the real Church's buildings, personnel, media and money to advance their cause.

(i)   The Self-Dispensers

Part of much of the hypocrisy is the tendency to dispense oneself from the obligation to follow a whole range of Catholic ideas and practices. Apparently, such men can decide for themselves when not to do their priestly duties. Even something as simple as Divine Office! Not praying it is a mortal sin. The self-dispensing attitude means that such Clergy put themselves above Scripture and Tradition and above obedience to the God who expresses himself in Scripture and Tradition. They are the proponents of what Benedict XVI called the 'manmade religion.'[287] This has been a constant problem throughout history but every so often it becomes the dominant culture in the Church. Some other times when it has become dominant were during the sexual revolution of the 1960s, and again after Vatican II. After Vatican II, there were those who thought that the council gave them the license to 're-do' the Church because the 'council said they could'. This misinterpretation of the council was accompanied by their sense that they are somehow privileged to know more than the Church does. Finally, the widespread moral corruption in the Church in the eleventh century ought never be forgotten as an object lesson.[288] The present situation of the Church does look like a replay of some of the events of that time.

(ii)   The Stand-Up Comedians

Another form of priestly hypocrisy is the priest who is an entertainer. In a weak culture, where there are few templates for a positive integrated male public presence, the priest has to dig deeply into the meaning of Christianity to find that. There one finds perfect templates for positive male presence and positive female presence. One has to wonder why a priest does not try to adopt the positive male public presence of Christ. Is Christ perhaps not that central to human life? When the priest does not do

---

[287] Benedict XVI, "The Church and the Scandal of Child-abuse," *Catholic News Agency*, https://www.catholicnewsagency.com/news/full-text-of-benedict-xvi-the-church-and-the-scandal-of-sexual-abuse-59639

[288] Cf. Peter Damian, *The Book of Gomorrah and St. Peter Damian's Struggle against Ecclesiastical Corruption*, Matthew Cullinan Hoffman trans., New Braunfehls Texas: Ite ad Thomam Books, 2015.

this, then he will adopt one of the cultural templates for how he presents himself to others.

One common template in the US is the stand-up comedian. The best stand-ups are where they are because of a phenomenal amount of work. But mediocre comedians are not the issue. The problem is that priests are meant to be other Christs. They are not meant to be entertainers. They need to derive their public presence from the image of Christ that is encountered in the Gospels. They need to derive their way of being present from Christ himself. John Vianney was a great practical example of how to do this.

Humor is a great thing in the right context. However, it is not the only way of communicating and it is not suitable for communicating some kinds of truth. It can indicate a flippant attitude to doctrine, for example.

(iii)   The Perfect

Hypocrites often have the illusion of personal perfection. Such people have some characteristics that in former times might have been found in the Cathars or the Illuminati. The Cathars thought that they were the perfect ones. They knew everything. They knew so much about the spiritual world that the material world was merely to be manipulated and hence one could do whatever one pleased. They were the Gnostics of their time, medieval Europe.[289] The modern Illuminati are free to behave in any way they choose, as arrogant, prideful and nasty as they wish because they are more perfect than those around them. They are a modern kind of Pharisee.

(iv)   Eradicator

Another practitioner of hypocrisy is the eradicator. In parishes or chaplaincies, one will sometimes be followed by someone who eradicates things that you have done. They might snub groups that have been cooperating with the priest in the growth of the parish and in its charitable work. They might destroy the architecture (assuming it has been done according to theological and historical principles, in the first place) or the art. They might nullify liturgical principles. They might cancel confessions or only do sick calls between nine and five.

The problem seems to be ego. The individual needs the parish to be an expression of his personal preferences. For him, the parish is not part of the universal Church. It is a personal fiefdom that mirrors his inadequacies and ignorance. Some of his 'improvements' might confuse the parishioners and make some them very angry. Now it is not to say that some people get angry or nasty for the wrong reasons. There are as many 20-minute Christians among the Laity as there are among the Clergy.

---

[289] Cf. Stephen O'Shea, *The Perfect Heresy – The Revolutionary Life and Death of the Medieval Cathars*, New York NY: Walker and Company, 2000.

Parishioners are entitled to stability and consistency in parish life from one pastor to the next. This assumes that Clergy have been trained to know that they are serving the local Church (diocese) and not themselves.

These are just a few of the forms of hypocrisy that one often encounters.

Chapter Fifteen The Male Priest and Same-Sex Attraction

"The number of men and women who have deep-seated homosexual tendencies is
not negligible. They do not choose their homosexual condition; for most of them it is a trial.
They must be accepted with respect, compassion, and sensitivity.
Every sign of unjust discrimination in their regard should be avoided.
These persons are called to fulfill God's will in their lives and, if they are Christians,
to unite to the sacrifice of the Lord's Cross the difficulties they may encounter from
their condition." (CCC 2358)

— — —

Introduction

The priesthood and the issue of same sex attraction has been a worthy concern for
theological reasons for two thousand years. In the twenty-first century, the political
pressure is on to avoid even considering the issue, but it is theologically significant.
Inside the Church, there is also a factor to be considered and that is that when one
does raise concerns some participants in the discussion have same-sex attraction.

First a definition: Homosexuality in a male "is a sustained condition or adaptation in
which erotic fantasy, attraction and arousal is predominately directed toward one's
own sex."[290]

(1) The Theology

The whole Judeo-Christian history involves two genders, male and female. This is an
intricate theological issue if one is not to settle on an ideology and then choose data
that substantiates one's decision. Obviously, this would not be truthful.

When considering gender, the fundamental principle, that recurs throughout the
history of salvation is, in the words of the moral theologian William E. May that:

> The more apparent anatomical differences between males and females, are as
> one contemporary writer puts it, 'not mere accidentals or mere attachments . .
> . [instead the] differences in the body are revelations of differences in the
> depths of their being.'[291]

Comprehending this sentence requires getting rid of the idea of a neutral ungendered
'humanity' because no actual neutral ungendered individual human being exists and
then (i) grasping the nature of ontological thinking itself and (ii) The meaning of the
phrase "in the depths of their being."

---

[290] J. Keefe, "Homosexuality," *New Catholic Encyclopedia*, 2nd ed., vol. 7, Detroit MI: Gale,
2003.
[291] William E. May, "Marriage and the complementarity of Male and Female," *Anthropotes*
VIII (1) June 1992, 45.

Ontological thinking is the mode of thought, where one considers being itself. It is this mode of thinking that grounds May's and the Church's moral thinking. In other words, it is thought drawing on the level of being and not at the far more superficial level of a political ploy or social fad. So, salvation history and all of the revelation that grounds the Natural Law approach are needed to find the meaning of human self-perception, participation in Christ's priesthood, human action in the specific issue of the priesthood and same sex attraction.

Many things about human beings simply cannot be known without divine revelation. The role of gender is one of those things. Now, the Natural Law approach essentially relies on human nature which is revelatory and is not decided by the exceptions. In contrast, the ideologically founded 'theologians' do not want to have the meaning of someone's self-perception and their actions lying outside of the control of the individual himself, or in other terms, they want the individual's self-perception to be under the control of a man-made ideology. This is odd because in every other field of human endeavor, except sexuality apparently, there is a larger field of meaning held by society, rooted in nature and revelation, to which the individual is expected to conform to some extent. One cannot run a business and ignore the rules of economics. One cannot construct buildings and ignore gravity. The list goes on. The rule applies to music and art and law etc. unless one is a leftist when nothing applies if they do not think it does.

As the best possible way for intellectual effort, John Paul II described the ontological kind of thinking:
[The] process of 'determining the meaning' would obviously have to take into account the many limitations of the human being, as existing in a body and in history. Furthermore, it would have to take into consideration the behavioral models and the meanings which the latter acquire in any given culture. Above all, it would have to respect the fundamental commandment of love of God and neighbor. (VS 47)
In other words, finding the meaning of actions, perceptions and situations of an individual inevitably involves more than oneself and one's own preferences. It involves the broad context of being itself. One must say again that theology is often only done based on the political currents in society, something that is not really theology—but that is a question for another time.

Above, John Paul II argued for the substantial role of ontology in the process of finding meaning. This mode of thought can be traced back into the Old Testament. Emmanuel Kant, for example, took the contrary and quite simply ideological position that ontology was *subjective* because Kant objected to getting knowledge from objects in general.[292] In other words, he rejected realism. He further did what leftists do, he accused his opponent of doing what he was doing, namely being subjective. In fact, Kant propagated the most extreme form of subjectivism! Once again, someone is following in the trend of Enlightenment thinking.

Back to ontological realism: According to the moral theologian, William May the Church's realist position more formally is that: "Ontology is a fundamental interpretation of the ultimate constituents of the world of experience. All these constituents—individuals with their attributes—have factors or aspects in common."[293]

The expression (ii) the "depths of one's being" requires some further examination. Aquinas simply speaks of the body being the expression of the soul but as was explained in Chapter Four, the person is most completely described as a body soul unity.

To start with, Catholic thought contributed the notion of person to the history of thought. Emmanuel Mounier, for example, formalizes the idea that already can be found in Jesus' teaching of love of God and love of neighbor. (Mark 12:30 - 31) This teaching includes a basically dynamic notion of being a person, going out of oneself in love. Mounier notes that the person "cannot do this by force of self-attention, but on the contrary by making himself available (Gabriel Marcel) and thereby more transparent to himself and others."[294] If this is true, then for the established homosexual male—'established' to get beyond the possibilities of unresolved gender dysphoria—there is a difficulty in loving in the Christian sense. (Note that I said 'difficulty'.) There is difficulty with achieving the selflessness of Christian love. This selflessness is not at the level of sexual attraction but at the level of conscious choice to the degree that it is free.

Sister Prudence Allen qualified this conclusion: "much of the identity [of the individual] is still set by biology and culture, [and] there is still a 'space' in which free will, choice, and capacity to change oneself can operate."[295] But ultimately the Church is not relying on a person's adaptability in the sense that an actor in a movie adapts to a role. He/she can switch it off when the camera's stop rolling. That is not the kind of person who incarnates Christ the Priest. (This was explained in Chapter Four.) This is because all of the 'layers' of his being do not move in the same direction. So, the

---

[292] Michelle Grier, "Kant's Critique of Metaphysics," *Stanford Encyclopedia of Philosophy*, Stanford: Stanford University, 2016.

[293] F. Siegfried, "Ontology," *The Catholic Encyclopedia*.

[294] Emmanuel Mounier, *Personalism*, Notre Dame: University of Notre Dame Press, 1952, 19.

[295] Prudence Allen, "Integral Sex complementarity and the Theology of Communion," *Communio* Vol 17.4 (Winter 1990), 535.

Church makes the distinction between a man *being* a spiritual father and *acting* like a spiritual father one occasion. Here, one might recall the words of Jean Galot cited earlier: "God is at work: he wants to gain possession of the whole person, and not only of the upper and visible layer, which is the person's activity."[296] In other words, the Church is relying on the ontological identity of the individual being compatible with the taking on of Christ.

(2) Spiritual Fatherhood

Obviously, the issue of identity can be expressed in terms of the capacity for spiritual fatherhood. (Also treated in chapter Four) The spiritual fatherhood of the priest is analogous to the physical and spiritual fatherhood of the male husband in the family. Now transpose the 'family' into the Church and the spiritual father into the priest and one has the direct analogy. Turning to the female gender complement of the spiritual father, one could say that: "God entrusts the human being to her in a special way, . . . precisely by reason of [her] femininity . . . always and in every way" (MD, 30). Here, the spiritual femininity of the Church is analogous to the female caring of a woman. As was noted earlier, the feminine also involves "that [which] makes a person secure in nature and in being."[297]

Following the analogy still further: when speaking of the husband, John Paul II says: "in many ways he has to learn his own 'fatherhood' from the mother." (MD 18) In the same way, the priest has to learn how to deepen his fatherhood using cues from Christ and his Church. Note Well: The making of the ontological analogies has all kinds of biblical exemplars at its base. The Bible is, after all, largely a collection of ontological statements.

The Vatican II document on priests simply states that "priests of the New Testament, in virtue of the sacrament of Orders, exercise the most outstanding and necessary office of father and teacher among and for the People of God." (PO 9)

To summarize: the Church has a theology of the presence of Jesus Christ in his Church that leads to understanding of the priesthood in Christ as spiritual fatherhood in a male individual who has been taken over by Christ. This chapter has only given the briefest sketch of some of the consequences of the maleness of Christ and its consequences as preparation for a consideration of Church teaching on the subject. (This was examined in detail in Chapter Four.)

(3) Church Teaching

Over the years, the Church has issued a number of disciplinary documents on the management of candidates with same-sex attraction. However, the teaching on the

---

[296] Jean Galot, 202.
[297] Ibidem.

issues with Clergy who have same-sex attractionis not merely disciplinary. The Catholic priesthood is theological in nature as was hopefully apparent in the preceding text.

The correct starting point for the theological argument is the role of the Church as the Body of Christ (Cf. I Corinthians 12) and as the context of the priesthood. Everything to do with priesthood happens in the ecclesial context. Hence, first of all: "Anyone who thinks he recognizes the signs of God's call to the ordained ministry must humbly submit his desire to the authority of the Church." (CCC 1578) Subsequently, the Church herself is responsible for conferring the sacrament and, in all of this, there is nothing like a right to ordination.

Moreover, various relationships in the Church involve sexual complementarity. So, when for example, in 1961, John XXIII issued a statement entitled: *Religiosorum Institutio*, "Careful Selection and Training of Candidates for the States of Perfection and Sacred Orders," it stated that: "Advancement to religious vows and ordination should be barred to those who are afflicted with evil tendencies to homosexuality or pederasty, since for them the common life and the priestly ministry would constitute serious dangers." (art. 30) Just to be clear—the evil present has to do with expressing these tendencies in actions. The instruction was prepared by the Congregation for Religious and they were very conscious that relating interpersonally is a central part of the life of religious men or religious women in community. Relating in an ordered way is also crucial to the men in priestly ministry.

Now on one level this is a psychological statement where certain theological realities (religious communities and priestly ministry) depend on certain underlying psycho-spiritual realities for their functioning. On another level, the theology says that there is the integral gendered complementarity in the relationships that are being discussed. In the case of religious communities, people with same-sex erotic attractions can wreak havoc in the operation of a same-sex community where relations between members are only to be based on the love of neighbor and love of God. Erotic same-sex relationships contain the thread of erotic 'love' that contradicts the unprejudiced love of neighbor. The contradiction lies in the nature of love itself.

Theologically, love is wishing for the good of the other, not wishing for exclusive relationship or the simulation of sexual involvement. The generation and progress of the community in Christ cannot be subordinated to the desires of one or two individuals—or in some places to a whole homosexual subculture. Individuals do not have the priority in the development of the whole Christian community for the mission of the Church.

Moreover, even from a purely sociological view, the common habitual dynamics of immature men's groups with the boy's clubs, the loners, and so on, create enough difficulties in the seminary and in presbyteries without looking at the problems of men forming couples, with all of the exclusiveness and self-centeredness that that entails. The problems simply multiply when one considers the problems caused by a whole subculture forming inside the hierarchy of the Church.

For priests, the same concerns ensue. The priest is to love his people and not only occasionally. This has nothing to do with erotic attraction at all—hence the term *spiritual* fatherhood. Fatherhood is a state of being. Demonstrating evangelical love—wishing for and working for the good of the other person according to God's will—actually gets sidelined by erotic attraction. Again, the needs of the man-who-would-be-priest do not have the priority in the mission of the Church. The priest showing Gospel love to the faithful is primary.

Lastly, in John XXIII's 1961 document, the authors left the responsibility for applying the various standards, that they had described, to the Bishop. They are not clear how this would be done. But it comes down to a judgement call just as it does for candidates with other issues. In conclusion then, the homosexual candidate is being held to the same standards as the heterosexual candidate. Each candidate has to be developed and able to show Gospel love as completely as he can and at least not to have major psychological issues or spiritual issues that will impair their work as priests. Laypeople do not deserve second-best just as the candidate does not deserve to be a priest unless called by the Church.

A later Vatican document added more detail to the psychological and spiritual picture regarding Clergy. From the Congregation for the Doctrine of the Faith (CDF), there came a very nuanced statement, the "Declaration on Certain Questions Concerning Sexual Ethics" (Dec. 29, 1975). The CDF said that: "A distinction is drawn, and it seems with some reason, between homosexuals whose tendency comes from a false education, from a lack of normal sexual development, from habit, from bad example, or from other similar causes, and is transitory or at least not incurable; and homosexuals who are definitively such because of some kind of innate instinct or a pathological constitution judged to be incurable." (n. 8) This is the Church's understanding of the homosexual orientation according to the best non-political research available. This formulation carries an enormous burden that is not stated and that is that the seminary is not the place for 'working on' these issues. Bishops desperate for pastors cannot be the disinterested authorities needed to keep their seminary focused on its original task and not becoming a therapeutic clinic.

In fact, the CDF did later qualify their statement by saying that: "Considerable difficulties still beset efforts to reach a sound understanding of the homosexual orientation itself from an authentically Christian perspective. Behavioral and social scientists offer no clear or uniform account of this orientation in terms of its genesis, exclusivity, permanence or other related questions. Confronted with obscure data and often conflicting interpretations from within the scientific community, the Church disowns any pretense at 'an exhaustive treatment' of the 'complex' homosexual question, remaining open to enlightenment from the human sciences while confident of its own "more global vision ... [of] the rich reality of the human person." (CDF 1986, n. 2) The phrase 'authentically Christian perspective' is the key to their words. Christian hermeneutics is where the Church is grounding its search for the meaning of its priesthood in the revelation in Christ. Either Christ is the meaning of the world or he isn't. The Church says that he is which means that political considerations about acceptance of candidates do not even enter the search for meaning on any issue including this one.

Consequently, theologians could and did say certain things, such as in the following summary of the doctrine in the same document: "God ... fashions mankind male and female, in his own image and likeness. Human beings, ... in the complementarity of the sexes, ... are called to reflect the inner reality of the Creator. They do this in a striking way in their cooperation with Him in the transmission of life by a mutual donation of the self to the other.... Homosexual activity is not a complementary union, able to transmit life; and so, it thwarts the call to a life of that form of self-giving which the Gospel says is the essence of Christian living." (CDF 1986, nn. 5-7). The unhindered self-giving is among the things being sought in candidates.

The Church's most extensive document on the *theological* aspects of homosexuality and priesthood came from the Congregation for Catholic Education, which is responsible for the regulation of seminaries. The document has the lengthy title of: "Instruction Concerning the Criteria for the Discernment of Vocations with regard to Persons with Homosexual Tendencies in view of their Admission to the Seminary and to Holy Orders." (4 November 2005) The document was signed and approved for publication by Benedict XVI.

First of all, the document describes the nature of affective maturity and spiritual fatherhood. Behind these words lies the fact that in the Incarnation, Jesus Christ is male, *and* he is the perfect human being, which means among other things that he can love in an ordered way in any situation. It is by participating in the being of Christ that the priest can function fully and not just on occasion. The way that the document portrays it: "Because of this configuration to Christ, the entire life of the sacred minister must be animated by the gift of his whole person to the Church and by an authentic pastoral charity." (art. 1) The phrases 'whole person' and 'authentic pastoral charity' get to the nub of the problem when considering someone who is dominated by erotic same-sex attraction.

Briefly: behind the phrase 'whole person', there lies the concept of the mature person who is able to bring all of his powers of body and soul to bear *for* others in any situation in an ordered fashion because of who he is (ontology). As Jean Galot said earlier: this argument is based on the fact that "God is at work: he wants to gain possession of the whole person, and not only of the upper and visible layer, which is the person's activity."[298] His loyalty is not divided by some personal affections that detract from what he can offer in a situation. The same would apply to a priest who has a mistress on the side or a drinking problem, or a gambling problem. Someone being at ease with a divided loyalty will show itself in other things, for example, when the priest does not pray the Office or celebrate daily Mass or put forward Church teaching.

Though the problem is deeper than that. As always, God features in the full comprehension of the relationship between a priest and the faithful. So, as Paul described it, in the adverse cases just mentioned: "They [have] exchanged the truth of God for a lie and revered and worshiped the creature rather than the creator, who is blessed forever." (Romans 1:25) The issue comes down to idolatry something rarely mentioned in discussions. In other words, the issue has a supernatural dimension. It is not merely a sociological issue. The Church cannot have Clergy setting up this-worldly religions (a problem already raised in the case where people hold counter-Catholic views. Chapter Nine) because they counter to the preaching of the Gospel by word or by example.

Paul gave us the basic principle of Catholicism that applies here: "None of us lives for oneself, and no one dies for oneself. For if we live, we live for the Lord, and if we die, we die for the Lord; so then, whether we live or die, we are the Lord's." (Romans 14:7-8) In other words, there are no 'compartments' in the psyche of the individual who is baptized.

The other phrase in the document refers to 'authentic pastoral charity', refers to the priest's commitment to love. Scripture deals exhaustively with the nature of evangelical love, which is the kind of love that is 'authentic'. Moreover, it is 'pastoral' in that it 'pastors' the recipients of this love. They know that they are relating to someone who is there solely for their good and who has the goal of their heavenly beatitude as his sole preoccupation. The priest himself does not have any other goal in life. He has no divided loyalties.

Next, the document treats homosexuality and the priesthood. Among other things, the Congregation for Religious Education states the teaching—one paragraph of which was subsequently used in the *Catechism* and was quoted at the beginning of this

---

[298] Jean Galot, 350.

chapter. The Congregation could not accept as candidates for seminary training, those who "practise homosexuality, present deep-seated homosexual tendencies or support the so-called 'gay culture'." (art. 2) These behaviors undermine so many aspects of Catholic teaching that they can only be stated here: the understanding of love; of manhood and womanhood; of the understanding of marriage; of the understanding of sexuality and sexual morality; of the understanding of community; of the understanding of Christian Church; of the understanding of the Incarnation and so on.

Thirdly, the document explains the 'discernment by the Church concerning the suitability of candidates. Evidently, there are two forces at play in the vocation of the priest: the gift of God and the graced freedom of the candidate. The former is guaranteed. The latter depends on many factors. So, at the foundation of the individual man's priesthood lies "the particular importance of human formation as the necessary foundation of all formation." (art.3) Again the Church is relying on its far-ranging knowledge of human beings that can only come from the scriptures and the tradition.

Moreover, the centrality of the humanity of the individual is emphasized in a perhaps unexpected way. The document is clear that: "It is understood that the candidate himself has the primary responsibility for his own formation." (art. 3) It is a sign of his maturity that he himself takes on his formation and all of the theological implications that go with it. The mature student recognizes the true nature of the priesthood means that "he must offer himself trustingly to the [repeated] discernment of the Church." (art. 3) The theology of the Catholic priesthood cannot be handled in terms of individual rights. The primary right is that of the Church to be so manned as to best be able to do its mission according to what it knows about the priesthood, the Church and humanity.

(4) Conclusion

In its conclusion, the document points to one final way in which the candidate's human development is involved: "It would be gravely dishonest for a candidate to hide his own homosexuality in order to proceed, despite everything, towards ordination. Such a deceitful attitude does not correspond to the spirit of truth, loyalty and availability that must characterize the personality of he who believes he is called to serve Christ and his Church in the ministerial priesthood." Honesty is a central trait when responding justly to the Church that is founded on truth and preaches the truth. This also applies to the situation of the homosexual candidate. It characterizes the presence of Christ in the world that the candidate hopes to participate in, in the unique way that it comes about in the Catholic priesthood in a man.

Chapter Sixteen A Nation of Priests

> Without priests the Church would not be able to live that fundamental obedience
> which is at the very heart of her existence and her mission in history. John Paul II

In an age when there is such confusion about what leadership is, even in the secular world, the concept of the priesthood has gotten muddled too. Some priests and bishops do not want to lead, either consciously or unconsciously echoing the Enlightenment conviction that the Church is not meant to lead because that is reserved for the cultural elite. Coupled with these problems there is the problem of a decreasing degree of the expression of fatherhood among men and the atheism that accompanies it in the culture.[299]

The confusion over leading either goes in the direction of the blind following of an elite (Enlightenment) or the complete denial of the need to acknowledge someone's leadership in one's life at all. (Sin) Strangely this occurs in people who will obey a clock, or a weather report but in matters of their salvation, they know more than the expert which is the Church. Paul VI called the Church "the expert on humanity" with good reason.[300] It is not because of any natural competence on the part of its members but because the Church is the custodian of the meaning of God's revelation in Jesus Christ. Through the fog of human error and sometimes deliberate obstruction, one can and will find, what is needed to live best before God.

The Catholic Church is the primordially humane institution in the world in the area of its competence which is faith and morals. It can even be the template for institutions that aim to give human beings their best chance of flourishing before God here on earth. *Ex corde ecclesiae* is just one text that suggests how possible this is. This proposition flies in the face of Enlightenment conviction that the Church is oppressive, evil and at best only useful for private devotion for those who are not fully developed. One only has to look at the streams of good people, good institutions and works of charity that the Church has contributed to human history. This does not even begin to cover the avalanche of prayer by the Church for people and situations, whose effects we will only learn at the end of time. Even more this proposal leaves out the millions of hours of worship of Almighty God and the corresponding flood of graces for humanity and the ordering of the world.

The word 'template' (above) does not imply that priests must run institutions. That would be stupid because that is not why they are ordained and there are all kinds of

---

[299] Paul C. Vitz, *Father of the Fatherless: The Psychology of Atheism*, Dallas TX: Spence Publishing, 1999.
[300] Paul VI, Speech to the United Nations, October 4, 1965.

specialized knowledge that priests do not have. Priests are called to lead the Church and convert the world to God which is where their competence lies. What priests do usually have is a knowledge of man, man before God, of the community before God, of the nation before God and of the world before God. This knowledge helps priests offer the sacraments, prayer and do pastoral work. If they don't have this knowledge, then they should leave the priesthood.

Correct knowledge is part of leadership. This book highlights the role of the intellectual dimension of the life of the Church. It is the Body of the Word of God, after all. Once one forgets trying to reframe the Church as a political agent, then the nature of the real role of presence of the Church comes to the fore. Politics does not handle the truth very well mainly because it does not have to. The seeking of power is more dependent on manipulating truth and people. The truth of the Church is the one dimension of the Church that throws light on the sinfulness and concupiscence of the clergy and laity.

Priests are called by Jesus Christ into a hierarchy, a sacred leadership in the Church. This leadership is by divine mandate and is structured according to the priesthood of Jesus Christ and only by the power of Jesus Christ who gave it its form by fulfilling the Mosaic Law. Then the Church becomes the central form of grace and truth out of a number of ways that the grace and power of Jesus reaches people in this world.

The Mosaic Law involved a moral law, a cultic law and a jurisdictional law. Christ fulfilled these three necessary ways of ordering human society under God's "mighty hand." (I Peter 5:6) They then continue to be applied in a Christological way in the life of the Church. A number of consequences follow from these events.

First, despite a lot of propaganda in the sixties about all religions being the same—a leftist fantasy by the way—the Church is not just one church among many. (See Vatican II and *Dominus iesus*.) The leftist's conclusion comes from an agnostic comparative anthropology born of Enlightenment thinking and is not what is known from revelation. (Cf. *Dominus iesus*) Vatican II never taught this idea. Levelling out the Church and ecclesial communities and making them homogenous does no credit to the nature and quality of God's revelation or the work of the Divine Missions. This kind of fatalism paralyses the priest in his pastoral work. Meaning no disrespect to ecclesial communities and religions, if he thinks this way, the priest cannot extend the reign of Christ "who is the Way, the Truth and the life." (John 14:6) If Jesus Christ is not the Savior of the world the priest might as well go and get a job.

If Christ is the Savior, then teachings like Vatican II's Dogmatic Constitution *Gaudium et spes*, Constitution of the Church in the Modern World begin to make sense. Hidden in this text is the fundamental fact that Catholicism is universal truth. It is true for all of humanity, all the time, in every circumstance. Losing the Catholicity of the truth undercuts the grand scope of the death and resurrection of Jesus. The priest has to operate with the clear vision that Jesus is meant to embrace the whole world because he holds the ultimate meaning for the whole world and the grace that it so badly needs. As was indicated earlier, the problem for clergy is when they—out of a false sense of their own superiority—try to mix Catholic elements of teaching and with doctrine from their political party, for example. Then, Catholicism merely becomes window dressing for what some other organization is really doing and that is executing a push for power and threatening society. The modern Jacobins are terrifying because they use common words and symbols for the destruction of the society that has a real grasp of what those words and symbols mean.

Embracing the whole world means countering sin in all of its forms. Hence the reason for beginning this work with a study of the mystery of iniquity. In that chapter, there is a lot of theological anthropology. This includes a proper understanding of what sin is. It definitely requires much more than good intentions to stamp an action as a good action, one worthy of a human being. A Catholic cannot choose a bad means to a good end, for example. This is where the way of true love parts company with the way of power. The way of power allows immature people to overlook some or all of the requirements of a good act. They let go of the demands of their humanity by doing this, where to be fully human, they really have to do the heavy lifting of evaluating all of the criteria of a potential action. They cannot follow politicians who they know are going to act badly or promote antihuman policies, for example. They cannot even know if the politician or his/her policies are bad *unless* they go back to the Church and at the very least get into the *Catechism*.

In thinking and behaving politically, there seems to be an attraction to vicariously living the life of people who hate, bully and insult. In the TV series called the Sopranos, Tony Soprano's wife has to warn off a priest who is hanging around the family. She understands why he does it because she knows what her husband does for a living and she warns him off. Today it is so odd to see priests who are ordained in Christ speaking about someone in the vilest possible way just like their congressional representative does. Perhaps it lets their egos out for a trot free of constraints? This is yet another way that a priest is separate. The priest is not free to do this. Once again, the 20 minute rule applies!

Catholicism is a way of conversion towards following the will of God 24/7. Hence, the emphasis on obedience in the caption at the top of the chapter. Secondly, as the presence of Christ, Catholicism is one important instrument for the healing of the communion of humanity, as well as the communion of the faithful. If someone is still as mean as they were five years ago, then someone else, a superior or a spiritual director is not doing their job.

Sin affects the operation of the intellect and the will. This has been repeatedly mentioned. Meeting so many Catholics who imagine that they have "arrived" and yet are vicious unforgiving people is a salutary reminder of this fact. In the minds of these individuals, they do not need to forego certain kinds of behavior and grow in grace. Hence, some grasp of what is sinful is essential for clergy. Sin means that people do not choose their true good. Meeting some of those who consider themselves perfect made it essential to mention the ways that evil distorts the intellect and the will. This discovery indicates that people are not as knowledgeable as they imagine, and they are never as loving as they imagine.

The study of the priesthood reaches into the heart of what Jesus came to do. At the same time, it grasps the core of what it means to be human. Jesus is perfectly divine and also the perfect human being. The Enlightenment reduction of Jesus Christ to just another human in history, perhaps not even very good, is an effort to give society a place in defining the human which it is never going to do very well. This is a powerful way to move beyond Christ and use notable figures of today as the 'Christ's' of today. The theology of the Catholic Church is most decidedly "in" Christ for all time. It is because of malice or a want of a proper comprehension of Christ that people reduce him to an artefact of the past.

Now they can meet him in the present in the episcopate and their priests. The fullness of the presence of Jesus Christ resides in the Catholic episcopate. The episcopate and their assistant priests are empowered as the face of the Father in Christ as he serves his people and the world at large. Once again, the theme of obedience and its accompanying humility enters in! This demands men who are both humble enough to follow the will of God and humble enough to lead others under the will of God.

Given the waves of scandals, the episcopate has an enormous task ahead of it, namely, to again manifest publicly what the theology of the bishop says it should be. The mix of the sceptical atmosphere engendered by the Enlightenment Age on top of the scandals trapped the Church in what looked like a self-fulfilling prophecy. The Enlightenment had been saying how predatory the Church is and here was proof. In the slippery way modern culture uses statistics, the bad actions of a few clergy look as if they characterize the entire priesthood. Of course, this is not to excuse even one act of abuse. The other unmentioned component in the modern moral situation is the high degree of abuse of kids in families. (Over 90% of abuse cases occur in families.)

This brings us back at the issue of leadership. The middle-class culture is seductive in that it allows clergy in general to take on the trappings of the middle-class and to blend in, in the process. This blending in includes allowing clergy to be deeply divided along political lines and again to resemble the culture and its godlessness. Theology calls for an undivided clergy because they are not much use if they follow an ideology of division or even if they merely allow it to occur. Also, they were not ordained to use Church positions and Church money to support political movements. Not only does it show that they do not get what their position in society actually is, but they also do not understand that they are separated in certain ways from that society. The priestly society has a different comprehension of morality which they can be expected to live out, both when it is convenient and when it is inconvenient. They have a different understanding of what it means to be human, what it means to be a community or a society. They have a different comprehension of what institutions are for, what a nation is for.

Thus understood, the priesthood does not stand between Christ and human beings in a kind of pictorial understanding that again was and is the caricature that the Enlightenment opposed. They sometimes had good reason for this where priests were using their roles for personal power i.e. not being true priests. However, the true priest is not 'in the way of' Revelation, rather he is drawn into the priesthood of Christ and so becomes transparent to the presence of his master. So much so, that others can see Christ in him.

The transparency of the priest only becomes possible to the degree that he is poor and humble of heart. The choice of Saint John Vianney as the Patron Saint of Pastors was not accidental. He comes forward as a Christlike figure and not as the presence of one of the cultural stereotypes of the age such as the omniscient one (like the cult of Steve Jobs), or the romantic one (like the cult of Che Guevara), like the wealthy one (like the cult of Bill Gates) or the celebrity (like the cult of some movie star). The authentic priest is simply Christ in this place and time—being listened to or not being listened to.

This priest is a man of Scripture. The presence of so many other books and media have displaced the felt primacy of Scripture. Just as other media take time so too does the reading of Scripture and the proper *lectio divina*. The priest is a man of the Eucharist. Not only is it central to his reason for being where he is, it is his most imminent encounter with his Lord. Vianney did not spend hours before the Blessed Sacrament for no reason. He was going to see a friend.

The personal mystery of the priest is that he is priest body and soul. He has all kinds of special graces, but he still is free to skim along the surface of life, to be just like pagan men of his age, seeking comfort and the good life.

Because he is priest body and soul, and not just occupationally, he will be expected to be like the Father of a family in many respects. He is generative in a masculine way, so he will have to motivate and lead as well as comfort and empathize with his flock. He is not doing this because he took a program but because that is what mature men do. They are sufficiently developed emotionally that they do not expect every situation to have a pay-off or to be encouraging for them. They have a certain self-sufficiency. As Theresa of Avila once said: "God is enough." They do enough prayer and meditation to find their support, even in very difficult circumstances, in that time with God. He is secure enough that he can learn new things if what he knows does not work. He is secure enough that a failure does not mean the total end of everything.

On the other hand, he is comfortable around women and men. He can listen to them and converse with them and not expect more out of the situation than he gets. He will be meeting people who have not had the opportunities for development that he has had. Yet, somehow with the insight that comes from Christ, he can leave people more graced than when he met them. His intense following of love of neighbour means in his case that he is selfless enough to focus totally on the other person.

The leadership role of clergy in society means using the 'apartness' of the bishop or priest to set up new dynamics in society. Clergy are a "people set apart." (Deuteronomy 7:6) The bishop or the priest is not in thrall to the rich and powerful so he can speak forthrightly whenever he finds a platform, even if it is only a street corner. Of course, he has to know what to say otherwise he is just another voice gibbering in the street. The author Georges Bernanos was fascinated by the struggle of the bishop or priest to bring some light into apparently frozen dark situations that people get themselves into. (*The Diary of a Country Priest* is just one example.) He also wrote copiously on Catholicism in relation to larger questions, some that lay people have to get involved in.

Leadership goes beyond having formal dinners and chasing after the rich. It means getting involved with local soup kitchens and feeding the poor. It means helping those in law enforcement and education and the other public services that make society a place where all people can flourish. There is a place for conversation with faculty and students at universities, and not just Catholic ones, although they are often in the biggest trouble. Catholicism is a meant for the marketplace, much like Paul's speech at the Areopagus.

I mentioned civilization in the chapters on pastoral work and also the one on the Laity. Working from the perspective of civilization again offers a thought-through addition to how people view their situation. The sense of the family as a school opens up all kinds possibilities for husbands and wives to appreciate each other and their kids as they look at things going on all the way from having fun to helping the homeless. It also helps husbands and wives to grasp how much time they owe each other and their children. It obliges people to challenge how their work and their social set structure the dynamics at the heart of their family. One highly successful comedian once said that to succeed in that business, you have to say to your nine-year old son: cheers I will see you again when you are thirty-one.

Having observed the scandals from the outside and the pandemic from inside, there is a lot to be said for the working of Church structures as they are. There is a momentum to the structure that is already established. Training and ordinations continue. Then too, some serious steps are being taken to improve reporting by seminarians and female religious so that they are heard and responded to. In some places some dramatic steps are being taken to deal with perceived flaws in the structure such as the Archdiocese of Freiburg in Germany that is going from 1000 parishes to 40 megaparishes.

Whether this makes sense or not, I have no idea, but at least we can see that the administration sees a problem and is trying to respond. However, dioceses are not filled with experts. Unless there is a good Catholic university there will not be too many orthodox theologians available. Usually the finance department of the diocese has some competent accountants. But in the specialized areas of demographics, architecture etc. again there are not too many people to whom one can turn. Reorganizing parishes is something to be approached carefully and with a lot of discussion and communication seeing that they are part of the heritage of the diocese. Being an ignorant outsider, I would just ask if the Archdiocese has even tried going out to find fallen-away Catholics and talk with them. Has the Bishop tried it? Have clergy tried it? Have Laity tried it? Talking with them would reveal a lot of information and it may be helpful in diocesan initiatives. It is a time when people can learn that they belong to a diocese and that it is not just an administrative unit but a community around the bishop.

Around the world, the Church is very evidently in some real pain right now: there are the crushing efforts of the Government of China to remake Catholicism there; there are the attacks on Christians in India and also various Moslem countries such as Egypt. There are attacks by gangs on Church communities in East Africa and West Africa. There are the burnings of churches across Europe and so on. Then, too every country is going to have to deal with the pandemic as we wait for a vaccine. The pain should take us back to the essentials: we follow Christ crucified as Paul did.

On top of these terrible things there is the subtle and not so subtle creep of leftist ideas into government and legislation. Since the governments that produce this legislation and administrative orders were always partially voted in by Catholics, one wonders if the old adage by Lenin is true: capitalists will sell you the rope with which to hang them. John Paul II's call for re-evangelization was not far off the mark.

God's injunction that "I will put my spirit within you so that you walk in my statutes, observe my ordinances, and keep them" (Ezekiel 36:27) is still relevant today.

Bibliography

Prudence Allen, "Integral Sex complementarity and the Theology of Communion," *Communio* Vol 17.4 (Winter 1990), 535.

Thomas Aquinas, *Commentary on the Sentences*, trans. Scott M. Sullivan, at https://scottmsullivan.com/AquinasWorks/Sentences.html

Thomas Aquinas, *Questiones disputatae de veritate*, https://dhspriory.org/thomas/QDdeVer10.htm#5

Thomas Aquinas, *On Evil*, Richard Regan trans., Oxford: Oxford University Press, 2003.

Augustine of Hippo, *Book of the 83 Questions*, Q. 12, *The Fathers of the Church 70*, Washington DC: Catholic University Press, 1982.

Augustine of Hippo, *Concerning the City of God against the Pagans*, London: Penguin Books, 2003.

J. Arendzen, "Gnosticism," *Catholic Encyclopedia*, Washington DC: CUA Press, 2006.

Hadley Arkes, "The Church and Socialism: The Fallacy that will not go away," *The Catholic Thing*, September 10, 2019, at https://www.thecatholicthing.org/2019/09/10/the-church-and-socialism-the-fallacy-that-will-not-go-away/

Johann Auer, Joseph Ratzinger, *Dogmatic Theology 6: A General Doctrine of the Sacraments and the Mystery of the Eucharist*, Washington DC: CUA Press, 1995.

Augustine, *Concerning the City of God against the Pagans*, London: Penguin Books, 2003.Augustine, Tractate 123 (John 21:12-19).

Augustine, *Tractates on the Gospel of John*, Nicene and Post-Nicene Fathers, First Series, Vol. 7. Edited by Philip Schaff. (Buffalo, NY: Christian Literature Publishing Co., 1888.)

Attorney-General William Barr, Remarks to the Law School and the de Nicola Center for Ethics and Culture at the University of Notre Dame, South Bend, IN, Friday, October 11, 2019.

Benedict XVI, Encyclical Letter *Deus Caritas Est* (25 December 2005).

Benedict XVI, "The Church and the Scandal of Child-abuse," Catholic News Agency, https://www.catholicnewsagency.com/news/full-text-of-benedict-xvi-the-church-and-the-scandal-of-sexual-abuse-59639

Bevil Bramwell OMI, *Laity: Beautiful, Good and True*, (Amazon: 2012).

Cambridge University, *Cambridge Business English Dictionary*, Cambridge: Cambridge University Press, 2018.

Center for Applied Research in the Apostolate, *Frequently requested Church Statistics*, Washington DC, CARA, 2019.

Ron Chernow, *Grant*, New York: Penguin Press, 2017.

Catholic Church, *The Roman Missal*, New Jersey: Catholic Book Publishing Corp, 2011.

Hillary Clinton, "There is only the Fight: An Analysis of the Alinsky Model." https://en.wikipedia.org/wiki/Hillary_Rodham_senior_thesis

Yves Congar OP, *The Word and the Spirit*, London: Harper & Row, 1986.

Peter Damian, *The Book of Gomorrah and St. Peter Damian's Struggle against Ecclesiastical Corruption*, Matthew Cullinan Hoffman trans., New Braunfehls Texas: Ite ad Thomam Books, 2015.

Michael Dauphinais and Matthew Levering, *Knowing the Love of Christ*, Notre Dame IN: University of Notre Dame Press, 2002.

Henri de Lubac, *Catholicism – A Study of the Corporate Destiny of Mankind*, New York. NY: Sheed and Ward, 1950.

Henri de Lubac, *The Splendour of the Church*, San Francisco, Ignatius Press, 1986.

Henri de Lubac, *Catholicism – A Study of the Corporate Destiny of Mankind*, New York. NY: Sheed and Ward, 1950

Denis Diderot, *Encyclopédie*, or its original title, *Dictionnaire raisonné des sciences, des arts et des métiers*. 1751-1772.

K.F Dougherty, "Atonement," *New Catholic Encyclopedia*, Gale Publishing: Detroit MI, 2003.

Avery Dulles S.J., "The Criteria of Catholic Theology," *Communio* (22), 1995.

J.B. Endres, "Appropriation," *New Catholic Encyclopedia*, Detroit MI: Gale, 2003.

A. Fortesque, "Liturgy," *The Catholic Encyclopedia*. New York: Robert Appleton Company. 1910.

Francis, motu proprio, *Vos estis lux mundi*, came out 7 May 2019.

Peter Fritsche, *Life and Death in the Third Reich*, Boston: Belknap Harvard University Press, 2008.

Jean Galot, *Theology of the Priesthood*, San Francisco: Ignatius Press, 1985.

Jonah Goldberg, *Liberal Fascism – The Secret History of the American Left from Mussolini to the Politics of Meaning*, New York: Doubleday, 2017.

Gregory of Nyssa, On the Making of Man, *Nicene and Post-Nicene Fathers*, Second Series, Vol. 5. Edited by Philip Schaff and Henry Wace. (Buffalo, NY: Christian Literature Publishing Co., 1893.)

Michelle Grier, "Kant's Critique of Metaphysics," *Stanford Encyclopedia of Philosophy*, Stanford: Stanford University, 2016.

Alois Grillmeier, "III Christology," *Encyclopedia of Theology – A Concise Sacramentum Mundi*, Karl Rahner ed., London: Burns and Oates, 1975.

Klaus Hemmerle, "Power," *Encyclopedia of Theology: The Concise Sacramentum Mundi*, ed. Karl Rahner s.j., London: Burns and Oates, 1975.

International Theological Commission, The Reciprocity between Faith and Sacraments in the Sacramental Economy, December 19, 2019.

John Jay College of Criminal Justice – The City University of New York, *The Nature and Scope of Sexual Abuse of Minors by Catholic Priests and Deacons in the United States 1950-2002* USCCB 2004, 24.

John Paul II, *Angelus* (Jan. 14, 1990), 2: *L'Osservatore Romano*, Jan. 15-16, 1990.
John Paul II, *Fides et ratio,* Boston MA: Pauline Books & Media, 1998.

John Paul II, *Pastores dabo vobis*, Post-Synodal Apostolic Exhortation, 1992.

John Paul II, *Veritatis splendor*, August 6, 1993.

John Paul II, *Letter to Families*, February 2, 1994.

John Paul II, Apostolic Letter *Rosarium Virginis Mariae* (16 October 2002), 21: AAS 95 (2003).

John Paul II, *Man and Woman He created them – A Theology of the Body*, ed. Michael Waldstein, Boston: Pauline Books, 2006.

Andrew Willard Jones, *Before Church and State: A Study of Social Order in the Sacramental Kingdom of St. Louis IX*, Steubenville: Emmaus Academic Press, 2017.

Kevin Jones, "Pennsylvania Grand Jury's Catholic Sex-Abuse Report Gets a Fact-Check", NCR, January 14, 2019.

Charles Cardinal Journet, *The Theology of the Church*, San Francisco: Ignatius Press, 2004.

Walter Kasper, "III. The Theology of History," *Encyclopedia of Theology – A Concise Sacramentum Mundi*, Karl Rahner S.J. ed., Burns and Oates: London, 1975.

J. Keefe, "Homosexuality," *New Catholic Encyclopedia*, 2nd ed., vol. 7, Detroit MI: Gale, 2003.

Philip Lawler, *The Faithful departed—The Collapse of Boston's Catholic Culture*, New York: Encounter Books, 2010.

R.T. Lawrence, "Conversion, II (Theology of)." *New Catholic Encyclopedia*, 2nd ed., vol. 4, Gale, 2003.

Matthew Levering, *Scripture and Metaphysics – Aquinas and the Renewal of Trinitarian Theology*, Blackwell Publishing, 2004.

Fr. Dwight Longenecker, "Why was the McCarrick abuse hushed up?", https://dwightlongenecker.com/why-was-the-mccarrick-abuse-hushed-up/

Alfred Marshall, *The RSV Interlinear Greek-English New Testament*, Grand Rapids MI: Zondervan 1968.

Bronwen Catherine McShea, "Bishops Unbound- The History behind today's Crisis of Church Leadership," *First Things*, January 2019.12.

Karen McQuillan, "Barack Obama populated the US Government with Communists," The American Thinker, https://www.lifesitenews.com/opinion/barack-obama-populated-the-us-government-with-communists

Alfred Marshall, ed. *The RSV Interlinear Greek-English New Testament*, Grand Rapids MI: Zondervan Publishing House, 1970.

William May, *An Introduction to Moral Theology*, Huntington IN: Our Sunday Visitor Publishing, 1994.

W.E. May, "Personalist Ethics," *New Catholic Encyclopedia*. Vol XI, Detroit MI: 2003.

William E. May "Marriage and the Complementarity of Male and Female." *Anthropotes* VIII (1) June 1992.

Alfred Monnin, *Life of Saint John-Baptist Vianney: Curé of Ars*, London: Burns and Oates, 1907.

Emmanuel Mounier, *Personalism*, Notre Dame: University of Notre Dame Press, 1952.

Bernard Nodet, *Le curé d'Ars. Sa pensée – Son cœur*, éd. Xavier Mappus, Foi Vivante, 1966.

Stephen O'Shea, *The Perfect Heresy – The Revolutionary Life and Death of the Medieval Cathars*, New York NY: Walker and Company, 2000.

Paul VI, Discourse to the Roman Clergy (June 24, 1963): AAS 55 (1963), 674.

Pius XII, *Miranda Prorsus*, September 8, 1947.

D.N. Power, "Ministry", *New Catholic Encyclopedia*. 2nd Edition, Detroit MI: Gale, 2003.

John Jay College of Criminal Justice - The City University of New York, *The Nature and Scope of Sexual Abuse of Minors by Catholic Priests and Deacons in the United States 1950 -2002*, USCCB 2004.

Joseph Ratzinger, *Introduction to Christianity*, San Francisco: 1990.

Joseph Cardinal Ratzinger, Declaration, *Dominus Iesus*, Congregation for the Doctrine of the Faith, August 6, 2000.

Joseph Cardinal Ratzinger, *Truth and Tolerance: Christian Belief and World Religions*, San Francisco: Ignatius Press, 2004.

Sacred Congregation for Catholic Education, "The Theological formation of Future Priests" (February 22, 1976), No.100.

Peter M.J. Stravinskas, Homily, April 5 2007, St. Thérèse of Lisieux: A guide to understand, appreciate the holy priesthood, *Catholic World Report*, April 22, 2019.

Simon Schama, *Citizens - A Chronicle of the French Revolution*, New York: Thrift Books, 1989.

Peter M.J. Stravinskas, Homily, April 5 2007, "St. Thérèse of Lisieux: A guide to understand, appreciate the holy priesthood," *Catholic World Report*, April 22.

Fr. Paul Sullins, "Is Catholic Clergy sex abuse related to homosexual priests?", Ruth Institute, 4845 Lake Street Suite 217, Lake Charles, Louisiana 70605.

Synod of Bishops, eighth ordinary general assembly, "The Formation of Priests in the Circumstances of the Present Day," *Instrumentum Laboris*.

University College of San Diego, "*High prevalence and adverse health effects of loneliness in community-dwelling adults across the lifespan: role of wisdom as a protective factor.*"
https://www.eurekalert.org/pub_releases/2018-12/uoc--sls121218.php

US Conference of Catholic Bishops, *The Charter for the Protection of Children and Young People*, (The Dallas Charter), June 2002.

US Conference of Catholic Bishops, *Program for Priestly Formation*, 2005.

US Conference of Catholic Bishops, "US Bishops' Catholic Campaign for Human Development continues to fund pro-abortion, pro-LGBT groups,"
https://www.lifesitenews.com/news/us-Bishops-catholic-campaign-for-human-development-continues-to-fund-pro-ab

Andre Vauchez, *The Laity in the Middle Ages*, Notre Dame: University of Notre Dame, IN. 1993.

Hans Urs von Balthasar, "Conversion in the New Testament," *Explorations in Theology IV: Spirit and Institution*, San Francisco: Ignatius Press, 1995.

Hans Urs von Balthasar, "On the Concept of Person," *Communio* 13 (Spring 1986).

Hans Urs von Balthasar, *The Christian States of Life*, San Francisco, Ignatius Press, 1983.

Hans Urs von Balthasar, *The Glory of the Lord I: Seeing the Form*, San Francisco: Ignatius Press, 1982.

Hans Urs von Balthasar, The Glory of the Lord IV: The Realm of Metaphysics in Antiquity, San Francisco: Ignatius Press, 1989.

Hans Urs von Balthasar, "Office in the Church," *Explorations in the Theology II: Spouse of the Word*, San Francisco: Ignatius Press.

Hans Urs von Balthasar, "Women Priests?" *New Elucidations*, San Francisco, Ignatius Press, 1986.

Hans Urs von Balthasar, *Theodrama – Theological Dramatic Theory III: Dramatis Personae: Persons in Christ, San Francisco: Ignatius Press, 1992.*

Hans Urs von Balthasar, *Theodrama – Theological Dramatic Theory V: The Last Act*, San Francisco: Ignatius Press 1998.

Paul C. Vitz, *Father of the Fatherless: The Psychology of Atheism*, Dallas TX: Spence Publishing, 1999.

George Weigel, "Joseph Ratzinger, Theological Reformer," Denver Catholic, Archdiocese of Denver, at https://denvercatholic.org/joseph-ratzinger-theological-reformer/

George Will, "Much of Today's Intelligentsia cannot Think," Washington Post, June 26, 2020.

Andrew Willard Jones, *Before Church and State—A Study of the Social Order in the Sacramental Kingdom of St. Louis IX*, Steubenville: Emmaus Academic, 2017.

World Religion News, https://www.worldreligionnews.com/religion-news/secularization-canada-set-shut-third-churches#.XJIpa4dem3U.twitter

Appendix One: Feelings, Nothing more than Feelings

One treasure of Catholicism is that it handles truth with integrity which means that it is faithful to the situation described. Not all Catholics do that or do it all the time but that is a story for another day. Functioning as fully realized human beings in grace requires truth—the truth that comes from studying every aspect of a situation. Sitting on the fence, grabbing any idea that comes along without checking it out against the situation makes a person "neither hot nor cold." (Revelation 3:15) And it gets worse: "because you are lukewarm, neither hot nor cold, I will spit you out of my mouth." (Revelation 3:16) Not my goal!

Deciding whether some action rebels against God or not involves knowing that "the morality of human acts depends on the object chosen; the end in view or the intention; the circumstances of the action." (Catechism) The act and its context *together* lead us to decide—Do I add to the world's communion of grace or the communion of evil? Then, some actions are always evil such as abortion, masturbation, contraception, homosexual acts, for example.

Catholics—those interested in truth— take a realistic view of actions. They note *everything* that is part of the real situation. Then an action can be evaluated. Since we are on earth to become more perfect, i.e. acting morally all the time, this definition is crucial. We 'capture' a piece of reality and handle it respectfully, valuing every component of the situation.

So, for a historical event, for example: to have any chance of grasping what the event means or at least coming close, one needs as many facts as possible. Only then can the event be accurately reconstructed to find what it meant for the people of that time. It is humbling that we will miss something. So maybe precipitate action can be held off for a day or a week until people are better informed.

The hurried actions, of mobs tearing down history and looting, are designed by their instigators to happen before reason can be exercised. Weaponizing peoples' feelings leads them up the garden path towards not-reflecting. Feelings become dominant. Then it is easier to just smash something, feel the elation of being part of a horde or follow one's lusts rather than reflecting.

Feelings are only a part of the whole human experience. The Catechism's formula for judging how to act aright, emphasizes how our intellects and wills are also deeply involved. "Feelings are too exclusively thought of as an isolated act alongside the intellect and the will, and too little understood as the integration of the person's whole life." (Hans Urs von Balthasar) Christianity involves integrity. Our feelings, when they have been schooled by right reflection and right action, become appropriate to the truth. The total experience then becomes "having within you the same mind that is in Christ Jesus." (Philippians 2:5) For Paul, 'mind' is more global than intellect. It is the complete disposition of the person.

Manipulated feelings never rise to the level of reason. Our feelings get hooked by words like 'justice' or equality' even when the user does not mean justice or equality but just wants to grab our loyalty.

Now we are getting to the heart of the matter: the baptized presumably are open to Jesus Christ and *his* way of being in the world which we would like to be our way of being in the world. Jesus' life was not about occasional good acts. It was the presence of full obedience to the Father all of the time—hence the mention of rebellion above! "Everything down to the foundation of a person has been put at the disposal of his ministry and made available for his work." (Von Balthasar again.) So, Christian life is not doing something good occasionally. Doing something good when it is convenient is a problem. That would be like seeing my family only when I need food. It is getting the whole relation to family completely wrong. For all Christians, following Christ is total just as his following of his Father is total. It arises out of his eternal filiation within the Godhead, namely as the adopted sons we aspire to be.

The total feeling of being *with* Christ inevitably coincides with *sentire cum ecclesia*, Ignatius of Loyola's phrase for feeling with the Church, the Body of Christ. One of his rules was "Always be ready to obey with mind and heart, setting aside all judgement of one's own, the true spouse of Jesus Christ, our holy mother, our infallible and orthodox mistress, the Catholic Church." In faith and morals, the Church gives people a complete grasp of what a situation means. So it is something more than feelings and then we cannot be easily manipulated.

Index

239

Printed in Great Britain
by Amazon